A Guide to Dating
English Antique Clocks

Eric Bruton FBHI

N.A.G. PRESS
an imprint of
ROBERT HALE · LONDON

ISBN 978 0 7195 0360 4

NAG Press
Clerkenwell House
Clerkenwell Green
London EC1R 0HT

NAG Press is an imprint of Robert Hale Limited

Printed and bound in Great Britain

Contents

Introduction *page 9*

The Wetherfield Clocks *17*

Technical Features *49*

The Plates *57*

Lantern and Hanging Clocks *59*

Bracket Clocks *71*

Longcase Clocks *121*

Notes concerning Makers of
the Clocks illustrated *237*

Appendix One: Marquetry and
Veneering *251*

Appendix Two: Cross-reference
Guide *254*

Index *259*

Bibliography *263*

Introduction

Near the end of the last century, Blackheath, in south London, through which the old Dover Road passed, was no longer a haunt of highwaymen and rebels; the riotous 'hog and pleasure' fairs had been stamped out by the government and the gravel pits had given way to pleasure gardens. The heath had become a resort and a fashionable place in which to live. It had tempted to itself a successful coal merchant named David Arthur Wetherfield, whose home, at No.8 Lansdowne Place, became a horological treasure house of English clocks known to collectors all over the world.

Wetherfield was for many years the senior partner of the firm of W.S. Partridge and Co., of No. 4 Billeter Street, London, E.C.3, coal exporters and marine insurance brokers, a firm that went out of business when he retired at an advanced age. His interest in collecting clocks, it is said, began when, in middle age, he wanted to own a grandfather clock, and employed an 'expert' to obtain a first class specimen for him; but 'he was deceived into buying a worthless imitation, and when he realised the fact, he decided, for moral solace, to acquire a collection of timepieces which would be unexcelled elsewhere'.[1]

Whatever may be the truth, there is no doubt that in his time he achieved that end, for, on his death in March 1928 at the age of 83, he had 232 fine specimens of English clocks in his house. Visitors were asked not to disclose his address because 'he had an abhorrence of opportunist dealers, plaguing fakers and persistent American millionaires'. It seems that some of the wealthiest men in the world had tried – unsuccessfully – to 'raid' his collection.

Every room except one in his house was occupied by clocks, 'the result of 30 years searching' according to one obituary, although it was certainly longer. A person who visited his house for the first time was entranced by a chorus of ticking, it was reported. Thirteen longcase clocks graced the dining room, 25 were in the drawing room, six or seven in the bathroom, while a boxroom was furnished with 45 bracket clocks. The only place where no clock, or even a watch, was allowed, was his bedroom.

Donald de Carle, who was for many years in charge of the clock and watch department of the Goldsmiths and Silversmiths Co., which later absorbed and became Garrard and Co., Crown Jewellers, writes[2] 'I met Mr. Wetherfield at his house in Blackheath, with Mr. Ilbert,[3] many years ago. The house was three or four storeys high with a sub-basement. Grandfather clocks stood on every other stair of a wide staircase. In a large room in the basement, grandfather clocks stood shoulder to shoulder against all the wall space; down

[1] *The Practical Watch and Clock Maker*, May 15, 1928.

[2] Letter of June 27, 1979.

[3] Courtenay Adrian Ilbert, of Chelsea, amassed a much more eclectic and technically interesting collection than Wetherfield's. After his death in 1957, almost the entire collection was acquired by the British Museum through the efforts of M.L.Bateman, Gilbert Edgar and the Ilbert family.

the centre of the room they stood back to back. In another room, on the ground floor, many bracket clocks, side by side, were arranged on shelves. Several special clocks, Tompions, Knibbs, etc., were in the lounge on the first floor'. Mr. de Carle added that as a rough calculation, he estimated that the clocks would have realised £1,970,000 in 1979.

The clocks were restored and put into working order by Daniel John Parkes and his son John William, who traded as D.J.Parkes and Son, at 51 Spencer Street, Clerkenwell, London, between Haswell's, the material supplier, and the chronometer maker, Thomas Mercer. A horse and trap was sent from Blackheath to collect one of the Mr. Parkes whenever his services were needed. The present Mr. Parkes, Daniel William, still carries on the business of restoration as Rowley, Parkes and Co., but from 17 Briset Street, in Clerkenwell. He says his mother always referred to Mr. Wetherfield as 'a very nice gentleman' and he recalls Sir John Prestige, another enthusiastic collector, saying that Wetherfield was a near neighbour of his.

On Wetherfield's death, his executors agreed to place the entire collection in the hands of W.E.Hurcomb, the auctioneer, valuer and estate agent, of Calder House, Piccadilly, London, for disposal by auction. Hurcomb had been acquainted with Wetherfield, as he explained in a two-page advertisement in editorial style in the *Horological Journal* of April, 1928, an account he afterwards edited and used as a preface to his book on the collection.

'Soon after the "Tupenny Tube" was opened (July, 1900), I attended an auction sale at Knight, Frank and Rutley's for the first time. The elder Mr. Knight was selling at the time, and gave me a warm reception from the rostrum. It had been noised abroad by a non-gentile dealer in a City Auction Room (Phineas Lazarus by name) that there was a bracket clock by the famous old Master, Thomas Tompion. The news acted like a magnet to a piece of steel, drawing me from the City Auction Rooms to the West, and Mr. Knight knocked down the clock to me. I paid for it, and took it away. I entered Oxford Circus Station, newly opened, and no sooner had I taken my seat "nursing my baby", so to say, than an immaculately-dressed gentlemen of about fifty-eight surprised me by saying, "Surely that is a Tompion." I was amazed, because ninety out of a hundred clockmakers (so-called) would not know who "Tompion" was, let alone a private gentleman. I told him so, and very meekly he said, "My name is Wetherfield". I understood at once, because I knew he possessed the finest collection of "Old Masters" (clocks) in the Kingdom. The clock changed hands, and a cheque on Coutts and Co. was drawn before we reached the Bank Station.'

In his advertisement, Hurcomb stated, 'It is the executors' wish – and I know it was the late Mr. Wetherfield's – that his collection should not be acquired for America. Nevertheless, I am quite sure the American competition will be very keen. I propose holding the sale two or three days towards the end of April. The whole collection will be offered first in its entirety, and, if the reserve I have advised the executors to accept is not reached, the sale will proceed and the lots sold separately. However, it is hoped that some millionaire will come forward and offer to buy the collection *en bloc*, enjoy the possession for his lifetime, and then bequeath it to the Nation.

10

'Let us try to keep it in the Homeland.'

The dates of the auction were to have been April 24 and 25, 1928, but were postponed until May 2 and 3. In the meantime. Hurcomb's appeal in his advertisement had elicited a response from Francis Mallett, of Mallett and Son, the Bond Street antique dealers, acting in collaboration with the well-known dealer-collector, Percy Webster, and an American furniture and clock dealer, Arthur S. Vernay, of No. 19 East 54th Street, New York. On May 1, the syndicate bought the whole collection for £30,000. The clocks now totalled 222, according to Hurcomb, who advertised 232, but his figures were unreliable. In fact, the lots numbered 222, and two extra, 60A and 75A, were inserted, making 224 in all. However, 60A was a framed mezzotint of Tompion, 166 comprised five clock movements and various brackets, and 167 was a clock movement, so 221 clocks and six movements were offered at auction and presumably all sold to the syndicate. It may be that, if there were more originally, the family decided to keep some.

It is curious that Vernay should have been accepted as a member of the syndicate, despite Hurcomb's declared intention to carry out the wishes of Wetherfield and his executors that clocks should not be sold to the USA. In fact, 96 of the clocks, somewhat less than half the collection, went to America. They are listed under Vernay in the chart on pages 254 to 258.

To squeeze the maximum publicity out of the sale, Hurcomb produced and published a picture book, entitled 'The Wetherfield Collection', in August, 1928. It was described as a 'handsome volume in a limited edition' for one guinea. The book sold out within a year and, despite the promise, the same edition was reprinted and republished just a year later. The pictures in the book are of the clocks prepared for auction because labels on the dials and cases can be seen, roughly touched out. Hurcomb used as an introduction an abbreviated version of the statement in his advertisement, part of which was reproduced earlier. The rest of the statement, strangely, has nothing to do with the collection and was merely 'puffing', as it was called at the time, to boost Hurcomb's reputation.

He wrote that the dealer mentioned earlier (Phineas Lazarus) told him that 'a certain nobleman living in Berkeley Square had sold three hundred pounds' worth of "junk" to a dealer in old clothing, who had removed it to another part of the West End, namely Greek Street, Soho, where it was sold by auction. Amongst the so-called junk was a Thomas Tompion grandfather clock sold for twenty-seven shillings. Phineas told me of the purchase, saying the name of the maker was "Thomas Tompion". That was good enough for me to visit a cellar in the East End of London, where he asked me to give him 35s. for his bargain. Even in those days I thought more of the vendor than of my own personal gain, and after paying him eight pounds for the clock – I did not wish to take advantage of his ignorance of its value – I sent him to the nearest rank for a hansom cab, and managed to prop it up in the cab and take it home. That was before I knew Mr. Wetherfield; the clock did not find its way into his collection. . . .' Despite this disclaimer, the clock has been confused with the famous Tompion clock, made for William III, in the Wetherfield Collection.

Vernay also published a hardback catalogue, entitled 'The Wetherfield Collection of English Clocks', in 1928, in which were illustrated 70 longcase,

26 bracket, and three lantern clocks. However, Cumming and Scott bracket clocks were illustrated twice, and an Adamson bracket clock was shown again with the wrong maker's name, so the total number of clocks was 96 and not 99 as listed.

In his preface, Vernay disclosed that seven years previously (in 1921), he had tried to buy the collection, but Wetherfield had declined to sell it, as he hoped it would go to the nation and remain in England. Vernay added, 'However, this year, owing to his decease, it was disbursed, and I obtained half of the collection. Consequently the breaking up of this collection has released many remarkable specimens. No other collection comparable either in size or importance with that of the late Mr. Wetherfield has ever existed in England. The collector will never probably again have such an opportunity of acquiring clocks such as the demise of Mr. Wetherfield has set free.'

Later, he commented, 'In many instances, the cases of longcase clocks have been restored to a certain extent, which is not surprising when one considers that a clock case 200 years old or more is bound to have suffered damage in the many removals it must have been subjected to. It will be found that some cases have had the base cut down or the top of the hood shortened, especially of tall clocks, to allow them to stand in a low room. . . .' Pointing out that the collection was rich in small and narrow longcase clocks by Tompion, Knibb, and Quare, he said he had obtained the majority of the smaller specimens and claimed that a Tompion clock in a plain walnut case would be worth 15 times as much as a poor quality clock in the same case. Wetherfield, or an advisor, seemed to have gone beyond the bounds of strict restoration. Ronald A. Lee, the fine art dealer of 1–9 Bruton Place, London, W.1., comments, 'I do believe that Wetherfield got Van Winsum[4] to make and extensively repair cases for him and, glancing through the collection, one can recognise much of his work. In the course of business, I have had many Wetherfield clocks through my hands, but many were pushed aside on grounds of considerable alteration.'

Hurcomb gave a brief description of how the William III clock came to light. He called it the 'gem of the collection' and added that, 17 years after it had been bought for 380 guineas, he 'fully expected to sell it for 1,000 guineas'. He called the clock 'The Record Tompion'. This name has stuck, unfortunately in the view of many horologists. The origin of the name is uncertain; it may first have been applied by Hurcomb simply for reasons of publicity.

The better description of the emergence of the William III Tompion is by R. W. Symonds, who became intimately involved with its future, in his book, 'Thomas Tompion, His Life and Work' (London, 1951). The second Duke of Cambridge, grandson of George III, had been given the clock by his cousin, Queen Victoria. Percy Webster bought it for 125 guineas at the sale of the Duke of Cambridge's effects at Christie's in 1904. The catalogue entry was 'Lot 284. A clock in a tall walnut-wood Case moulded with chased ormolu',

---

[4] Van Winsum was a cabinet-maker in the Euston Road, north-west London, who carried out case repairs for Wetherfield before about 1920, after which Percy Dawson took over the restoration from his workshop at 15 Warren Mews, not far away. There were two timber yards in the vicinity. Van Winsum's work has been described as 'fine craftsmanship, but carried out without historical knowledge'.

with no reference to Tompion. A newspaper account at the time called it 'an old grandfather clock' that had been overlooked in one of the bedrooms and had been included in the sale at the last moment.

Percy Webster sold the clock to George Dunn, the book and clock collector, of Woolley Hall, Maidenhead. When Dunn died in 1914, it was rebought by Webster at auction for 380 guineas and was later acquired by Wetherfield. After the Wetherfield sale, it was sold by Mallet's for £3,000 to an American collector, Francis P. Garvan, and exhibited for some years at the Pennsylvania Museum. Francis Mallett is reported[5] to have said at the time, 'I shall undoubtedly receive even higher offers, but I should like the nation to have it. All the authorities can find is £1,500. The National Art Collection Fund Committee is being approached, but it is for the public to assist. The Museum (Victoria and Albert) has no specimen like this, and I am ready to let the authorities have it at the sum offered me.'

In 1934, it came back to England, having been bought for £4,000 by J.S.Sykes, a merchant involved in trade with the Near and Middle East, and in October, 1955, it was exhibited at the 'Five Centuries of British Timekeeping' exhibition, where it looked magnificent in the drawing room of Goldsmiths Hall, London, and was probably on show for the first and only time in Britain. In 1956, Mr. Sykes, then in his eighties and living in Grosvenor Square, London, resold the clock privately for £11,000, to Colonial Williamsburg, the 18th century museum town in Virginia, USA. His intermediary was R.W. Symonds, and energetic efforts were made by honorary officials of the Worshipful Company of Clockmakers and others to trace the specialist packers into whose care the clock had been placed. The object was to prevent export of the clock on the grounds of its being a national treasure. The packers were traced, but too late. The time had been chosen with care, when several members of the committee concerned with the export of national treasures were on holiday and it was not possible to assemble a quorum at short notice, but, in any case, as R.A.Lee points out, the committee would have been unable to prevent its sale for the second time to the USA under what is called the '50 year rule'.[6] Ironically, there was a dock strike in New York at the time, and the ship brought the 'Record' Tompion back to England once more before it arrived eventually in New York.

The clock is at Williamsburg today. For some years it graced the Upper Middle Room of the Palace, where 'Spanish leather wall covering, c.1680, specified as "gilt Leather hangings" in a 1710 "Proposal For rendering the new House Convenient as well as Ornamental" forms a sumptuous backdrop for the magnificent tall case clock, c.1699, made by the famed clockmaker Thomas Tompion'. At the time of writing, this superb year clock has been removed from display. From the time of the Wetherfield sale, it was hoped that the Victoria and Albert Museum would eventually be able to acquire the

[5] Horological Journal, June, 1928.

[6] A licence to export an antique is normally granted if the article was imported into the United Kingdom or Isle of Man within the previous 50 years. A notice to exporters of antiques, collectors' items, etc. explaining the controls and how they have developed since 1952, is issued by The Department of Trade, Export Licensing Branch, Sanctuary Buildings, 20 Great Smith Street, London SW1P 3DB, and The Reviewing Committee on the Export of Works of Art, c/o Office of Arts and Libraries, Elizabeth House, York Road, London SE1 7PH.

William III clock. This hope, as well as the wishes of Wetherfield and his executors, was an instant casualty in the scramble for the clocks.

F.J.Britten referred to Wetherfield as the owner of many of the clocks illustrated in his standard work, 'Former Clock and Watchmakers and their Work', the first edition of which was published in 1894. In 1907, a book entitled 'Old English Clocks (The Wetherfield Collection)' was published in London by Lawrence and Jellicoe Ltd. with an introduction and notes by F.J.Britten, in which he commented, 'Such an array of choice examples as Mr. Wetherfield has gathered, affords an opportunity of obtaining information never before presented, and the large number of excellent photographic reproductions here given enables one to compare the styles in vogue as well as the conceits of different makers throughout the whole period. Again and again I have gone over this collection with delight and profit, and I think no one who has a regard for the work of our old craftsmen could inspect these clocks without being amply repaid for his trouble.'

In the 6th edition of 'Old Clocks and Watches and their Makers', published in 1932, Britten wrote in his preface, 'Since the last edition Mr. D.A.F.Wetherfield has passed away. Many of his clocks have crossed the Atlantic including the "record" Tompion made for William III'. Many of the clocks in the sale, including the 'record' Tompion were not in Britten's book on the collection. Also, two Tompion eight-day longcase clocks, one in oak and the other in walnut, and a bracket repeater clock by Moore of Ipswich, were illustrated by Britten, but did not appear in the sale catalogue. A movement by Williamson had acquired a case by the time of the sale.

Curiously, another classic work, 'English Domestic Clocks', by Herbert Cescinsky and Malcolm R.Webster, published in London in 1913, contains only half a dozen references to Wetherfield and does not identify pictures of Wetherfield clocks as such, although the authors acknowledged 'great indebtedness to Mr. Britten' and the 'invaluable' advice of Percy Webster, father of Malcolm Webster, and one of the syndicate that bought the collection.

It was in the 1940s (I believe) that Arthur Tremayne, publisher of 'Practical Watch and Clock Maker', acquired a wooden box containing a number of photographic plates, mostly 12 inches by 10 inches, showing longcase and other clocks. Some were silvered, but only a few were cracked. Tremayne said they were the originals of the Hurcomb book, but in fact they turned out to be the originals for Britten's book on the collection, and they included a number of photographs not used. I acquired them in the early 1950s. It is possible that Tremayne bought them from Malcolm Gardner, the dealer and antiquarian bookseller.

Nearly a quarter of a century later, in 1977, I happened to be talking to Charles Allix, successor to Malcolm Gardner, and mentioned the 'Hurcomb' plates, at which Mr. Allix told me he had recently purchased an ordinary snapshot album containing prints of all the pictures in Hurcomb's book. They were genuine, because they showed the retouched labels on dials and cases. By an amicable arrangement, I was able to purchase this album also. The coming together of the two collections of pictures suggested the compilation of this book, selecting the best from each group. In general, the album

14

pictures, although smaller, are better for the cases, and those from the negatives better for dials.

Britten attempted to show the clocks in chronological order, which is of considerable benefit to anyone interested in dating clocks, from the antiquarian horologist to the furniture dealer. Hurcomb followed the order of the sale catalogue, which was random. In the present volume, the chronological pattern has been followed, but many of the clocks have been redated, generally slightly earlier, in the light of present knowledge.

It soon became evident that there were inaccuracies in the catalogue, some obvious, like Elliott instead of Ellicott, but a nuisance when there was a maker named Elliott, and Elsworth for Ebsworth. Some were amusing, such as Alexander Cunning, instead of Cumming (Hurcomb corrected some errors in his book), Madderman for Maclennan, and Diverriburns for Dwerrihouse. Hurcomb's illustrations had some transpositions that caused plenty of trouble. A plain case he described as marquetry was manifestly not so, and what he described as a burr walnut clock by Daniel Quare was said in the sale catalogue to have a marquetry case. There were more errors and ambiguities. Britten was much more accurate, but nearly all of the clocks in question did not feature in his book. A magnifying glass used on the best prints solved some of the puzzles. For example, the longcase clocks of Edmund Day and Corn. Herbert were transposed by Hurcomb, and a clock he attributed rightly to Daniel Quare was shown also on the previous page in the book attributed to Edward East. Going times given by both Hurcomb and Britten are in a few cases incorrect, to judge by the dials.

In the attempt to make sense out of conflicting facts and attributions, I enlisted the help of someone who knew many of the clocks well. He spent some weeks compiling a chart with the object of reconciling the catalogue descriptions, album pictures, prints from the plates, Britten's descriptions, and Hurcomb's descriptions, and eventually gave up because there were still so many loose ends, that, to tie up, would require years rather than months of research. For that reason, he does not wish his name to be mentioned, but I have to record my indebtedness to the substantial start he made by re-dating so many clocks. To bring the work to publishing stage, I have tried to carry on where he stopped, with the help of horological friends.

At a final stage, Beresford Hutchinson, who was responsible for the horological collection at the British Museum and is now Keeper of Astronomy at the Old Royal Observatory, in Greenwich Park, where there is a fine collection of chronometers and precision clocks, cast his eye over the manuscript and page proofs to spot any false assumptions. He is in a good position to do so, because, after he left college, he went to work for Percy Dawson, the specialist case restorer, where he handled a number of movements from Wetherfield clocks. His suggestions were of great assistance. Charles Allix, too, having a special interest in this book, as well as a wide ranging knowledge of the subject, was kind enough to read through the text for heresies. Neither of them, of course, is responsible for any residual errors or omissions. I am also much indebted to Ronald Lee.

The pattern adopted by both Britten and Hurcomb of appending short biographies has been followed, with the advantage of additional facts from

G.H.Baillie's 'Watchmakers and Clockmakers of the World', now designated as Volume 1, and Brian Loomes's Volume 2 of the same title (see footnote on page 17).

Because the collection was so representative of early English clocks, and its presentation in chronological order with more information will assist dating even to those unversed in horology, an introductory chapter has been included for the non-specialist. It deals mainly with superficial features that may indicate a date of making, or perhaps where a marriage of case and movement may be suspected. This again follows a precedent set by Britten.

Although the collection and this book include lantern, bracket, and longcase clocks, most of the clocks are in the last category, which also has a wider span, and that is where most value will be found by readers. However, the gaps in the bracket clocks have been filled by sketches in a dating chart on pages 72 to 76.

Clocks are serial numbered, and to find a clock by any particular maker, it is only necessary to refer to the short biographies beginning on page 239, where each entry is accompanied by the serial numbers of the appropriate clocks.

The Wetherfield Clocks

The way in which a date is ascribed to a clock can be set down as a discipline, which will help in general, but not in particular because the particular needs specialised knowledge. This is the usual pattern of procedure:

(1) Examine the clock (or picture of it) to see if it appears to be original and that the movement fits the case.

(2) If the maker is named, and his location given, try to find a record in 'Watchmakers and Clockmakers of the World', volumes 1 and 2,[1] and, if necessary, one of the more or less specialised books listed in the bibliography.

(3) If the maker is identified, see if the style fits into his period of working and when. If there are several makers of the same name, try to determine which overlaps the estimated date of the clock by its style.

(4) If the maker's name cannot be identified, try to date the clock by its features and make comparisons with other clocks of the same period, remembering to compare London clocks with London clocks and provincial clocks with provincial clocks.

Although this volume is produced as a historical record, its format will give a good start to someone attempting to learn about English clock styles, especially if the basic information recorded is amended and corrected as more facts come to the reader's attention.

Lantern Clocks

Wetherfield's clocks were representative of the three classic earliest styles of English clock, the lantern, the bracket, and the longcase. Although it included very few lantern clocks, the bracket clocks and longcase or grandfather clocks – the most English of all – were particularly illustrative of changes in style over the years.

Before about 1600, makers in England, many of continental origin, were constructing weight-driven iron chamber clocks and spring-driven table clocks with box-like cases on short feet with hand and dial on the top. The chamber clock was built in a three-dimensional frame with four corner posts and was commonly called a 'bird-cage' or a 'bed-post' clock, because the vertical bars in which the wheel pivots worked made the whole frame look like a cage, or because the corner posts were reminiscent of those of a four-poster bed. It was hung on a hook in the wall, driven by weights hanging below it, showed the time by a single hand turning once in 12 hours, and sounded the hours on a bell at the top.

The lantern clock was an English version of the chamber clock, particularly of the style from southern Germany, which became more or less standardised

---

[1] Published by N.A.G. Press Ltd., 93–99 Goswell Road, London EC1V 7QA.

around 1600. English makers began to introduce brass in the construction, first, possibly, for the dial, as an early example of an iron lantern clock with a brass dial is known. The iron church buttress-shaped corner posts were forged in square sections of symmetrical design, still of iron, then replaced by cast and turned brass pillars, with feet and finials made similarly. Brass was used for the top and bottom plates and for more and more parts of the movement (as the mechanism is called).

The lantern clock was always enclosed by plates all round, the side ones being hinged and latched. The brass annular ring on which the hour numerals are engraved, known as the chapter ring, was attached to the front and a single iron hand with a long tail showed the hour.

In an English lantern clock, the corner posts are united to the top and bottom plates by the feet and finials which act as nuts, having female threads. Each post has a threaded portion at each end, which passes through a hole in the corner of the plate. Continental makers of lantern clocks, mainly in France, usually avoided the difficulty of cutting threads by making pillars integral with their feet and finials and slotting squared sections of the pillars to take the corners of the plates, which were pinned in place.

Since the lines of the joints are easily visible, for example in the Closon clock numbered 1, this is easily noticed evidence of origin, but it must be remembered that some English makers used the continental construction, like Joseph Knibb as well, in the clock numbered 2.

The four ornamental finials at the top also hold the ends of two curved straps in a crossed arch, from which the hour bell is suspended, being fastened by a fifth finial acting as a nut. Ornamental frets fill the gaps at the front and sides between the top plate and bell. The most common designs were twin dolphins, foliage, and heraldic emblems, but the patterns of frets do not belong to any period and are therefore of no real value in ascribing a date.

The chapter ring is marked by engraved Roman numerals outside two concentric rings divided into 48 spaces representing quarter hours. Half hours are indicated by ornaments engraved between the hour numerals and projecting from the quarter hour ring. There are no outside divisions on the chapter ring of any one-hand clock. The hand itself is thickly wrought in iron with a simple arrow head and long tail. The central boss is oval or round with a square hole to fit over the square end of an arbor (axle), through which a taper pin is passed to keep the hand in place. The tail is there to allow the hand to be turned like a wingnut when setting the hand to time. In alarm clocks, it also has the function of indicating the alarm time.

An early lantern clock has, riveted to the rear of the top movement plate, an iron stirrup, almost semi-circular in shape, for hanging the clock on a large L-shaped hook. At the bottom, projecting horizontally from the feet are two spiked spurs that dig into the wall and prevent the clock from swinging when being wound. The spurs may also be found riveted to the back protective plate.

These clocks were called 'hanging clocks' at the time, but also referred to as 'brass clocks'. As French still influenced bureaucratic language and *laiton* or *latten* was used for brass in, for example, some inventories, it is surmised that the name became corrupted to lantern, since the clock is similarly shaped.

The expression 'Cromwellian clock' is a misnomer of Victorian times; the design pre-dated Cromwell by nearly half a century.

Below the clock hang two heavy weights, suspended from ropes. That on the left to the front is for the going train, the train of gears that turns the hand; the other, which is on the right towards the back of the clock, is for the striking train. Each rope passes over a grooved pulley and a small weight is hung from the free end to keep the rope from jumping out of the groove, which is also spiked for the same purpose. To wind each train, the rope end with the small weights is pulled down.

The going train of a lantern clock made before about 1660 has three wheels: the great wheel, to which the driving pulley is attached by a ratchet, the second wheel, and the escape wheel. The escape wheel has a rim like a band with pointed teeth cut in one side and is called a crown wheel because of its resemblance to a crown. Above the top plate of the clock, under the bell, is a large circular wheel known as the balance. It has a single spoke and its arbor passes down into the clock, across the crown wheel. Two small plates, called pallets, attached to the arbor, are positioned in the path of teeth on each side of the crown wheel so that it cannot be turned without swinging the balance first one way and then the other. This arrangement, called a 'verge escapement', controls the rate at which the going weight falls to the ground, and therefore the timekeeping.

It is obvious that the higher the clock is hung on the wall, and the longer the driving ropes, the longer it will run. The practical limit is about 12 hours, so early lantern clocks had to be wound morning and night. There was little or no provision for regulation except by increasing or decreasing the driving weight. A banking pin was also provided to intercept the spoke of the balance, should it swing excessively with risk of damage to the crown wheel. This also tended to control the timekeeping.

The great wheel of the going train also drives the hand. (In clocks and watches, all the larger toothed wheels are called, simply, 'wheels'. The small ones they engage are called 'pinions'.) The arbor of the great wheel passes through the front of the frame and its end is formed into a pinion which drives a larger wheel above it. This one is called the 'hour wheel' because the hour hand is attached to it. The hand is fastened to an arbor connected by a friction washer to the hour wheel, so that the hand can be set to time without damaging the clock movement.

The striking train, behind the going train, is quite independent of the going train, but is released by it at each hour. In a one-hand clock, this is done by a star wheel with 12 points, mounted behind and fixed to the hour wheel. At every hour, a point of the star lifts a lever and drops it to release the striking. The great wheel of the striking train has a pulley with ratchet drive like the going train, so that the weight can be pulled up without trying to turn the train backwards. It drives clockwise, in the opposite direction from the great wheel of the going train, so that the weights are kept apart and do not foul each other.

The striking train great wheel is also the pin wheel that operates the bell hammer. It has around it 13 (usually) pins, projecting sideways. When striking, a pin pushes the tail of the hammer against a spring and then releases it so that the hammer on the other end strikes the bell. To prevent the bell being struck in rapid succession, an air brake, known as a 'fly', is provided. Two other wheels and pinions, driven by the great wheel, increase the speed ratio so that a final arbor carrying a rectangular plate (the fly) is made to spin rapidly and slow down the rate of striking. The plate is attached by a friction spring so that no damage results when the train is abruptly stopped.

Control of the striking is a little more complicated. The arbor of the striking great wheel projects through the back of the frame and is formed into a pinion, like that of the going train. It also turns a large wheel, which runs on a stud and has attached to it a circular plate with 11 slots cut in its edge, called the 'locking plate'. An ⌐ -shaped locking lever is arranged over the locking plate so that the end rests on the rim, or in a slot. As the clock strikes, the locking lever is raised and dropped at every blow. If it drops into a slot, striking stops; if it comes down on the land between slots, striking continues. The length of the land between the slots therefore decides the number of blows. There is no land for one o'clock, because the lever has to fall into the same slot. A description of the releasing mechanism can be found in a practical clock book. Because the locking plate does not in fact lock the striking train, despite its name, it is usually called the 'count wheel' today.

Although the release mechanism for striking is not described, because this is not a technical book, it is worth noting that it is more sophisticated and accurate than most earlier systems, where the gradual lifting of a lever released the striking train. In the early lantern clock, this occurs a few minutes before the hour; the train is initially released, but is immediately held up again. The lever drops exactly on the hour to start the striking. The same or a similar system was continued for bracket and longcase clocks. The holding-up action is known as the 'warning'.

Many early lantern clocks incorporated an alarm as well as striking, and occasionally instead of striking. They are immediately recognisable by the disc numbered from 1 to 12 behind the hand. The disc can be rotated, and has knobs around the edge to assist in this. The time on it indicated by the tail of the hour hand is the time of alarm. The disc is mounted on a pipe, which also carries a plate with a projecting pin, behind the dial. The disc and plate rotate with the hour hand and the pin lifts a lever at the time set to release the alarm.

The alarm mechanism itself is usually mounted on an iron plate at the back between the pillars. It comprises a crown wheel combined with a ratchet pulley wheel. A cord over the pulley has a fairly small driving weight at one end and a small counterweight at the other, which hang behind the clock. There is a verge with pallets across the crown wheel, like that of the escapement, but instead of swinging a balance, the arrangement oscillates a small horizontal hammer mounted inside the bell. (The hour hammer is larger and vertically mounted on the right inside the bell.) The lifting lever at the front of the clock lifts a similar one (called a 'detent') at the back. When the detent is down, a pin on the crown wheel rim buts on it, to prevent the weight from rotating the crown wheel.

On some clocks, but mainly continental ones, the alarm is on one side. Lantern clocks with alarms and no striking were primarily for use when visiting. They were commonly made with short pendulum. The alarm crown wheel and pulley are positioned where the striking work would normally be, behind the going train, and not on the back plate.

The lantern clock remained in this first, more or less standardised, form until about 1660, when a major change took place. Such early clocks are extremely rare in their original state for a reason that will appear later. The change was the introduction of the pendulum, which greatly improved timekeeping.

Many fine lantern clocks with short pendulums appeared from c.1660 until well throughout the 18th century. Clockmakers realised that it was not difficult to alter the design of a balance with crown wheel and verge to short pendulum with the same escapement. The main change was to plant the crown wheel horizontally instead of vertically, so the original crown wheel was replaced by one with ordinary teeth on the edge of the band rim. This is known as a 'contrate wheel' and was used to drive a pinion on the end of a vertical arbor with the crown wheel on top of it, under the bell, where the balance used to be.

The verge was now mounted horizontally across this, with the pendulum rod fastened at the back end, at right angles, to hang down. The pendulum bob was a small, pear-shaped brass knob, threaded on so that it could be screwed up and down to alter the rate of the clock. To avoid the difficulty of making a long, thin female thread in the bob, a piece of wood was inserted in a hole and the threaded rod screwed into this.

At some time in the life of the short pendulum lantern clock, some makers placed the pendulum between the going and striking trains, in the middle of the movement. Others retained it at the back, but within the case. Extremely rarely, the pendulum was hung outside on the front, continental style, instead of outside at the back. A central pendulum sometimes has a banana-shaped bob, each end of which appears through slots in the side of the clock when it is going. The 'Tompion' clock numbered 5 has such slots. Such clocks were often provided with wings each side, triangular pieces behind the slots, from the later 17th into the second half of the 18th century. They were enclosed at the front by transparent horn or they were glazed.

The greatest change came about 1670, with the introduction of the anchor escapement, in which the escape wheel was like a flattened crown wheel, so that the teeth were on the outer edge like the normal gear wheel, except that they were of special pointed shape. This allowed the use of pallets at the end of an anchor-shaped piece of steel instead of a verge. The advantage was that the pendulum did not have to swing so widely, so a long one could be used. This miraculously improved timekeeping over the short bob pendulum. It was relatively easy to convert old balance wheel clocks, by removing the verge and balance, replacing the crown wheel by a flat escape wheel, and adding the escapement.

The incongruity of a long pendulum hanging behind a lantern clock did not seem to worry some owners, and almost all the original circular balance wheel clocks seem to have been converted to anchor escapement and long pendulum. Unfortunately, because the pendulum was hung on the outside at the back, the alarm mechanism was removed and thrown away, along with the entire back plate.

The arbor carrying the lifting lever and alarm detent was pivoted in the dial plate at the front, near or at 11 o'clock, or in a hole behind the chapter ring. The other pivot was in the iron back plate. When a clock was converted to anchor escapement, the back plate was replaced, and the arbor removed, but the pivot hole remains. The alarm setting disc on the dial was usually retained because the zone underneath was not engraved or had practice cuts in it.

Another sign of conversion is a bridge (a ♭ bracket fastened at both ends) riveted on the middle frame bar, through which the verge passed. This was usually retained to hold one pivot of the escape wheel.

The more accurate long pendulum encouraged the use of two hands in clocks other than lanterns, which meant the incorporation of the 12 to 1 gearing between minute and hour hands known as 'motion work'. The single hand persisted in lantern clocks, and also in longcase clocks with lantern clock style (posted) movements made outside London, as well as later ones with plated (see page 50) movements, until the end of the next century, mainly because there was little demand for timekeeping to the minute except in the more industrialised towns. Few were made with two hands.

Some lantern clocks (and many posted frame movements in long cases) made with one hand were converted to two and conversion sets were readily available. The motion work is the same, whether the clock was made with it or converted, which causes difficulties in judging originality.

One benefit, the endless rope drive, an invention credited to Christiaan Huygens, provided the opportunity of making clocks that would run for about 30 hours, so that they needed winding once a day instead of twice. Only one weight is required, but it is heavier. It hangs from a pulley in the loop of the endless rope, which passes over the pulleys of both going and striking great wheels, so that only one of them needs a ratchet drive. The other loop has either a small counterweight on a pulley, or is threaded through a lead ring.

The endless rope provided what is called 'maintaining power', because the weight continues to drive the hands while it is being pulled up during winding. The clock stopped while winding the earlier system.

To increase the going time, the great wheels were designed to run in the same direction (anti-clockwise). The going great wheel turns in $2\frac{1}{2}$ or 3 hours instead of one, and the striking great wheel has twice as many pins to operate the hammer, which is placed on the other (left hand) side of the clock.

Early lantern clocks driven by two weights were easily made to be operated by one, without mechanical alteration. An endless rope was placed over both great wheel pulleys in such a way that the driving weight turned the striking great wheel clockwise and the going great wheel anti-clockwise. The ratchet (clockmakers refer to it as a 'click') was removed from the going pulley, which was fixed to the great wheel, so that maintaining power would be provided.

Dating Lantern Clocks

Below are summarised some of the facts that help in dating a lantern clock, used in conjunction with the maker's biography, if he is known.

An original lantern clock made before *c.*1660 will have a circular balance under the bell. Unconverted clocks like this are extremely rare.

One with a long pendulum and signs of conversion such as holes that appear to serve no purpose, and perhaps a re-engraved dial centre where there was an alarm disc, may be a clock made before 1660 and converted.

A lantern clock with a short pendulum can be dated from *c.*1660 to late in the 18th century, depending on other features.

A clock constructed as a long pendulum clock was made after *c.*1670 and up to some time in the 18th century, depending on other features.

Chapter rings were, at the beginning, very narrow overall and across the band, and smaller than the width of the clock.

In the early years of the 17th century, they became a little wider overall than the clock, and about an inch (2.5 cm) across the band.

Some were flattened slightly at top and bottom, to fit, so this is not necessarily a sign of a 'marriage' (a part from another clock).

Chapter rings (which were silvered) gradually grew wider and bigger from the last quarter of the 17th century. By 1700, they were substantially wider and by about mid-18th century, some were so large and wide that they completely covered the corner posts of the clock. These are called 'sheephead' clocks.

Before the end of the 17th century, some lantern clocks were appearing with square dials (like the unusual one by Wm. Clay numbered 8).

These also appeared in a new guise from *c.*1680 or even earlier, as hooded wall clocks, enclosed in a case like the hood of a longcase clock. There is an example numbered 7.

A few years after the turn of the century, some lantern clocks were fitted with break arch dials. They were relatively common, but no example appeared in the collection.

Lantern clocks with one hand and no minute divisions on the chapter ring continued to be made through the 18th century. A chapter ring with minute divisions and one hand indicates a 'marriage'.

A bell striking hammer on the right (from the front) indicates a clock made before 1660.

If the left hand rear part of an endless rope or chain has to be pulled down for winding the single weight, the clock has been converted from two weight drive. If the right hand rear rope of chain has to be pulled down, the clock was made with endless winding, i.e. after *c.*1660.

Driving ropes were being replaced by chains at about the time of introduction of the pendulum. A pulley for rope may have spikes in the groove. One for chain may have the grooves shaped to the links.

Lantern clocks with long pendulums, after *c.*1670, were sometimes stood on tall wooden pyramid-shaped stands because less fall of weight was needed. The stands are generally not contemporary.

Lantern clocks were commonly used as the movements of longcase clocks going for 30 hours, until *c.*1700 in London, and until at least *c.*1800 by some provincial makers. The pillar frames were plain and later made of iron again, like the earliest clocks, because brass had become more expensive.

A signature on the front fret of a lantern clock is indicative of a very early date. Signing in the upper part of the zone (the area inside the chapter ring) soon became the usual practice, until the break-arch dial was introduced, when the signature was on a circular plate in the arch.

Early clocks were engraved in the zone and on corners of the case outside the chapter ring, with tulips, Tudor roses, or acanthus leaves. In later clocks, the zone was matted (roughly textured).

First hands, made of wrought iron, had simple unpierced arrow heads and long pointed tails. Sometimes the tail was decorated by a groove or band. Hands became more decorative as time passed, developing with the hour hand of bracket and longcase clocks.

Traditionally, the lantern clock was a one-hand clock and remained so through the years, although some were made with, or converted to, two hands.

A lantern clock with two hands and minute divisions on the dial could possibly be original, but is far more likely to be a conversion. One with two hands and no minute divisions is a conversion.

At all periods of their manufacture, some lantern clocks were made with alarm dials.

The height of lantern clocks was usually between about 14 inches (36 cm) and 16 inches (41 cm), but some miniatures were only 9 inches (23 cm) high, and are very rare.

Large numbers of clocks especially made for the Turkish market, particularly in the second half of the 18th century, included lantern clocks. There is an example numbered 9.

Finally, there are many reproduction lantern clocks in circulation. Often the lacquered brass of the case is not so yellowish as old brass. Most are made of commercial rolled brass, not cast brass.

Bracket Clocks

Some space has been devoted to lantern clocks despite their small representation in the collection, because the construction and development is intimately linked with those of bracket and longcase clocks. The first of these two English clock styles followed the introduction of the pendulum into England. The inventor was the remarkably able astronomer, mathematician, horologist and artist from the Netherlands, Christiaan Huygens. He related that the idea of how to apply a pendulum to a clock, so that it controlled the timekeeping, came to him on Christmas Eve. He obtained a patent for the clock in 1657, and commissioned Salomon Coster, a clockmaker working in The Hague, to make the first model.

This first pendulum clock contained several other inventions, including the endless rope drive, already alluded to, a separate suspension for the pendulum (by cord; a length of clock spring was used in English clocks), and a separate link with the escapement, called the 'crutch'. The pendulum was introduced into England by Ahasuerus Fromanteel, a London maker whose son, John, had gone to work for Coster eleven weeks after Coster had been granted the right to make pendulum clocks for 21 years. Ahasuerus Fromanteel advertised house clocks with pendulums that kept better time than any other clocks and that 'go either with springs or weights' and 'may be made to go a week, a month, or a year, with once winding up, as well as those that are wound up every day . . .'. The advertisement was published in English news sheets in October and November of 1658.

The truer successor to the lantern clock was the longcase clock, which was weight-driven, but the bracket clock is being dealt with first because makers of it continued to employ the traditional crown-wheel and verge escapement with simple short bob pendulum, fastened to the verge arbor, instead of Huygens's more sophisticated separate suspension and crutch.

The major constructional difference between both bracket and longcase clock movement and the lantern clock movement is in the frame. The lantern clock frame comprises two horizontal plates united by four corner posts. The so-called plate frame, is the same turned on its side – two vertical plated united by four corner posts. The main advantage is that the pivots of the wheel arbors can be planted anywhere in the plates, whereas, with a pillar frame, straps have to be placed between the pillars for pivot holes. The old continental table clock with a dial on the top had pivots in the plates, and this, on its side is the same construction as a plate frame.

Trains of gears can be placed side by side in a plate frame, instead of one behind the other. This has particular advantages with a spring-driven clock because the winding squares for the key can be made easily accessible from the front or back.

Spring clocks had been made for about a century and a half when the bracket clock appeared, but the flat, coiled spring could still not be made to provide even power for any length of time. The spring was therefore coiled in a drum, called the 'barrel'. The inner end is hooked to a fixed arbor and the other end to the inside wall of the barrel. A gut line is fastened to the outside of the barrel and wound round it. The other end of the gut line is attached to a trumpet shaped pulley with a spiral groove in it, known as the 'fusee'. The fusee itself is fastened through a ratchet and click to the great wheel.

Winding the fusee winds the gut line round its groove, thus turning the barrel and winding the spring inside it. When released, the spring barrel drives the fusee in the opposite direction. Gut changed in length with humidity, which caused problems and a better alternative in the form of a special chain, was introduced by a Swiss maker, living in London, at about the same time as the pendulum appeared. From about 1690, a cottage industry making fusee chains developed in Christchurch, Hampshire, to supply the trade in London and elsewhere.

The purpose of the tapered fusee pulley is to increase the leverage as the spring's power decreases, so that the power output remains more or less constant. In this, it is very efficient and goes a long way towards explaining why bracket clocks were successful, although they retained the outmoded verge escapement and rigidly fixed pendulum. Because the fusee, mounted above the spring barrel, is turned by key to wind the clock, the winding holes are always high in the dial of a fusee clock. A fusee barrel is always 'set-up' (given the correct pre-tension) by pre-adjustment of the barrel arbor, which is provided with a ratchet wheel and click. Fusees were used for striking and chiming trains for the same reason of overcoming the failing power of the spring.

One of the first points to note about a clock wound through the dial is, then, the number of winding holes and their position. If there is one hole which is central or asymmetrical, the 'clock' is a fusee timepiece. Although the word 'clock' is used in a generic manner today, strictly it implies a clock that indicates the time by a bell (Latin *clocca*, a bell). One that only shows the time is a timepiece. One that makes a sound, flashes a light, or trips a mechanism to tip you out of bed (such a clock was patented), is an alarm.

Traditionally, the going train of a timepiece is placed centrally, with the winding hole below the centre of the hands, as in the clock numbered 24, but occasionally, especially in a regulator, the winding hole may be displaced (see numbered 55). A regulator is a timepiece designed for high timekeeping accuracy, but is almost always weight-driven as described in the next section.

Traditionally, in an eight-day clock, the going train is positioned on the right, and the striking train on the left. In 30-hour plate frame movements, and in some going a month, the positions are reversed. When a chiming train is incorporated, this is placed to the right. Thus a clock with three winding holes is a striking and chiming clock. When an alarm is incorporated, the winding hole is not infrequently placed unsymmetrically on the dial. There is an example numbered 23. Almost all bracket clocks were wound from the front. The reason was that if a clock on a bracket or mantle had to be turned to wind it from the back, the timekeeping would be disturbed because of the pendulum control. Modern clocks with a lever escapement can be turned or lifted up without affecting the timekeeping and are usually wound from the back.

'Bracket clock' does not seem to have been the original name, although the clocks were often supplied with a matching wall bracket. Examples may be seen numbered 57 and 63. In most cases, however, the bracket has been lost or the clock never had one, because it became customary to stand the clock on a broad mantelshelf or a heavy table. The bracket is best for timekeeping because the clock is not disturbed. A substantial marble mantelpiece was as good, except if fires in the hearth made it warm, which could dry out the lubricating oil. If a clock stops and is rewound but the back is inaccessible, it is best started by lifting one side of the clock gently and lowering it back into place.

Bracket clocks were introduced about 1660, shortly after the adoption of the short pendulum. Most were designed to run for eight days, so that they could be rewound weekly, with some reserve time for late winding. Occasionally one was made to run longer at a winding, for a month, and even in rare cases, a year, but not as often as with weight-driven clocks, because the problem of providing a spring strong enough was much greater than using a heavier weight. One designed to run for a year is more likely to be a timepiece because the striking train also presents problems of providing enough reserve energy for so many blows of the hammer. There exists, nevertheless, a spring driven striking and chiming clock (which never had a bracket) by Thomas Tompion that runs for a year at a winding – it was not in the collection – as well as others.

There is sometimes confusion between what is meant by chiming and striking, mainly because there is also a valid expression 'quarter striking'. A chime implies more than one note and more than one pitch. The simplest chime is called the 'ting-tang', and is struck on two bells of different pitch, the higher one being struck first. An example is numbered 13. One of the latest chimes is the Westminster, on four bells (or gongs). It became popular after the Westminster clock, 'Big Ben', was set going in 1859, so a clock with Westminster chimes is unlikely to have been made before this date, although the chime, which was modified from the fifth bar of Handel's 'Messiah', 'I know that my Redeemer liveth', was first used in the clock of St. Mary's Church, Cambridge in 1793–4. It became fashionable, however, to add Westminster chimes to ordinary striking clocks.

Bracket clocks that sound the quarters generally do so on more than one bell, so have quarter chiming, or quarter striking, to use the more correct term. The standard French clock strikes the hours and one blow at the half hours, so has half hour striking.

There is also some confusion over musical clocks. A chime on more than one bell is musical, but the term musical clocks is reserved for those with a separate train of gears for music at the hour only or for music at other times, such as the quarters, as well. In general, a musical clock has a pinned barrel, like a musical box (except that it operates bell hammers) and offers a choice of tunes. A good example is to be seen numbered 56. Another difference is that a chiming clock plays a sequence of five musical phrases, one at the first quarter, and two more at the second quarter. The third quarter is marked by two further phrases, followed by the repetition of the first quarter. The hour consists of a repetition of the two phrases used at the half hour, plus the first two phrases of the three quarter hour.

Some striking, many chiming, and probably all musical clocks have a means of silencing them. This is achieved by moving the end of a lever across a slot marked S at one end and N at the other, meaning strike and not strike. Later it was more common to have a small subsidiary dial in a corner of the dial or in the arch with a strong hand with a tail. Two positions are marked Strike and Not Strike, or Strike and Silent. The hand is turned like a turnkey to indicate one or the other. Musical clocks usually have a tune indicator on the same principle.

Often, the strike/silent auxiliary dial is balanced by another in the opposite corner, with a similar hand but marked 0 to 30 or 0 to 60, which could be mistaken by the uninitiated for a seconds dial, but seconds dials are very rare on bracket clocks and then mainly on late ones of provincial make. It is in fact a pendulum regulator for the clock; increasing the number makes the clock gain and decreasing it, lose.

Large numbers of clocks were made with pendulums rigidly fixed to the verge arbor and the only way of regulating these was to screw the small pear-shaped bob up or down from the back of the clock. A pendulum regulator dial implies a clock with a pendulum suspended from a spring, because the regulator moves the pendulum up or down between two 'chops' that fit closely each side of the suspension spring. This effectively alters the length of the pendulum and therefore its rate. The escapement may be verge or anchor.

The going train of a bracket clock has an extra wheel and pinion, and is a four wheel train compared with the three wheel train of the lantern clock. The great wheel, attached to the fusee, drives a centre wheel, which drives a third wheel, which drives a contrate wheel to drive the horizontal crown wheel through the centre, contrate and crown wheel pinions. The verge, across the crown wheel, is pivoted in the front, but at the back, where the pendulum is attached, terminates in a knife edge that rests in a V-shaped slot. The knife edge end is prevented from jumping out of its slot by an ⌐-section plate known as an 'apron'. The apron was sometimes elaborately pierced and engraved, as on the back plate of the Gretton clock numbered 46. Obviously this clock, which has a glazed door at the back, as was usual, was not meant to spend its life on a wall bracket.

With the introduction of the crutch, the arbor was pivoted at both ends and the apron became superfluous.

One more comment should be made on the anchor escapement. It was common practice to convert bracket clocks from verge to anchor. A lenticular (lens-shaped) bob was used with an anchor escapement instead of a pear-shaped bob. For carriage of the clock, a means of fastening the pendulum was often provided. With bob pendulums this is a form of hook screwed into the back plate to one side. The wire pendulum rod had enough springiness to be bent under it without damage. With lenticular pendulums, which often have flat strip rods, there was usually a piece into which a thumb screw could be placed to fasten the pendulum. A few special clocks had auxiliary dials with hands, which, when turned, brought down levers to lock the pendulum centrally. The clock numbered 22, has such an arrangement.

The bracket clock, unlike the lantern clock, is essentially a two hands clock. In the lantern clock, the hour wheel with its hand was driven from a pinion on the great wheel arbor. In the bracket clock, the minute hand is turned by the extended arbor of the second wheel, known as the centre wheel, which is centrally positioned and geared to turn once in an hour. Fitting over the part of the centre wheel arbor extending beyond the front plate is a short pipe, to the front of which the minute hand is attached. The other end of the pipe, behind the dial, is integral with a toothed wheel. The hour hand is carried on a similar pipe fitting loosely over the minute pipe, and is integral with a larger toothed wheel. A wheel and pinion, mounted together on a post, connect the two so that the overall gear ratio is 12 to 1. A friction washer between the minute wheel pipe and the centre wheel arbor enables the hands to be turned for setting without damaging the movement. The gearing between the hands is known as the 'motion work'.

Clocks designed to run for a month or more have one or two wheels and pinions interposed between the great wheel and centre wheel, the centre wheel becoming the third or fourth wheel in the train.

Early bracket clocks had count wheel (locking plate) striking, like the lanterns. By 1680 William Barlow had invented a new method of control, the toothed rack. At the hour, this rack drops on to the edge of a snail-shaped cam, and is wound back a number of teeth that corresponds to the number of blows to be struck. The snail is fixed so that it turns with the hour hand and therefore the striking cannot become out of phase with the time shown by the hands, as happens with count wheel striking and is a nuisance to correct. Rack striking had another great merit, especially at the time, when lighting was by candle. The clock could easily be made to repeat the hour previously struck. It was only necessary to have a lever and cord to release the rack when required. In fact, it is likely that Barlow's invention was primarily intended as a repeating mechanism, and that rack striking followed.

Many clocks were repeaters from around 1680. Some strike the hours and can be made to repeat them. Others have quarter striking which can be repeated. A popular system was to have the clock strike the hours, but only sound the quarters at will, a type generally known as a 'quarter repeater'. One later design that was made in some numbers sounded hours and quarters, and another design the hours only, by a repeater action. In this and the previous system, pulling the cord winds up a spring to operate the repeating mechanism so that an extra train driven by a mainspring is not needed, i.e. the quarter repeater only has a going and hour striking train, and the repeater timepiece has a single train.

Bracket clocks in the Wetherfield collection, dated from *c.* 1665 to *c.* 1820 and embrace the main styles of case. The very first seem to have been of two patterns. One is like the hood of a longcase clock, an example being the Markwick clock numbered 17. The other is architectural, like the East clock numbered 15, which has pillars, or the Stanton clock numbered 13 without them. The design became more or less standardised around 1675, which is the date of the earliest typical bracket clock in the collection, by Tompion, numbered 18.

The majority of these early clocks were ebonised, i.e. the cases were black. In general, the carcase was of another wood and veneered with ebony, but sometimes the blackness was obtained by staining. In the captions, it has been impossible to differentiate positively, because terminology was unsystematic in the past (and still has many anomalies). Cases were sometimes made of other woods, such as walnut, until mid-18th century, when mahogany was most favoured. Tortoiseshell veneer was not uncommon (number 19), but marquetry and lacquer, both common for long cases, were rare for bracket clocks.

The standardised bracket clock has a glazed and hinged front door, at first square and later taller than it was wide, opened by a key, for winding and hand setting. There is a similarly glazed door at the back, so that the pendulum can be reached for adjustment, or to fasten it for carriage. The back plates of earlier movements were often beautifully engraved with tulip or acanthus designs because they could be seen.

At the sides of the case are glass panels, or frets of wood or metal with coloured silk behind them, to allow the sound of the bell to escape. It has been suggested that glass is a replacement for broken frets. A number of clocks before the introduction of the break-arch dial, had a fret in the top bar of the door to allow sound to escape. The most characteristic feature, after the earliest styles, is the carrying handle at the top. It is not advisable to carry a bracket clock today by its handle, at least without support from underneath.

The top of the case is a guide to the time in which it was made, but a difficulty of description or nomenclature arises. A domed top is easily understood. It is a convex top suited to the case, so that it is rectangular in plan. Cescinsky and Webster[2] referred to it as a 'basket top', but the shape is

[2] 'English Domestic Clocks'. London, 1913.

not like a basket unless it is inverted. An example is the top of the clock by Joseph Knibb numbered 21. A bell has concave sides, and so therefore has a bell top such as that of the Emery clock numbered 63. A convex-sided top, as on the Trubshaw clock numbered 29, is called an 'inverted bell top'. The very decorative brass domed top, they called a 'brass basket top', and a brass one shaped like a cushion, a 'bell basket top'. To confuse the descriptions even more, a cushion-shaped brass basket top with a domed addition was called a 'double basket top'.

Other shapes they included were described with accuracy – the arch, broken arch (with shoulders), lancet and balloon, but various others that appear on longcase clocks were omitted. Other authors have tended to follow Cescinsky and Webster with variations. So that there will be no confusion, the names adopted here follow the illustrations on pages 72 to 76, to which some comments have been added. (There are sufficient pictures of longcase hoods not to require such drawings.) The same illustrations provide a date guide to the periods when the styles were in fashion.

Earlier clocks often had brass ornaments applied to the case, sometimes to the front of the top, sometimes to the sides of the door frame or top and bottom as well. The simplest form was a decorative keyhole on the left with a similar mock one on the right. When the case top was extra decorative, the handle was made so, too. The inverted bell top appeared around the turn of the 17th century. After a few years of the 18th, the broken arch dial and door aperture appeared, often used with a bell top. It was a major change in style and was followed by the broken arch top to the case, following the lines of the top of the dial.

Although the top of the dial appeared to have a broken arch, it was the aperture in the door that made it so at first; the dial plate was rectangular. The next major change was to the round dial, a few years before 1750. Again, the dial was at first square or rectangular; the domed glass in the door was round. From this developed, in the later 19th century, the round door, or brass bezel with a hinge.

The true arch top was later than the broken arch, not appearing until around 1770. At about the same time there was a more radical departure in style, to the so-called 'balloon' case, which followed an outline introduced in France at the end of the Louis XIV period and beginning of the Regency, around 1715, and today most commonly known by its Swiss name, the Neuchâteloise clock. The English produced a few too, and that by MacLennan numbered 65, in a later variant, produced for the Turkish market. The most popular derivation of the shape in England, the balloon, was not given that name until many years later, when the Montgolfier brothers' hot air balloons caught the public's imagination. The earliest of the two examples in the Wetherfield collection was noteworthy because of its original bracket (number 58).

The shape became so popular after the bracket clock age, that hundreds of thousands of small low-priced versions were turned out by Swiss and French factories for the English market. The cases themselves were often made in England, the movements being imported and fitted here.

Towards the end of the period, when styles altered during the Regency, the lancet top came into fashion. It was one of the periodic revivals of the Gothic arch motif. This, too, was turned out later by factories in a smaller size in large quantities. The flat top, the chamfer top, and the gadrooned top (not represented in the collection) came into favour at about the same time in the beginning of the 19th century.

The dial of the traditional bracket clock is constructed of two main parts, the dial plate and the annular chapter ring. Both are of brass, but the chapter ring is silvered. The dial plate is attached to the front plate of the movement by four pillars, and the chapter ring attached by studs pinned to the dial plate. The very earliest clocks had the corners of the dial plate engraved and the central zone, inside the chapter ring, finely matted or engraved.

Within a very short time of the introduction of the bracket clock, the engraved corners were superseded by cast and gilded ornaments called 'spandrels', which remained until the introduction of the one piece dial, later in the 18th century. Spandrels are a good guide to the age of a clock, but as each was fastened by a single screw from the back, they were easy to replace and should be considered with other features. All early spandrels were of the same design, of a cherub's face or mask in the centre of a pair of wings. An early spandrel of this pattern is recognisable by its high relief and fine finish. There are further comments in the longcase clock section.

Fire gilding is a method of applying a surface of ground gold to the brass by mixing the powdered gold into a paste with mercury, rubbing it on, and then burning off the mercury. It is a highly noxious process and rarely, if ever, used today, even in good restoration. Modern electro-gilding is a more convenient and less hazardous process and uses less gold. Later spandrels were just left as cast and lacquered, as were the rest of the exposed brass parts. Occasionally silver ornaments were used on a case with silver spandrels on the dial.

The zone on an early clock might be engraved with a Tudor rose in the centre and perhaps some tulips on a polished surface that was lacquered. It was soon superseded by matting, which was coarse at first, then fine and silky, but soon became more commercial. Matting was at first produced by the laborious process of using a hammer and punch. The process was speeded up by the use of a knurled roller, the track of which may usually be seen if the chapter ring is removed.

The chapter ring was from the start engraved with an inner double line divided into quarter hours and an outer one divided into minutes. Every five minutes was numbered within the minute ring. The hours were invariably engraved in Roman numerals, with ornaments between them marking the half hours. The engraving was filled with a hard black wax and glossed.

There are comments on dial changes in the longcase clock section, including half-quarter markers, such as those on the Gretton clock numbered 46.

A common indication in the zone of a bracket clock is what is called a 'mock pendulum', as in the Gretton clock just referred to. A moving disc in a slot in the upper part of the zone indicates that the pendulum is swinging. The slot is usually curved like a smile, the disc being attached to an arm fixed to the pallet arbor. Occasionally a clock is seen with a downturned 'mouth' for the disc, in which case, the disc is above the arbor. A day of the month indicator is sometimes seen on a bracket clock, but it is not a common feature, as it is on the longcase clock.

Dating Bracket Clocks

Here are some aids to dating bracket clocks, in addition to what the maker's history, if known, indicates.

The first bracket clocks appeared about 1660 and they were made until at least the First World War.

Many were made without wall brackets and are more accurately described as table clocks, and all later ones, up to the First World War, are in this category.

The universal pattern is a wooden case containing a movement with fusee and spring drive, two hands, and a handle on top of the case.

From the beginning, a short bob pendulum with crown wheel and verge escapement were employed in a plate frame.

Although bracket clocks were made with anchor escapement and short pendulum (with lenticular bob) after the introduction of the escapement, c.1670, many continued to be made with verge and bob pendulum until well after mid-18th century.

Anchor escapements gradually overtook the verge in the later 18th century.

Clocks made from c.1660 to c.1670 are rather like the tops of longcase clocks and larger and wider than what became the standard pattern. They have either Parthenon type tops or flat tops with twisted pillars.

Handles were not used on the tops of the earliest clocks, and when they first appeared, they were of simple cranked shape.

The domed top came into fashion at about 1670, being shallow at first.

The first cases were of veneered ebony or walnut, although a few were in olive wood. Ebony became the standard veneer for most bracket clocks, although walnut was still used.

Other finishes seen occasionally are tortoiseshell from about 1700, marquetry from about the same time, and lacquer from perhaps a few years later. Mahogany was used for a number of clocks from about mid-18th century, but ebony continued to be popular until the 19th century.

Ball feet, usually on stems, are seen on some clocks made a few years after c.1670. Some dating from this time, without feet, may have tell-tale holes in the base of the case.

Small bun feet are seen in some clocks dated before about 1685, although shallow square feet, or none at all, became standard practice.

Tops of cases are a helpful guide. See the diagrams on pages 72 to 76.

All bracket clocks had square, or later rectangular, dials until c.1720, when the break arch first appeared and became increasingly popular, at first slowly.

Most clocks after about mid-18th century have break arch dial apertures.

The round dial aperture appeared around 1760.

The break arch top began to accompany a break arch dial from c.1770, although isolated examples appeared much earlier.

The break arch top with a round dial is a combination that did not appear until later in the century and became popular in the early 19th century.

The band width of the chapter ring was narrow until about 1670. The hour hand for such a ring is of simple design with the pierced part having a flattened appearance and being near the tip. The minute hand is a plain pointer.

From *c.*1670, chapter rings began to grow in band width. The pierced part of the hour hand was made larger, triangular, and more elaborate. The minute hand was still a pointer, but with characteristic piercing near the boss.

The earliest clocks have engraved decoration on the corners of the dial plate, but applied spandrels soon became universal.

The sequence of spandrel design is a useful guide to date. Some examples are shown on page 54.

A Tudor rose is sometimes seen engraved in the centre of the dial of a clock made before *c.*1675.

The minute numerals are engraved between the two circles of the minute divisions of clocks before *c.*1680, when they were moved outside and became bigger over the years.

Quarter hour divisions, inside the chapters, began to disappear from about mid-18th century.

Mock pendulums are commonly seen on clocks from about 1680 to about 1770.

Auxiliary dials came into use about 1680.

The 1770s were years of considerable production of clocks with Turkish numerals for the Turkish market.

The balloon shape was introduced *c.*1770, but did not become very popular until some years later.

At the end of the first quarter of the 19th century, the traditional bracket clock was still being made in large numbers, but by embryo factories in London and Birmingham, mainly, and supplied to 'makers' all over the country with their names engraved on the movements and painted on the dials. They are commonly in cases veneered with mahogany or ebony with break-arch top and round dial. The side frets are usually of pierced brass with a fish scale pattern. Some are repeaters.

Towards the end of the century, the table clock with chamfer or gadrooned top appeared. There was also a return of fashion to the flat top. These clocks have no handle on top, but often handles on the sides.

Longcase Clocks

The longcase clock was an innovation of an English clockmaker, most likely Ahasuerus Fromanteel, who, despite his Dutch name, was a third-generation Englishman of Flemish origin, before the long pendulum made a long case essential. Fromanteel advertised pendulum clocks in October and November, 1658, so the longcase clock probably originated in that year or the next. The earliest known longcase clock is ascribed to A. Fromanteel, and Ronald A. Lee vouches for its authenticity.

Wetherfield did not own a clock by Ahaseurus, but did have one by his nephew, John, who brought the right to make pendulum clocks to his family in England while he was working for Salomon Coster of The Hague, licencee of the inventor, Christiaan Huygens.

The movement of an early longcase clock is very much like that of a bracket clock, except that it is weight-driven. It has a horizontal crown wheel, verge escapement, and bob pendulum about $10\frac{1}{2}$ inches long. The case was to enclose the weight or weights, and was therefore narrow, the clock in most cases being quite short, not far off 6 or $6\frac{1}{2}$ feet (2 m). The square dial was 10 inches (25.5 cm) or less across, and the chapter ring narrow, with simple hands, as described under bracket clocks.

It has been suggested that the longcase clock standing on the floor was derived from the hooded wall clock, into which some lantern clocks had developed. It was an obvious move to support the much heavier weights of the two-train eight-day clock. The case also prevented interference by children. Wooden standing cases had been made years previously on the continent, but none anything like the English development.

The parts of a longcase clock and their names are shown in the diagram on page 120. Bob pendulum longcase clocks have rising hoods. The hood has a fixed glass and two grooves up each side at the back, so that it will slide up and down on the backboard of the case. When raised, the hood is held up by an iron hook, so that the clock can be wound through the dial. When the hood is lowered, closing the door presses back a spoon-shaped metal lever, which locks the hood. The door itself is then locked by a key. It is necessary, therefore, to open the trunk door in order to wind or set the clock. This also encourages the owner to see that he does not wind on until jerked to a stop.

The invention of the anchor escapement, c.1670, introduced the long pendulum of about 39 inches (1 m) and beating seconds, i.e. swinging from one side to the other in a second. It was known at the time as a 'Royal pendulum', because of its dominance over the clock, probably to commemorate the restoration of the monarchy. Trunks of cases had to be wider to accommodate the swing of the pendulum, and clocks grew taller in proportion, so that it was difficult to raise the hood, or there was insufficient height to do so. The hood was redesigned with a glazed door that could be opened to wind the clock or set the hands, and to slide forwards, if access were needed to the movement. Some rising hoods were converted and given a glazed door.

The bob pendulum and verge movement of a longcase clock from 1658 to c.1670 differed from that of a bracket clock in that the fusees were replaced by barrels wound with gut lines carrying driving weights, and the spring barrels were omitted. Some had Huygens's endless cord system with a single weight driving the going and striking trains, but the general practice established was to use independent weights. The gut line is attached, not to the weight, but to the seatboard carrying the movement, and the weight hangs from a pulley in the loop. This doubles the time it takes the weight to fall, and therefore doubles the going time of the clock, but it means the weight has to be twice as heavy to produce the same power.

The layout of the plated frame is orthodox, with the going train on the right. Very early clocks had the top corners of the plates cut away so that they have concave shoulders, which seems to have been the original design of Fromanteel that other makers copied, but the practice was soon abandoned and the rectangular plate became universal. The movement is wound from the front, using a cranked key with a rotatable wooden knob handle. Clocks with pull-up winding, i.e. endless cord, may be spotted by the absence of winding holes in the dials. They run for about 30 hours, being intended for daily winding. Thirty-hour clocks with long pendulums in the next century became the longcase 'cottage clocks', made in hundreds of thousands all over the country. London makers concentrated on those going for eight days or longer.

The escape wheel for an anchor escapement and long pendulum was made with 30 teeth. The pendulum releases one tooth at every swing, but it jumps only half a tooth distance before another tooth is stopped. The wheel therefore turns once in 60 seconds, so makers attached a hand to the escape wheel arbor that indicated seconds on a small dial and this became common practice on longcase clocks with long pendulums. The first seconds hands were a central boss with a short pointer, and remained so until one with a tail was seen occasionally. The tail did not become popular until late in the 18th century.

Weights were made of lead, which was sheathed in polished brass cylinders for the better clocks until *c.*1740. Cast iron came along at the beginning of the industrialised 19th century, especially for clocks produced in quantity.

The system of weight drive did not provide maintaining power like Huygens's endless cord. This is particularly disadvantagous on a clock with short bob pendulum, because it tends to stop, but also with long pendulum clocks, in which the hands stop although the pendulum keeps swinging. Clockmakers devised a separate form of maintaining power, known as 'bolt and shutter'. It can be recognised on a clock by the shutters behind the winding holes preventing the insertion of a key.

Pulling a cord inside or outside the clock, or moving a lever at the side of the movement, lifts the shutter or shutters and at the same time causes a spring-loaded piece (that looks like the bolt of a lock) to press against a tooth of the centre wheel to keep the clock going during winding. When this wheel has moved sufficiently, after one or two minutes, the bolt jumps out of engagement and shutters close over the winding holes, the key having already been withdrawn (page 51).

Regulator clocks that were made after *c.*1760 have a different form of maintaining power, devised by the man who made the first accurate marine timekeeper, John Harrison. This arrangement has no apparent outer feature by which it may be recognised. A spring is interposed between the barrel and great wheel. The weight has to compress this spring in order to drive the clock. While the barrel is being turned backwards during winding, the compressed spring, prevented from moving back by an extra ratchet wheel and a click attached to the movement, continues to drive the clock.

Bolt and shutter maintaining power was fitted to many bob pendulum clocks and to better long pendulum clocks. The more often a clock has to be wound, the more it is liable to lose time without maintaining power, of course. Nevertheless, it was often incorporated in month clocks.

A relatively large number of month clocks was made from just before 1700 for ten years or so. To enable a clock to run for this time from the fall of a weight, the gear ratio of the going train has to be increased by interposing another wheel and pinion between the great wheel and centre wheel, which requires a heavier weight, and also means the clock has to be wound contra-clockwise. Month clocks are usually more carefully made so that excessively heavy weights are not necessary.

The striking train has to run correspondingly longer because at least four and a half times the number of hammer blows are needed. Joseph Knibb neatly side-stepped the problem by introducing Roman striking to England. Every hour can be sounded by no more than four strokes. One blow on the lower pitched of two bells represents V and a blow on the higher one represents I. Thus the hour of IV is *ding-dong*, that of VII, *dong-ding-ding*. Two blows on the bell indicate X, so XI is *dong-dong-ding*. Clocks with Roman striking have IV engraved on the dial, instead of the usual IIII.

Quarter chiming was not incorporated in the earliest clocks; when it was introduced later in the 17th century, the two bell ting-tang was employed. By the turn of the century, some clocks had chiming on as many as six or eight bells, the hammers of which were controlled by a pin barrel. It was most usual to run through the scale at the first quarter, run through it twice at the half hour, and so on. Some clocks did the same with a simple tune. One clock in the collection has the simplest system of all, commonly used in French clocks. It strikes a single note at every half hour, and the maker had a French name, I. Papavoigne.

A few clocks were built with Dutch striking, in which two bells with different notes were employed. At the hour, say two o'clock, the clock sounds *dong-dong* on the lower bell. At half past two, it sounds *ting-ting-ting* on the higher bell. In other words, it sounds the next hour on a higher bell at half hours.

A few longcase clocks were fitted with *grande sonnerie* during the first 30 or so years of the 18th century. These are straightforward chiming clocks, but, in addition, strike the previous hour after each of the first three quarters. Musical trains were occasionally incorporated in the 18th century, but not as often as in bracket clocks. The 'Tulip Tompion' bracket clock numbered 22 has *grande sonnerie*, and is earlier than most at 1680–1685. There are longcase clocks by W. Kipling of *c.*1735 and G. Lindsay of *c.*1770 with musical trains, numbered 183 and 192.

Striking was at first controlled by a count wheel (locking plate), situated on the back of the back plate until about 1680, when it was moved to the side of the great wheel of the striking train. An outside count wheel (or locking plate) may be seen on page 52. Rack striking, which prevents the striking from becoming out of step with the time indicated, a fault of the earlier system, was invented between 1675 and 1680. It was introduced fairly quickly by London makers, but many provincial ones were using count wheels until at least 1750.

Repeating work, common on bracket clocks with rack striking, is not so on London-made longcase clocks, but two in the collection were fitted with it, by C. Gould (*c.*1700) and I. Nickals (*c.*1740) numbered 129 and 187. It is, however, fairly often found on provincially-made clocks from the later 18th into the first quarter of the 19th century.

There was a short period after the introduction of the long pendulum during which several leading makers, including William Clement, who is credited with the invention of the anchor escapement, experimented with extra long pendulums of about 61 inches (1.55 m) beating 1¼ seconds.

Sometimes such a clock can be recognised at a distance by a lenticle (circular or oval glass) in the plinth, instead of the door.

Auxiliary control dials, common on bracket clocks, first as sectors – as with the Tompion bracket clock numbered 22, and then as circles, do not appear to have been used on longcase clocks until the break-arch was introduced about 1710, and then mainly as a circular dial with a stiff hand having a tail.

What became almost universal in longcase clocks was a date aperture. Numbers 1 to 31 are engraved around an annular ring that has 31 corresponding saw teeth on the inner periphery. Over a period of a few hours before midnight, a tooth is moved by a pin on a 24-hour wheel. Ends of shorter months are adjusted by hand, taking off the hood and reaching behind the dial. Some date rings have small indentations under the numbers so that they can be moved from the front with the aid of a pin.

To avoid the nuisance of making such adjustments, some clocks, such as that by F. Gregg numbered 168, have annual calendars. A much larger disc has all the months and dates for an entire year engraved around the outer edge. It is turned a tooth daily in the same way as the month disc, but over 365 days, so that it has only to be adjusted by hand on leap years, to show February 28 twice.

The Gregorian calendar was adopted in England on September 2 in 1752, so the calendar of the Gregg clock, made before that date, would have been moved on 11 days that night, to September 14, and thereafter only adjusted on leap years.

A few clocks were made with calendars that adjusted themselves by adding another day to February on leap years. They are correctly known as 'perpetual calendars' (although to be truly perpetual, they would also have to omit the correction every century year that is not evenly divisible by 400; the next is the year 2000).

In the past, the terms 'annual' and 'perpetual' were used indiscriminately for year calendars.

As there was no time service, clocks had to be set to local time (Greenwich Mean Time was not introduced until 1880) by comparison with a local sundial, and it was not uncommon for a clockmaker to supply a garden sundial with a high quality clock. A sundial shows hours of different lengths throughout the year, but the clock shows what used to be called 'equal hours'. In other words, 24 hours by the sundial may be longer or shorter than 24 hours by the clock. During the year, the sundial can 'drift' to as much as $16\frac{1}{2}$ minutes ahead of the clock to about $14\frac{1}{4}$ minutes behind it. To equate the two, 'Equation of Time tables' were available, the first having been published in 1672. They were accurate enough for the time, and, of course, showed the old calendar before the end of 1752. Occasionally, an equation table is found pasted on the inside of the trunk door of a longcase clock.

With the publication of such figures, it became obvious to clockmakers that an annual calendar could be engraved with the minutes to add to or subtract from solar time on any day of the year. This is a feature of the Gregg dial, and is known as an 'equation dial' or 'equation clock'. Daniel Quare's year clock of c.1700 numbered 126 shows the Equation of Time on one subsidiary dial and an annual calendar on another.

A later mechanism operated a hand moving backwards or forwards over a small circular dial, or more usually over a sector in a break-arch dial, to indicate how much the sun was fast or slow of the clock at any time. The hand was operated by a kidney-shaped cam that turned once in a year, another invention that can be credited to the remarkable Christiaan Huygens, in 1695. However, Joseph Williamson claimed the invention and to have produced every equation clock made in England up to 1719. He worked for Quare and made the equation work for Quare's clocks. An equation clock by Williamson of c.1725 is shown numbered 173.

Dials showing the phase and age of the Moon are almost as early as clocks showing the hours. There is a clock with such an indication dated c.1700, by Fromanteel and Clarke, numbered 127, but they were not often incorporated in longcase clocks before the introduction of the break-arch dial, which was well shaped for their location. London makers do not seem to have been much concerned with Moon dials, but they were popular with country makers, particularly after about mid-18th century.

A lunation is approximately $29\frac{1}{2}$ days. Since it is impossible to have $29\frac{1}{2}$ teeth turned a tooth a day, twice that number, 59, was cut and a tooth moved every 12 hours. A Moon face behind a circular aperture shows the phase and a number near the edge of the disc, the age. A Moon dial in an arch has 118 teeth, which is advanced a tooth every 12 hours, so that the disc turns once every two lunations. It has two Moon faces painted on it, diametrically opposite each other. The aperture in the break-arch (see the Hawkins clock of c.1775 numbered 191) is shaped so that it conceals both Moon faces at New Moon. The Moon on the left then gradually waxes until the central position, when it is full, and wanes behind the semi-circular hump on the right, when the other face is due to follow.

The same moving dial will give not just the Moon's age, but the state of the local tide, because the varying gravitational pull of the Moon according to its age is mainly responsible for the tides. Another factor is the configuration of the local estuary or harbour, so a tidal clock was often made for a particular place. However, some makers discovered that the ring with the tidal times only had to be made friction tight to provide a universal dial that could be set for any place. Tidal times are usually in roman figures to avoid any confusion with the Moon's age in arabic figures. The Isaac Nickals clock of c.1740 numbered 187 has a tidal dial.

The purpose of auxiliary dials on musical clocks is self-evident, to select the tunes and to silence them at will, and sometimes to repeat a tune. There are often seven tunes, one for each day of the week, including perhaps a religious one for Sundays.

From the beginning, the brass dial of the longcase clock was made of two pieces, a square dial plate and a circular band bearing the hours or chapters, the chapter ring. Very soon four ornamental spandrels were added, by screwing each to a corner of the dial plate by passing a screw through a hole in the dial plate into a threaded hole in the spandrel. The dial plate was first polished and engraved. Very soon it became the standard practice to matt the zone, the central area, and gild the dial plate and spandrels while the chapter ring was silvered or occasionally made of silver.

The chapter ring is attached to the dial plate by four short pillars (the dial feet), the shouldered ends of which pass through holes in the dial plate and are secured by taper pins. The dial plate is fixed to the front plate of the movement in the same way. From about 1770, specialist dial makers began to supply one-piece painted iron dials. To overcome the lack of standardisation, they sometimes introduced a false plate made of iron, to which the dial was attached by the usual four feet. The clockmaker could then use three or four feet on the false plate where he wished, to avoid striking and other work on the front plate of the movement. False plates are not ordinarily found on London clocks.

The sequence of changes in style of dials is much the same as with bracket clocks, except for the size, which is much more significant with longcase clocks. It increased from under 10 inches (25.5 cm) square and, in most cases, to about 11 inches (28 cm) before 1700, and then grew to about 12 inches (30 cm), and in some cases 14 inches (36 cm) as the years of the square dial passed. The break-arch, which was gradually introduced from about 1710 or a little later and became the most common shape before mid-century, was usually about 12 inches wide by 16 inches tall (30 by 41 cm).

Early dials have chapter rings with narrow bands and hands to suit. Between the Roman numerals are decorations representing half hours. Twin circles engraved inside the chapters are divided into 48, four divisions between each hour, to represent the quarters. Outside the chapters, another twin ring is engraved and divided into 60 to represent minutes. Usually these are numbered every five minutes, but occasionally the maker of an early clock numbered every minute, as on the John Knibb clock of c. 1676 numbered 73.

Minutes were at first numbered by small figures appearing within the ring of minute divisions, but as the chapter ring was widened, from about 1680 to 1685, the minute numerals were moved outside the minute divisions, which is a useful dating point. Thereafter, minute numerals became bigger and bigger, until they reached their optimum size about 1725. Minute divisions were retained throughout the longcase period, but the numerals were omitted occasionally towards the end.

Quarter hour divisions, a relic of the one-hand clock, were important to an early owner, it seems, because he would read the quarter from the hour, and not the minute hand, being confused by two concentric hands. They persisted for many years, to 1750 and beyond in many clocks, until, it seems, even the most unsophisticated owner had become used to reading quarters from the minute hand.

Because the quarter was a much used interval of time, the next division that came into common use was the half-quarter. Some makers appear to have thought it important enough to mark half-quarters outside the minute ring from about 1690 to, say, 1710. It may have been a fashionable London fad without much significance. Usually the pattern is related to that of the half hour ornament.

Half hour ornaments do not vary much, usually being a *fleur-de-lys*, or some modification of it, a diamond, three balls in a triangle joined by lines, or an ornamental H-shaped design. They overlapped and appeared at different times, but some makers favoured one or another. All clocks had them until about 1725, and most continued to do so until about 1750, when not only half, but quarter hour divisions were often omitted. Usually a single engraved line was left where the hour divisions used to be, but even that began to go around 1790.

The two-part dial was gradually superseded from around 1770 by a one-piece dial, which was simply a dial plate with all the dial information on it. There were two types, a brass dial silvered all over with the indications engraved on it and filled with black wax (such dials were used by Graham for his 'regulators' from c.1740 on), and the iron dial with painted indications and decoration. The first was more expensive and used by a few of the later London makers. The Vulliamy clock numbered 209 and Mudge and Dutton clock of c.1790 numbered 210, are examples.

The painted dial was at first plain with simple ornamentation based on the previous brass dials, which became more elaborate and scenic as the years passed. Painted dials were seldom a feature of London clocks. There was one in the collection bearing the name of C. Haley, London (c.1780) and another by a West Country maker, C. Moore, dated about 1790.

True enamelled dials, i.e. finished by vitreous enamel fired on the surface, including the indications and decorations, are rare on longcase clocks, but there are two examples in this book, by R. Comber (c.1778) and T. Clare (c.1790) numbered 199 and 206. One of the problems of manufacture was to fire such a large surface without blemish and without warping, which was usually countered by enamelling both sides. Another problem was that the enamel was easily chipped around the winding holes. Comber overcame this hazard by locating the winding squares below the dial.

Spandrels passed through several distinctive design phases that are useful guides to date. Some are shown on page 54. It must be remembered that, as they were screwed on, they could easily have been changed. The same remark applies to hands. Some makers had their own hand designs before specialist hand makers 'flooded the market', but spandrels seem to have been the product of a specialist trade much earlier. Early spandrels are in high relief and have obviously been well finished by filing and burnishing before gilding. The relief became less as the spandrels became more elaborate, and with foliage designs there was rarely much attempt, if any, to clean them up at all after casting. The twin cherub designs are in two main patterns, as illustrated, the main difference being that one has a wider crown and the cherubs hold crossed maces as well as the crown. The idea of having two figures undoubtedly came about because William and Mary were on the throne. Their reign was from 1689 to 1702, which gives a starting date for the fashion of about 1690, but it continued until about 1730 or so. The examples in the collection are nearly all of the crossed mace style, which is to be expected as it was most favoured by London makers. The use of other patterns can be followed by reading the captions.

Early hands, already mentioned under bracket clocks, are easily recognised, especially when associated with narrow chapter rings. They were made to fit the chapter rings, the lengths being exactly right for the scales. This attention to detail soon went with the change in style of the hands and the wider chapter rings. The major changes in style were to the cross-over pattern of the hour hand, still with a pointer minute hand, about 1770, and to matching hands, where the tips of hour and minute hands were the same, about 1800.

Signatures of makers were at first engraved along the bottom edge of the dial plate, with their locations, and Latinised, as in *Chr Gould Londini Fecit*, but some soon favoured English, and by about *c.*1700, Latin had been almost abandoned, although the Gould example (no. 167) is an exception, the clock being dated 1715. Tompion liked to sign his clocks on a panel or cartouche on the zone, from at least *c.*1680, and was followed by others.

The day of the month aperture is usually square and somewhere in the lower part of the zone, although there was a fashion for round holes for a period from *c.*1680 to 1700 or later in London. This was a time when decorative engraving was being used to embellish the area around spandrels. Early dial plates had engraved borders, a feature that did not survive long into the 18th century on London-made clocks.

The zone, as mentioned, was at first polished. When matting took over, as with many other features, it was at first well executed, but soon deteriorated. Generally it is finer on quality clocks. Winding holes are most of the time plain, but a ringed hole appeared about 1680 and can still be seen on some clocks dated *c.*1730. One distinctive feature that had a short, but apparently popular life, was the skeletonised chapter ring. There are several examples in these pages dating between *c.*1675 and 1680.

Fromanteel's first cases were constructed on a carcase of oak, veneered with ebony or with pearwood stained black to resemble ebony, the process known as 'ebonising'. Oak and pine were also stained to ebonise them. The long case was panelled on the sides and door, which is long with three panels, the middle one being shorter than the other two. Such a case was usually short, around 6 feet (1.8 m), and narrow, because the pendulum was only about 10 inches (25.5 cm) long, with an architectural (portico) top hood with plain pillars and brass capitals. Fromanteel's casemaker was a Joseph Clifton of Bull Head Yard, Cheapside, London, the only casemaker of the time of whom a record has been found. The style followed that of Dutch and German cabinets. Edward East followed the architectural style of Fromanteel and his partner Thomas Loomes, but soon other makers began to favour the flat hood with barley twist pillars, the same trend as with bracket clocks, as well as other woods, and the ebonised architectural style vanished.

There is a clear distinction outwardly of clocks made before and after *c.*1670–1675, mainly in size, because that was when the long pendulum came into universal favour. There was, however, another major style change that makes an invaluable dating point and is purely stylistic. Below the hood is a moulding attached to the top of the case, to lead the eye from the narrow trunk to wider hood. Before about 1700, this was convex. Afterwards, over a period of only a few years, it became concave and remained so through many fashions and other changes of design.

The longcase clock, being a dominant feature of a room, was usually regarded as much a piece of furniture as a clock, much more so than the average bracket clock. It was therefore more susceptible to trends in fashion, particularly in woods and case finishes, although not usually in step with furniture. It is unfortunate that so little is known of the casemakers, whose work is sometimes more admired than that of the clockmaker whose signature appears on the dial.

The first ebony veneering and ebonising was followed by walnut and enjoyed no real revival. Burr walnut, in which the grain makes attractive complex patterns was a favourite for fine clocks, but olive wood, mulberry, burr elm and amboina (sometimes spelt amboyna) were also used.

There are two means of making veneers. One, the earliest, but still used for certain woods, is to cut four sides off a tree trunk to leave a thick baulk. One side is shaved to produce veneers in much the same way as a board is planed. The other method is to shave a trunk in a form of lathe, so that the veneer comes off like a roll of paper being unwound, and larger sizes of veneered sheet become available. Grain patterns almost repeat themselves by veneering, so that mirror image panels, known as 'book-matching' are possible.

When the part of a trunk where a branch joined is cut to produce veneer, a V-pattern of grain appears. If a tree has been heavily pruned, the grain becomes knurled, and a pollarded tree is cut back so hard that the knurled grain produces the attractive patterns in burr walnut, burr elm, and one or two other woods. Olive wood is naturally whorled because of the stunted growth of the tree and makes a fine veneer that was employed from the last quarter of the 17th century. Young olive wood trees were sometimes cut across the grain to provide small circular or oval pieces of veneer with close concentric ring patterns. They were used to make an all-over pattern with other veneers filling the gaps. Such cases were called 'oyster cases' because of the likeness to patterns on oyster shells.

Walnut was sometimes used in the solid, but it was usually laid as a veneer on a carcase of oak. Carcases were sometimes made of pine, and increasingly so as the years passed. Sometimes an oak carcase has a pine backboard. Walnut, although in the background during the marquetry period, still retained favour for some fine clocks into the 1760s.

The early ebony cases sometimes had metal ornaments, such as swags across the top of the hood, applied to them. These were abandoned with the new woods, but carved wooden cresting became a popular alternative to the unadorned flat top until nearly the end of the 18th century. In the meantime, from around the 1680s, a domed top to the hood was challenging the earlier styles. With the dome, metal ornaments were often reintroduced, in the form of finials. Nearly all these cases had barley twist pillars. Before the end of the century, a great variety of hood designs was appearing, and straight pillars re-emerged. The flat top continued, but on taller cases and often with finials. Domed tops became taller and more elaborate, again often with finials. A form of break arch combined with the dome appeared, and also the exaggerated bell profile style, that became more popular later, and was called a 'pagoda top'.

Until about 1710 or just after, hood tops were of the styles referred to, or true bell (which is convex in the front as well as the two sides, as distinct from the pagoda top, with a flat front and curved sides), or inverted bell. The break-arch top, introduced about this time, was employed by Tompion in a clock of *c.*1710 in the pure form with a break-arch dial, but most other makers, for some years, combined it with other shapes to create what were somewhat overbearing hoods, such as that on the T. Clift clock of *c.*1730, numbered 180.

After mid-18th century, hoods were less elaborate, but still following classical styles, flat top, dome, break-arch, pagoda, and even an occasional architectural. The only new styles were rare and introduced under the influence of the furniture designers, such as the Chippendale case of J. Holmes, *c.*1775, numbered 198.

The art of laying a veneer led naturally to cutting veneers into shapes to make patterns. The first were geometrical patterns of light, dark and coloured woods as well as other materials such as ivory, sometimes stained. The patterns included the rosette, star, and fan shapes, laid in small areas and known as 'parquetry'. At the same time, or even earlier, panels of veneer were separated by thin lines of a differently coloured wood veneer known as 'stringing'. Stringing commonly followed the edge of a door or edges of a case. Wider lines of veneer are called 'banding'.

Parquetry was introduced about 1670 and was superseded in London about 1680 by the more complicated marquetry. It had a revival in provincial clocks of the later 18th century. Patterns in marquetry are applied in the same way as those of parquetry. On clocks, they represent stems, leaves, scrolls, flowers, birds, and often human or mythical figures.

A pattern was drawn in outline on a large sheet of thin paper, which was placed on a sheet of veneer of, say, a light coloured wood, and the design pricked into the wood with a steel needle along the outlines. The points were joined up with a marker. Four sheets of light-coloured wood were made into an eight sheet sandwich with sheets of dark-coloured wood and fastened in a special sawing donkey so that the sandwich was vertical in front of the operator. The donkey holds a fretsaw with an extremely thin blade in a jig so that it is always square to the work and the operator can saw round the lines directly in front of him.

Sawing produces four sets of marquetry, light on a dark ground and dark on a light ground, to make four cases. For every case of a certain pattern, there should be another, somewhere, with the same pattern, but the woods reversed. (See Appendix).

At first, marquetry was applied in panels, often of oval shapes on the trunk door, as may be seen by looking through the illustrations. The ovals grew in size and began to join up around 1685. It is curious that the art of marquetry seems to have arrived in England fully developed, because it had no heritage. There was a history of development in Holland, however, so that there is little doubt that early English cases were made by Dutch immigrant cabinet makers. With William of Orange and Mary on the throne, there was little obstacle to Dutch craftsmen wanting to work in London.

Gradually, casemakers became more ambitious, applying marquetry not only all over the trunk, including the sides and moulding under the hood, but all over the hood itself. Flowers, foliage and birds continued to be the most popular themes, but often with human figures in scenes, like the warrior slaying a dragon on the clock by C. Bonner, *c.*1701, numbered 151. Marquetry pieces with human figures are called 'grotesques'.

Makers of marquetry cases began to show their skills with more and more complicated designs. Flowers and birds gave way to more complex designs of foliage and stems that looked rather like interwoven seaweed, so that it became known as 'seaweed marquetry'. An example is the clock by Windmills, *c*.1700, numbered 124. The interlacing of foliage, stems, scrolls, spirals, zig-zags, knots, and so on, is also called 'arabesque marquetry'.

Marquetry cases were well represented in the Wetherfield collection, and its decline in the years before about 1715 may be seen in the pictures. Walnut again became the main veneer for good clocks. After the introduction of marquetry, a quite different kind of finish, lacquering, was applied to many longcase clocks. Few seem to have been collected by Wetherfield; such cases do not withstand the attrition of use and climate over the years as well as other finishes, although modern central heating is now taking its toll of veneering and marquetry. 'Lacquering' was invented some centuries BC by the Chinese who used a hard, waterproof varnish from the sap of a tree. The process was introduced into Japan, where craftsmen changed to another varnish derived from the lac insect, hence the names 'shellac' and 'lacquering'.

The process introduced into England for clocks from *c*.1695 to *c*.1715 or later, was that of the Japanese, and should properly be called 'Japanese lacquering' or 'japanning'. A ground of gesso (plaster of Paris) is applied to the case and coloured black, usually, or red, but sometimes blue, green, yellow, cream, or buff. Decorative scenes, almost always oriental, are built up in relief in gesso and painted in various colours, almost always including gold. The whole is covered with transparent lacquer. There was a period, from 1715 to 1745, according to Cesinsky and Webster, when cases were sent to Japan in the old tea ships to be lacquered, but this has not been substantiated.

A new wood, mahogany, found favour with furniture makers, but not at first with clock case makers, perhaps because of the difficulty of veneering it. A change in the import regulations in the 1720s provided cabinet makers with a choice of woods that had previously been too expensive, the most pleasing of which was so-called 'Spanish mahogany', because it came from the Spanish colonies in the West Indies.

Mahogany was increasingly used for clock cases from *c*.1755, at first in the solid and then increasingly as veneers on oak cases, like other woods, as well as on softwood carcases. The earliest Spanish mahogany was heavy, straight-grained, hard, had a dark red or brown colour, and was resistant to woodworm. It was supplemented by mahogany from Cuba, which was lighter in colour and could have a wavy grain. Both were largely superseded by Honduras mahogany, also a red-brown in colour, but lighter in weight and more suitable for furniture that was moved. Feathered patterns were obtained by veneer cut from where a branch had joined a trunk. Curved patterns on some veneers, typical of Cuban mahogany, are called 'Cuban curls'.

Solid oak was very occasionally employed for London cases, and often for country productions. London oak cases were usually made for technical clocks. Oak was no favourite with Wetherfield, although represented. Oak was sometimes veneered on a carcase of the same or another wood. Pollard oak, which has a grain of short straight lines and broader wavy, light coloured feathers across it, was most often used as a veneer.

Later solid mahogany and solid oak cases were often inlayed with simple fan, shell, or other patterns in the centre of the trunk door and its corners, as well, perhaps in the plinth. If the clock case is veneered, the same decorations would have been laid as veneers. An inlay comprises chiselling the intaglio pattern in the wood in order to glue in the shaped inlay pieces. Ivory or bone was used as well as woods. As well as the usual narrow stringing, cross-banding was popular. This is a wider band of a quarter of an inch (6 mm) or more, cut as a veneer across the grain.

After, say, *c*.1760, mahogany was the most popular wood in London. Styles became more functional, like the regulator clock, but with an orthodox dial. Mahogany was the last wood used by London makers, when they gave up longcase clockmaking, except for a few isolated makers. The time was soon after the end of the 19th century. The furniture designer, Thomas Sheraton, wrote in 'The Cabinet Maker' of 1805 that 'these pieces (longcase clocks) are almost obsolete in London'. Production in the provinces was still substantial, however, and there was a steam factory in Clerkenwell, London, turning out large numbers of traditional longcase clocks for country clockmakers, as well as a long-established partnership in the same area producing 'bread and butter' bracket and longcase clocks for London and country makers, whose names were engraved on the movements and marked on the dials. The most prolific clockmaking counties of the later period, after 1770, say, were Yorkshire and Lancashire, but by no means the only ones. There were clockmakers in most towns of any size over the whole kingdom, who gradually became retailers, many still in business as such today.

As a broad guide, woods for long cases fall into the following periods:

Ebony and ebonised, solid and veneered (usually)
1668–1675 and at intervals rarely until at least 1735

Parquetry, at first in laburnum and olive wood – 1670–1680

Marquetry in panels – 1675–1700

Marquetry all over – 1690–1725

Walnut, solid or veneered (usually), and veneered burr walnut for high quality
1670–1730 and then occasionally in the south to end of period

Solid oak, later veneered pollard oak
1690 and at intervals rarely in London to end, but very commonly outside London to end. Carved oak in provinces, 1760–1790

Japanese lacquer
1695–1715 and at intervals to at least 1775, later versions usually outside London

Mahogany
1720, but rarely until 1750, and then very commonly to end

Olive wood, olive oyster pieces, laburnum, burr elm, rosewood, amboina, yew, mulberry, satinwood and cocus wood, all veneered, as well as tortoiseshell
1675–1700, but only very rarely

Solid pine wood, painted or grained and perhaps decorated
1750 to end, but outside London and for cheap productions only

Regulators

The regulator, or regulator clock, was built solely for accuracy and acquired a case and dial style of its own. There were five fine examples in the collection. George Graham was amongst the first to make regulators, which originally had standard long cases – usually of oak – and orthodox dials. The difference was that they were timepieces, so that there was no striking to interfere with the accuracy of the going train, which had a dead-beat escapement, an accurate version of the anchor escapement perfected by Graham c.1715. They also had maintaining power (usually of the Harrison type), and a temperature-compensated pendulum. The mercury compensating bob was invented by Graham in 1721, and gridiron compensating pendulum rod by Harrison in 1726. The dead-beat escapement has no recoil, unlike the anchor, the seconds hand of which may be seen recoiling.

The regulator acquired a different style of dial to eliminate the motion work, a source of friction and sloppiness in the drive. This coincided with the introduction of the one-piece silvered brass dial. Each hand is separate, with its own ring of numbers. Usually, the long central hand shows minutes, with a smaller seconds hand in the top of the dial and a smaller hour hand in the bottom. Sometimes the hour is shown by a moving disc engraved with the chapters and showing through an aperture in the dial, as with the Graham regulator of c.1740 numbered 186. The minute hand is usually counterbalanced internally and the seconds hand has a tail to counterbalance it.

Dating Longcase Clocks

Here are some notes on dating longcase clocks, apart from what the maker's dates and history may indicate.

In general, the shorter and narrower the case, the older the clock.

Cases panelled in the cabinet style were made from c.1660 to c.1690.

From c.1660 to c.1670, side windows in the hood were the same depth as the front window of the hood.

The architectural or portico top lasted from the beginning to about 1685, and reappeared towards the end of the 18th century.

The flat top was introduced soon after the longcase and was the most popular style until about 1710. It was popular again nearer the end of the century in London and throughout the century in the provinces.

Carved cresting on the front of the flat topped hood (and very occasionally on the sides also) was popular from c.1670 to c.1690.

The domed hood appeared about 1680, being shallower at first, and continued in popularity during the first quarter of the 18th century.

46

Some clocks had a fret backed by coloured silk above the dial opening from *c.*1675 for a few years.

The rising (lift-up) hood, used on the earliest clocks, that were short, persisted to about 1700, even on some 7 feet (2.13 m) clocks with long pendulums.

Some rising hoods were converted to forward sliding ones with doors, however.

Barley twist (spiral) columns, introduced about 1660, went out of fashion *c.*1690 in London, but persisted in some clocks by provincial makers until *c.*1715.

Before about 1700–5, there was convex moulding underneath the hood. After then it was made concave.

Plain pillars were almost universal throughout the 18th century.

A flat or domed top with ball or other finials was fashionable from *c.*1700 to *c.*1710, but was made at other times.

Many case doors had lenticles of plain glass, or bullseyes, in the case doors from *c.*1670 to *c.*1715.

The break arch hood top with a break arch dial gradually became popular after *c.*1720 and was common in the second half of the century.

Swan's neck cresting was introduced before 1750, but not favoured by London makers, although it became very popular with provincial and colonial makers of longcase clocks.

Case doors had straight edges until a few years before 1750, when wavy edges were introduced by some casemakers.

Woods used and their periods are listed on pages 45 to 46.

In general, the narrower the chapter ring the older the clock.

Earliest clocks with narrow chapter rings had distinctive hour hands with pierced spade-like hands and minute pointers, with no seconds hand. The hands fitted the scales of the chapter ring exactly, unlike almost all later hands.

Every minute numbered usually indicates a date before 1680, but some were made as late as 1700.

Half hour ornaments were introduced from the beginning, but by 1720, some makers were omitting them. After about 1750, few makers, except some in the provinces, retained them.

Quarter hour divisions, used from the beginning, began to disappear from about 1720 (Graham started the trend before then), and were used by some provincial makers after about 1750.

Half-quarter ornaments had a short vogue from *c.*1670 to *c.*1690.

Minute numerals were moved outside the divisions ring about 1680–5 and became larger and larger on most clocks until about 1725.

Seconds hands, introduced with the long pendulum, *c.*1670, were pointers without tails until *c.*1710–15, when they began to 'sprout' tails.

Skeletonised chapter rings had a vogue from *c.*1670 to *c.*1690.

Spandrels developed fairly consistently from the original simple winged cherub's head. See page 54.

Ringed winding holes were often used from *c.*1690 to *c.*1710, but also appeared at other times.

Break-arch dials were almost universal for London clocks after *c.*1725, although introduced by Tompion as early as 1695. They became very popular with provincial makers in the later century, although square dials were still made.

One-piece silvered dials were introduced about 1770, and one-piece painted dials at the same time. The first were of brass and the second of iron.

Matching hands also came in about 1770. Before then, the minute hand was always a pointer. See page 55.

Vitreous enamel dials are rare and usually of the last quarter of the 18th century.

The earliest movements had shouldered tops to the plates.

Very early movements may have 'Dutch' bell hammers, moving in a horizontal instead of a vertical plane.

All longcase clocks made before *c.*1670, and many until *c.*1675, had short bob pendulums, about 10 inches long.

After the long pendulum was introduced because of the invention of the anchor escapement, *c.*1670, a few makers experimented with very long pendulums reaching almost to the bottom of the case.

Bolt and shutter maintaining power was used from the beginning, but gradually went out of favour in the first quarter of the 18th century.

Before *c.*1680, count wheels were on the outsides of back plates, and after then between the plates.

Rack striking was rapidly introduced after *c.*1680 in London, but at a much slower rate outside, where some provincially-made clocks still had count wheel (locking plate) striking after 1750.

The dead-beat escapement, a more accurate anchor, was invented in 1715, and the temperature compensated pendulum in 1721 (mercury bob) and 1726 (gridiron rod).

Always note where the makers worked. There can be as much as a half a century difference in dates for the same style, particularly in technical features. Case features frequently recur in provincial clocks after having been abandoned by London makers. In general, provincial makers were more prolific after mid-18th century, with peak production in the 1770s and 1780s.

This completes the brief and elementary survey of clock features. It should be emphasised that most of the remarks apply to London clocks (and Wetherfield ones in particular) which set the fashions. Styles outside London have been referred to where relevant, but not in detail, because that is a separate study. Finally, because of the dispersal of the clocks and the almost impossible task of discovering facts about most of them, this volume must inevitably be incomplete. It is hoped, however, that it will stimulate those who do know of their present whereabouts, to add to the fund of information.

Technical Features

Frames and Plates

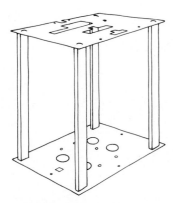

1600 onwards The posted frame originated from the 13th century. The brass frame of the lantern clock, with turned pillars, was developed from it. It reverted to the earlier form, as shown, for many country-made 30-hour longcase clocks.

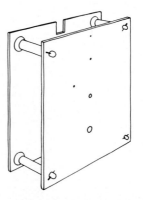

1660 onwards The plated frame of the bracket and longcase clock allowed more freedom for planting the trains, which could now be side-by-side. Although a more rigid construction (apart from a brief habit of splitting the front plate, *c.*1670–1675), it made assembly more difficult.

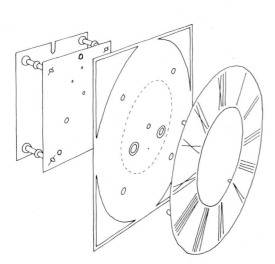

1660–1800 Separate dial plate and chapter ring, held by studs and taper pins, for longcase and bracket clocks.

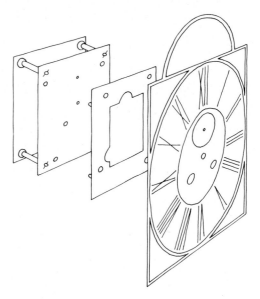

1775–1860 A false plate was often used for one-piece dials, so that they could easily be fitted to movements by various makers. Such dials are usually painted on iron.

Power Sources

1600–1670 Direct weight drive for lantern clocks, with separate weights for each train.

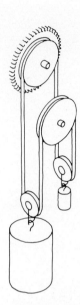

1660 onwards Huygens endless rope (or chain) with weight and pulley drive, for lantern and 30-hour longcase clocks. Known as 'pull-up winding'. One weight provided power for both trains.

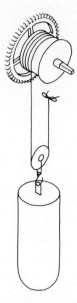

1660 onwards Weight and pulley drive, for longcase clocks going for eight days or more. Wound by key.

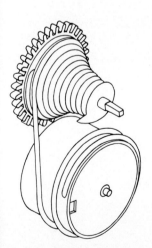

1660 onwards Spring barrel and fusee drive, for bracket clocks, adapted from the same kind of drive for table clocks from about 1475 onwards. Wound by key.

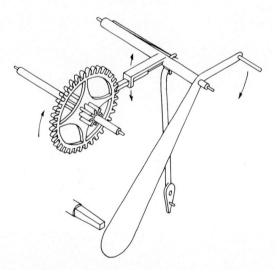

1660–1700 Bolt and shutter maintaining power for weight-driven longcase clocks with short or long pendulums.

Mechanisms

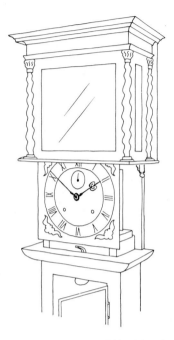

1660–1700 Rising (lifting) hood, used mainly on longcase clocks under 6ft 3in (1.91m) tall regardless of whether the escapement was verge of anchor. It was locked when down by closing the trunk door and latched when up, to allow winding.

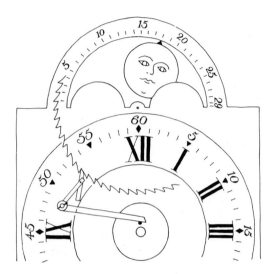

1740 onwards After the introduction of the break-arch dial, Moon dials became popular in the arch.

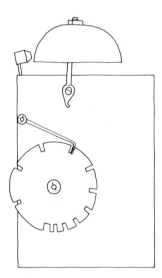

1640–1680 Outside count wheel (locking plate), used on the back plate of a bracket or longcase clock before *c*.1680, after which it was located between the plates, except on provincially made longcase clocks.

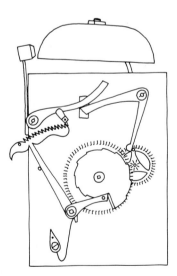

1680 onwards Rack striking replaced count wheel striking for most London clocks and was gradually adopted by other makers, sometimes as much as half a century later. All repeating clocks have it. The rack was first placed inside the plates (internal rack), but commonly found mounted on the front plate by 1690.

Escapements

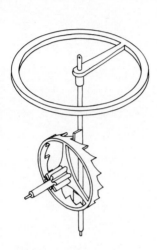

1600–1660 Verge and crown wheel escapement with unsprung circular balance, used on lantern clocks before the pendulum. The escapement originated in the 13th century.

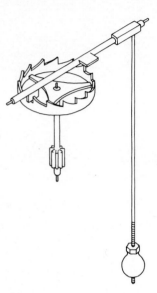

1660–1750 The verge and crown wheel escapement with a bob pendulum, used in all bracket clocks to *c*.1670 and most for a long time later, and in longcase clocks only until 1670–5. Lantern clocks were made with it *c*.1660–1750.

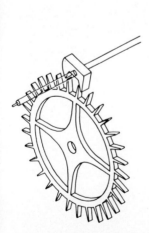

1670–1680 The tic-tac escapement was designed to provide the wide swing, and insensitivity to being moved, of the verge escapement with the benefits of the anchor.

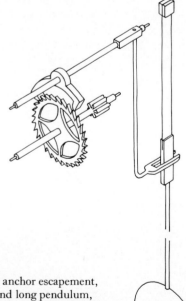

1670 onwards The anchor escapement, used with a crutch and long pendulum, made the longcase clock, accurate to within seconds, possible. It was gradually introduced in bracket and table clocks from 1780 onwards, but is rare before then.

Dials

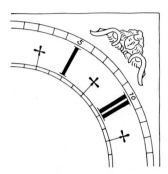

1660–1670 Earliest type of winged cherub spandrels for bracket and longcase clocks, with narrow chapter rings and numerals between minute divisions.

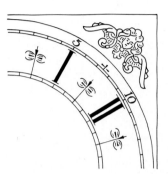

1690–1710 Chapter rings were divided into quarter hours and minutes with half hour ornaments. Half -quarter – $7\frac{1}{2}$ minute divisions – were usual.

1690–1725 Twin cherub spandrel style, influenced by William and Mary reigning.

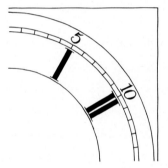

1740–1800 Quarter hour divisions omitted and generally large minute numerals.

1700–1750 Head or mask spandrels, but not used much on London clocks after 1725.
1730–1770 Urn spandrels.

1760–1785 Scroll spandrels.
1760–1785 Leaf and scroll spandrels. A number of other designs was used.

Hands

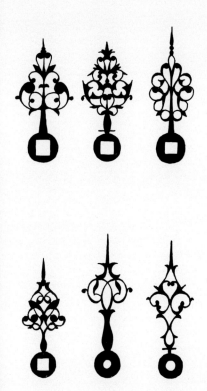

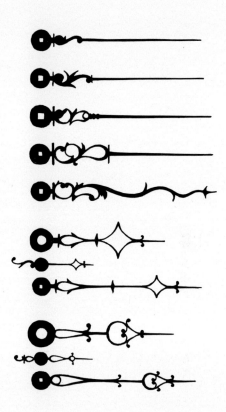

Hour hands, some of various designs, dated in sequence across from the top down: *c.*1675–1700, *c.*1680–1700, *c.*1680–1720, *c.*1700–1780, *c.*1725–1780 (cross-over), *c.*1725–1780. The earliest were pierced and more spade-like and may be seen in illustrations on pages 79 and 128.

Minute hands dated from before *c.*1690, after *c.*1690, and after *c.*1715 when the piercing became bigger and bigger.

Two typical sets of matching hands, dated *c.*1790 and *c.*1830.

The Plates

The cases of Wetherfield's clocks were often altered or added to during 'restoration'. Many such changes are indicated in captions and the informed reader will notice others about which he may have doubts.

Lantern and Hanging Clocks

1 P.Closon,
London. *c*.1650.

Brass 30-hour striking lantern clock with alarm, signed 'Peter Closon neare Holborne Bridge Londini Fecit'. Prependulum style with striking hammer on the right. The hour hand has an oval boss, and a tail to indicate alarm time on the central disk, which can be turned by the knobs on its edge. The dial has no minute ring, but indicates hours, quarter hours, and half hours by ornaments. Dolphin frets below the bell. Pull-up winding with separate weights. Height 15in (38cm).

2 Joseph Knibb, Oxon. *c.*1670
Small brass 30-hour lantern clock with alarm. Converted to two
hands and chapter ring with minute ring. The hour hand
should have a tail to indicate alarm time. Pull-up weight drive.

3 N.Coxeter, London. *c.*1675.
Brass 30-hour striking lantern clock with alarm, signed
'Nicholas Coxeter Neare Gold-Smiths Hall Londini Fecit'.
Hour hand with oval boss and tail to indicate the time at which
the alarm is set, by turning the central disk. No minute
divisions on chapter ring. Dolphin fret. Pull-up winding. Bell
hammer on the left. Height 14in (36cm).

4 Charles Gretton, London. *c.*1680.
Brass 30-hour striking lantern clock. No alarm. Circular boss to hand and wider chapter ring than earlier lantern clocks. Foliage fret. Pull-up weight drive. Top finial broken at the tip.

5 'Thomas Tompion', London. *c.*1680.
Brass 30-hour lantern clock. No alarm. Narrower chapter ring than previous clock, with tulip engraving on zone. Striking hammer on the right; therefore there were two weights. Bell the wrong size. Slots in the sides of the case were for a banana-shaped central pendulum bob. The single hand has a long tail: Lantern clocks were set by turning the hand like a key. Authenticity doubtful. Height 14in (36cm).

5

6 John Knibb, Oxon. *c.*1680.
Small hooded 30-hour hanging clock with arch top. Tulips are engraved on the zone and corners of the brass dial plate. The case is much later and the spandrels over the engraving were added later still.

6

7 Joseph Knibb, London. *c.*1680 m/m. Walnut-cased hanging clock with arch top. The brass dial plate is engraved with tulips on the zone and corners. Hours, half hours, and quarters only are shown on the silvered chapter ring. Pull-up winding.

8 William Clay, King's Street, Westminster, *c.*1680
or possibly 1660.

Brass 30-hour alarm clock with pull-up weight drive. The hour
hand is fixed to the central dial and its three-arm pierced frame.
The 12 pointers on the outer edge indicate minutes on the
sector marked 0–60 at the top. The smaller hand at the centre is
for setting the alarm time on the smaller dial, which rotates
with the hour hand.

9 Markwick Markham, London. *c.*1730(?).
Small gilt lantern-style two-day timepiece (i.e. non-striking, so
that the dome is a decoration and not a bell). The clock was
made with two hands as there are minute divisions (and no
quarter hour divisions) on the chapter ring. Turkish numerals
and mock pendulum. Authenticity doubtful. Height 7in
(18cm).

10 'Daniel Delander', London, *c.*1730(?).
Eight-day spring-driven hanging timepiece in a gilt frame.
There are large minute numerals and half-quarter ornaments
outside the chapter ring, but early winged cherub spandrels.
Authenticity doubtful.

Bracket Clocks

Bracket (Table) Clock Styles

1660–1670 Dutch Architectural

A case with Dutch influence. The French rapidly adopted the pendulum and variations of this case became the *religieuse* case.

1660–1675 Early Architectural

The architectural case was made with or without plain pillars which had elaborate metal capitals.

1660–1675 Hood Style

Spiral columns were applied to architectural cases and to domed top cases like the hoods of a longcase clocks.

1675–1685 Flat Top

A severe style usually made in walnut. Edward East used it for at least one of his night clocks.

1670–1720 Domed Top

The first true bracket clock, with a handle on top and no pillars, in an ebony or ebonised case.

1675–1695 Domed Top (decorated)

Metal decoration was applied at times. A few special clocks with four finials turned on a spigot in the base.

1675–1700 Basket Top
Pierced metal domed tops with applied
decoration had a vogue.

1675–1700 Cushion Basket Top
One variation of the basket top with
more appled decoration.

1675–1700 Double Basket Top
Some basket tops became exceptionally
elaborate.

1695–1755 Inverted Bell Top
The inverted bell top has a concave
form on top of a convex one. See BELL
TOP for comparison

1710–1760 Break-Arch Dial (with
inverted bell top)
The break-arch dial opening appeared
with an inverted bell top.

1750–1800 Bell Top
The true bell top (convex on concave)
with a break arch dial.

1750–1850 Break-Arch Top
(Hepplewhite)
The break-arch top naturally suits the break-arch dial. It was introduced earlier, but did not then become popular

1750–1780 Break-Arch and Turret Top
Elaborate and large musical clocks were made for the East in break-arch cases with various fanciful tops.

1760-1850 Break-Arch Top with Round Dial
The break-arch top lent itself to a round dial, a style employed in great numbers later.

1785–1850 Break-Arch Top with Arch Dial and Spire
The true arch came into fashion long after the break-arch. This style employs both. Sometimes a spire was added.

1760–1790 Pagoda Top

A true pagoda top. The same name is
used for a longcase clock top with a
somewhat similar outline as seen from
the front. (See page 180).

**1750–1800 Inverted Bell Top with
Round Dial**

Round dial openings may have been
used first with inverted bell tops.

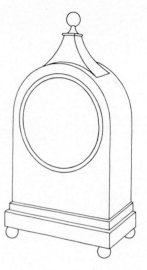

1785–1914 Arch with Spire

The arch top was sometimes used with
a round dial, in this case with a spire as
well.

1785–1914 Arch (Sheraton)

The true arch dial was eventually used
with a true arch case.

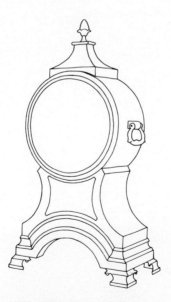

1760–1785 Early Balloon

The balloon case first looked like a
drum on a stand.

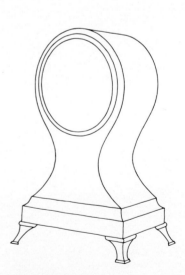

1780–1914 Balloon

The balloon later became sleek, at first
with metal feet.

1760–1790 Louis XIV Style

An English version of one of the most typical French clocks.

1790–1914 Lancet or Gothic Top

The Gothic arch became more popular than the true arch, usually with a round dial.

1800–1914 Chamfer Top

The chamfer top was popular for mahogany cases.

1800–1914 Gadrooned Top

Another favourite shape for mahogany was the gadrooned top.

1800–1914 Ogee Top

The inverted bell shape appears again, but in a simplified form with flat front and back.

1830–1914 Four Glass

A case with glass panels, usually bevelled, for the four sides. The wood was mahogany, rosewood, or ebonised.

'Bracket clocks' is incorrectly used today to describe any English spring-driven pendulum clocks that fit into a general style, but most were made without brackets and were stood on tables, mantelpieces, dressing tables and elsewhere. Some originally had brackets, it is true, but they were in the minority. Earlier all were called 'house clocks', 'English spring clocks', 'portable clocks' and similar names. There is a reference by E.G. Wood in 'Curiosities of Clocks and Watches' (1866) to 'ordinary-sized bracket-clocks' but he probably meant just what he said, i.e. clocks that stood on brackets.

11 Edward East, London. *c.*1665–1670.
Ebony eight-day striking bracket clock. Phase and age of the Moon dial in the zone and a
date aperture over XII. Architectural style of case with Corinthian built-up front capitals
(one missing). The brass dial plate is engraved with 'Sun rays' and has no corner
spandrels. The silvered chapter ring is narrow and the hand is of lantern clock style, but
without a tail. There are no winding holes; the clock is wound from the back. Pendulum
control. Height 21in (51cm).

12 Robert Seignior, London. *c.*1670.
Ebony and tortoiseshell veneered eight-day striking bracket clock with date aperture.
Architectural style case with a key drawer in the base. Engraved centre to the dial zone,
narrow chapter ring, winged cherub spandrels, and an early lantern clock style hand
without a tail. 'Robert Seignior Londini' engraved along the bottom edge of the dial
plate. The fine movement has a beautifully engraved back plate, bob pendulum, outside
locking plate, and sideways bell. Height 21in (53cm) and dial 10in (25cm) square.

13 Edward Stanton, London. *c.*1670.
Ebony eight-day three-train quarter striking bracket clock. It has three bells, an hour bell and ting-tang quarter bells. Architectural style case. The dial has a matted zone with winged cherub spandrels, a narrow chapter ring, and early lantern clock style hand without a tail. 'Edward Stanton Londini' engraved along the bottom of the dial plate. Height 17in (43cm).

14 Joseph Knibb, London. *c.*1670.
Black wood eight-day striking bracket clock. The architectural style case has a key drawer in the base and satinwood pillars with made-up Corinthian capitals. The dial has no spandrels and a slightly wider chapter ring and more elaborate hour hand than previous clocks, but still with a plain pointer minute hand. 'Joseph Knibb, Londini' engraved along the bottom of the dial plate.

15 Edward East, London. *c.*1670.

Ebony eight-day striking bracket clock with double inverted
bell style case top, but no handle. Barley twist pillars with
quarter pillars and splats at the back. Matted dial zone,
engraved corners, narrow chapter ring, and more elaborate
hour hand. 'Edward East Londini' along the bottom edge.
Height 17in (43cm).

16 Samuel Betts, London. *c.*1670–1675.
Walnut 30-hour striking bracket clock. 'Samuel Betts Londini'
engraved along the bottom edge of the dial plate. The case style
is orthodox except for the flat top, which was a style used by
Henry Jones, but may be a modification here. It became
popular much later in Regency times. The chapter ring is later,
*c.*1730.

17 James Markwick, London. *c.*1670–1675.

Walnut and ebony eight-day striking bracket clock with domed
top, but no handle. Barley twist pillars at the front only. There
may have been four. The dial has a matted centre and winged
cherub spandrels. 'Jacobus Markwick Londini' engraved along
bottom of dial plate.

18 Thomas Tompion, London. *c.*1675.
Ebony eight-day striking and pull repeating
bracket clock. The dial has a date aperture and
winged cherub spandrels. Ornate minute hand.
Maker's name not engraved on the dial. Domed
top to the case with a handle. Tompion has
introduced his own style of hands, but the case
was probably made by Joseph Knibb's
casemaker. Ronald A.Lee believes that when
Tompion first came to London, he worked in
Knibb's workshop, or nearby.

19 Humfry Adamson, London. *c.*1680.
Eight-day striking bracket clock in veneered red
tortoiseshell, with a gilt repousse domed top.
The dial has a pierced chapter ring over the
matted dial plate, with applied diamond-shaped
half hour ornaments, and a date aperture. No
maker's name on the dial. Brass claw and ball
feet. Height 12in (30cm).

84

20 Richard Jarrett, London. *c*.1680.
Ebony eight-day striking bracket clock with a silver repoussé
basket top. The hour hand is elaborately pierced and there are
2½ minute markers in the minute ring. No maker's name on the
dial. Height 11in (28cm).

21 Joseph Knibb, London. *c.*1680.
Ebony eight-day three-train striking and
chiming bracket clock. 'Joseph Knibb
London' engraved along the bottom edge of
the dial plate. There is a fret in the top of the
door frame, backed by silk, to allow sound
to escape. The case has a domed top. The
feet are too big, and therefore wrong.

21

21 (detail)

22 Thomas Tompion, London. *c.*1680–1685.

The 'Tulip Tompion'. Ebony eight-day striking and chiming bracket clock with a gilt basket top and tulip pattern finials. It will strike, and if required repeat, the hours and quarters at each quarter (grande sonnerie). There is no auxiliary spring for repeating. The movement is very complicated. Gilded brass frets at the sides of the case and door ornaments. Mock pendulum with the signature engraved below 'Thomas Tompion Londini Fecit'. The dial plate is decoratively engraved outside the chapter ring. The top subsidiary dials are for rise and fall pendulum regulation, and to silence the striking. The two bottom corner hands are to lock the lenticular pendulum from each side before the clock is carried. The back plate is not engraved, unlike most clocks of the period. A similar movement, but with alarm as well, belongs to the Institution of Civil Engineers, and was bequeathed to them by the Royal clockmaker, Benjamin Lewis Vulliamy, who had removed it from its all-gilt case and replaced it by a movement of his own. There is at least one other Tulip Tompion case extant.

23

24 (detail)

24

23 Thomas Tompion, London. *c.*1680–1685.
Ebony month repeating bracket timepiece (i.e. non-striking), with an alarm, set by turning the central engraved dial to set the time for alarm against the tail of the hour hand. The timepiece is wound through the zone, and the alarm by a square at the top right-hand corner. 'Tho Tompion Londini fecit' engraved along the bottom edge of the dial plate. Domed top case with appled decoration and finials. The movement is numbered 85. (There is another genuine Tompion with the same number.) Height 12in (30cm).

24 Thomas Tompion, London. *c.*1680–1685.
Ebony eight-day striking and pull repeating bracket clock with one main train of wheels. It strikes a single blow at the hours. The dial at the top, from which the hand is missing, is for pendulum regulation. 'Tho Tompion Londini fecit' engraved along the bottom edge of the dial plate. Domed top case with applied decoration. Height 12in (30cm). The back plate (detail) has suffered considerable alteration.

25 Joseph Knibb, London. *c.*1685.
Ebonised eight-day striking bracket clock. Dial with calendar aperture and minute numerals still engraved between the divisions, which are wider than previously. Winged cherub spandrels becoming slightly more elaborate. Maker's name and 'Londini' still along the bottom of the dial. The domed top case has applied ornaments and finials.

25

25 (detail)

26 John Knibb, Oxford. *c.*1685.

Walnut eight-day repeating bracket timepiece (i.e. non-striking) with
a going train only. The dial plate is engraved between the simple
winged cherub spandrels and along the bottom edge with 'John Knibb
Oxon fecit'. Date aperture under XII. Domed top case.

27 (detail)   27

27 Thomas Tompion, London. *c.*1690.
Ebony eight-day striking and repeating bracket clock
with mock pendulum and date aperture. Auxiliary
dials for rise and fall pendulum regulation (left) and
N or S, meaning strike or not strike. Elaborate mask
spandrels and minute numerals outside the division
ring. Maker's name engraved at the top of the dial.
Domed top case. Height 14in (36cm).

28 'Thomas Tompion', London. *c.*1690.
Ebony repeating bracket timepiece with a single gear
train. Ringed winding hole and engraved date
aperture under XII. Simple cherub spandrels with
minute numerals engraved inside the wide minute
ring. The 'T.Tompion' engraved at sides of VI is
almost certainly forged. Domed top case with urn
finials. The style does not look like Tompion's.
Height 13in (33cm).

28

29 John Trubshaw, London. *c.*1690.
Ebonised eight-day striking bracket clock. Ringed winding holes and engraved date aperture. The minute numerals moved outside the minute ring. No maker's name on dial. The case has a bell top with elaborate handle and ball and spire finials as well as applied decoration on the door. The pierced side frets (to let out the sound) are in the fish scale pattern that became very popular later and are a replacement. Also, the top of the case suggests a later date. Height 15in (38cm).

30 Jonathan Lowndes, London. *c.*1690.
Eight-day striking and repeating clock.
No strike/strike slot above XII and date aperture under it. Minute numerals still within the minute ring and maker's name along the bottom of the dial plate. The case has a deep pierced brass basket top and applied decoration around the door. Vernay shows it with urn finials. Height 13 in (33cm).

31 Thomas Tompion, London. *c*.1690.
Ebony eight-day striking and repeating bracket
clock with mock pendulum. Minute numeral outside
the minute ring. Auxiliary dials for rise and fall
regulation (left) and N/S (no strike/strike). 'Tho
Tompion Londini fecit' along bottom of dial plate.
The domed top case is a standard Tompion case that
he modified because the door opening has been
increased at the top to expose the subsidiary dials.
Probably the first with auxiliary dials.

32 Thomas Taylor, London. *c*.1690–1695.
Ebony eight-day three-train striking and chiming
bracket clock with a basket top, elaborate handle,
acorn finials (two missing), and applied cast
decoration. The winding holes are ringed, the
minute numerals are still within the minute ring and
the simple winged cherub spandrels are retained.
There is no name on the dial. Height 15in (38cm).

33 Thomas Herbert, London. *c.*1700.
Eight-day striking bracket clock in red tortoise-shell veneered case with a domed top. Minute division outside the minute ring and the half hour decorations are elaborate. 'Tho Herbert WhiteHall' engraved at the sides of VI on the chapter ring and early winged cherub spandrels retained.

34 John Martin, London. *c.*1700.
Eight-day striking and repeating bracket clock in a fine inlaid satinwood arabesque marquetry case with a domed top. The mock pendulum is engraved with a Sun motif and behind it is engraved 'Jn Martin London'. Date aperture and ringed winding holes. Minute numerals outside the minute ring and elaborate half hour ornaments. Authenticity doubtful. Height 13in (33cm).

35 Thomas Martin, London. *c.*1700.

Eight-day striking bracket clock in a red tortoise-shell case with a
domed top and silver handle. Mock pendulum with a Sun motif and
'Tho Martin London' engraved behind it. Ringed winding holes and
date aperture. The numerals outside the minute ring have become
larger than those on earlier clocks and the spandrels a little more
elaborate. Finely pierced hour hand.

36 Daniel Quare, London. *c.*1700.

Ebony three-train striking and chiming bracket clock chiming quarters on six bells. Mock pendulum and date aperture. Auxiliary dials at the top are for pendulum regulation and (not determined) and at the bottom for chime strike/silent and chime repeat/not repeat. The minute numerals are within the minute ring. 'Dan: Quare London' engraved at the sides of VI. Back plate superbly engraved with acanthus leaves. Domed top to case with bud finials. Height 15in (38cm).

36

36 (detail)

37 Thomas Tompion, London. *c.*1705.

Eight-day striking clock in continental style red tortoise-shell and white metal Buhl inlay case, which appears to be French, although the hinge seems English. When the door is opened, the dial plate is shaped, with straight sides and scallops top and bottom. At the top is a subsidiary dial for pendulum regulation, normally hidden. The area outside the chapter ring is engraved. The back door is of metal and is engraved on the outside and inside. The back plate has the same engraved pattern as the inside of the door. Lenticular pendulum bob and mock pendulum.

38 William Tomlinson, London. *c.*1705.

Ebony eight-day three-train striking and quarter chiming bracket clock. Mock pendulum and date aperture. The auxiliary dials are for regulation and silencing the clock, and between them is engraved 'W Tomlinson London'. Height 14½in (37cm).

39 James Markwick, London. *c.*1705.

Ebony eight-day striking and repeating bracket clock with double basket top and two sets of four finials. Engraved mock pendulum, date aperture, and no strike/strike above XII. Minute numerals outside the minute ring. 'Markwick London' engraved at the sides of VI. Applied ornaments (part missing) on the case door. Height 16in (41cm).

40 Charles Goode, London. *c.*1705.

Plain black eight-day striking and repeating bracket clock with mock pendulum and date aperture. The slot above XII and under the maker's name is marked 'N–S', meaning no striking or striking. Elaborate foliage spandrels. Slightly larger minute numerals outside the minute ring than previously and half-quarter hour markers also outside the minute ring. Height 14 in (36cm).

41 George Allett, London. *c.*1710.

Ebony eight-day striking bracket clock with mock pendulum, and date aperture immediately under the centre. Maker's name engraved between the auxiliary dials, which are for rise and fall pendulum regulation and for striking or not striking. Elaborate cherub mask spandrels. Fairly large minute numerals and half-quarter ornaments outside the minute ring. Very fine engraving on the back plate. The whole is very much in Tompion's style. Height 15in (38cm).

42 Samuel Watson, London. *c.*1710.

Ebony eight-day three-train bracket clock, striking and chiming on three bells. The unusual mock pendulum with reversed curve is mounted above the pendulum. A lever slot marked 'S–N' at the very top is for silencing the clock. Minutes engraved outside the ring, with half-quarter ornaments, and with an early style of hour hand, which is too short, and probably a replacement. Height 17in (43cm).

43 George Graham, London. *c.*1715.
Ebony eight-day striking bracket clock. Mock pendulum
and date aperture. Between the auxiliary dials for
pendulum regulation and silencing the striking is
engraved 'Geo Graham London'. Typical Graham half
hour diamond ornaments. Minute numerals outside the
ring have become larger. Elaborate foliage spandrels.
Height 13in (33cm).

44 George Graham, London. *c.*1715.
Ebony eight-day striking and repeating bracket clock
with a mock pendulum and date aperture. The silver dial
mounts show cherub faces and foliage. 'Geo Graham
London' is engraved between the auxiliary dials for
pendulum regulation and strike/no strike. Inverted bell
top case.

45 Jonathan Rant, London. *c.*1720.

Ebony eight-day repeating bracket timepiece (i.e. not striking but
repeating the hours on pulling a cord). Auxiliary dial at the top shows
the date. Crown and crossed baton spandrels. Very large minute
numerals. Break arch dial and inverted bell top case. Maker's name
and place engraved at sides of VI.

46 (detail)

46 Charles Gretton, London. *c.*1720.

Ebony eight-day striking and pull repeating bracket clock. Mock
pendulum, and auxiliary dial in the arch giving the date. Half-quarter
diamonds outside the minute ring. Crown and crossed baton
spandrels and the maker's name and place engraved in an oval
cartouche. Inverted bell topped case with glass 'inverted exclamation
mark' side panels. The movement has an elaborate pierced apron to
retain the rear knife edge bearing of the verge. Note the saw teeth of the
date indicator. Height 17in (43cm).

47 Joseph Windmills, London. *c.*1720.
Black eight-day striking bracket clock with mock pendulum and date
aperture. Early integral shallow dial arch engraved 'Windmills
London', but engraved border to dial plate and winged cherub
spandrels and minute numerals and half-quarter ornaments outside
the minute ring. No strike/strike slot above XII. Two glass panels
each side of inverted bell top case with elaborate handle.

48 Daniel Delander, London. *c.*1720.
Ebonised eight-day striking bracket clock with mock pendulum and
date aperture. Foliage spandrels. Large minute numerals. One
auxiliary dial is for pendulum regulation and the other is engraved
'strike/silent'. 'Daniel Delander London' is engraved between them.
Inverted bell top case. Height 16in (41cm).

49 Richard Peckover, London. *c.*1735.
Miniature eight-day striking and repeating bracket clock
in gilded metal case. Double arch dial with an auxiliary
dial for strike/silent. Large minute numerals with half-
quarter ornaments. No quarter divisions inside minute
ring. Maker identified on cartouche on the dial. Inverted
bell top to the case.

50 William Jackson, London. *c.*1740.
Walnut striking and pull repeating bracket clock with
strike/silent control in the break arch. Mock pendulum
and date aperture. Large minute numerals and no
quarter hour divisions. A plate on the dial is engraved
with 'William Jackson London'. The acanthus leaf
spandrels were used in many clocks from about this time.
Inverted exclamation mark wooden side frets. Inverted
bell top to case with a plain handle.

51 George Tyler, London. *c.*1740.
Walnut eight-day striking bracket clock with pull repeat
on six bells. Auxiliary dials in the arch are left,
strike/silent; centre, phase and age of the Moon; and
right, pendulum regulation. The maker's name is
engraved behind the mock pendulum, in an earlier
fashion, and there is a date aperture. Large minute
numerals with half-quarter divisions. Quarter hour
divisions inside the chapter ring retained. Crown and
crossed baton spandrels. Inverted bell top to case with
foliage feet. Height 13in (33cm).

52 John Ellicott, London. *c.*1740.
Black wood eight-day striking and pull repeating bracket
clock. Strike/silent in break arch, mock pendulum and
date aperture. Cherub mask and foliage spandrels.
Quarter hour divisions retained and maker's name
engraved in a cartouche on the dial. Inverted bell top
case with break arch side panels and gilded metal feet.
Height 13in (33cm).

53 John Ellicott, London. *c.*1760.

Mahogany eight-day striking and pull repeating bracket clock. The
all-over silvered dial is square and appears round because of the
circular glass in the rectangular door. Large minute numerals with an
engraved ring around them, but no quarter hour divisions or half hour
ornaments. Inverted bell top case with gilt metal feet.

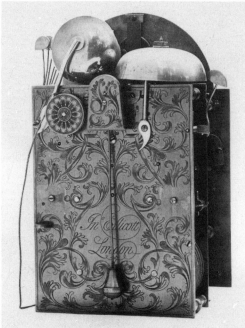

54 (detail)

54 John Ellicott, London. *c.*1760.
Eight-day striking and pull repeating bracket clock in green lacquered
case with strike/silent control in the break arch of the dial, mock
pendulum and date aperture. Large minute numerals and no quarter
hour divisions. Maker's name at the bottom of the chapter ring. Early
style cherub mask and foliage spandrels, cross-over hour hand, and
inverted bell top case with inverted exclamation mark side frets.
Note the apron covering the pendulum suspension, and the repeater
winding wheel. Height 18in (46cm).

55 John Shelton, London. *c.*1760.
Mahogany eight-day table regulator. All-over silvered dial. Aperture
for hours, top ring for seconds, lower one for minutes, through the
edge of which the winding square projects. Inverted exclamation
mark side frets and stop/start knob at the bottom of the case. Feet with
level adjustment screws. Height 17in (43cm).

56 George Clarke, London. *c.*1770.

Painted and gilded eight-day three-train striking and musical bracket clock designed for the Turkish market, with crystal domes and pillars, star and Moon finials and Turkish hour numerals. The 12-tune indicator in the dial arch is engraved: Princess Amelia, A Turkey Tune, A Gallen of Crayden, A Minuet, A Greeke Song, A Riga:doon, A March, A Riga:doon, A Minuet, A Greeke Song, A Minuet, A March. Auxiliary dials for strike/not strike and chime/not chime. The earlier quarter hour divisions and half hour symbols have been retained. Signed in the arch: George Clarke Leaden Hall Street London. The clock is now in Goldsmiths Hall, London. Height 39in (100cm).

57 Thomas Mudge and William Dutton, London. *c*.1770.

Ebonised and gilded eight-day striking and repeating bracket clock with its bracket. Break arch dial in a break arch case with glass side panels. Auxiliary dial for regulation in the arch with a lever slot for strike/no strike below it. No quarter hour division on the chapter ring. Foliage spandrels. Signed on a silvered cartouche on the dial. Height 21in (53cm) including the bracket.

58 John Johnson, Grays Inn Passage, London. *c*.1770.

Ebony eight-day striking bracket clock in balloon style with its carved sun motif bracket. Handles on the sides, pineapple finial and gilded metal feet. Circular enamelled dial with matching hands based on the earlier beetle and poker style, and dots for minute markers. Circular hinged bezel (instead of a rectangular wooden door). Pin wheel escapement for the pendulum. Height 27in (69cm) including the bracket.

59 Edward Tutet, London. *c.*1770.

Mahogany eight-day striking bracket clock with an enamelled dial behind a door with a circular glass. Wavy minute hand and no quarter hour or half hour indications. Inverted bell top case. Height 16in (41cm).

60 Alexander Cumming, London. *c.*1770.

Black wood eight-day striking bracket clock with three enamelled dials on a brass dial plate with acanthus spandrels. The left auxiliary dial is marked strike/silent and the other is for pendulum regulation. The maker's name and location are on these dials. No quarter hour divisions or half hour ornaments. Cross-over style hour hand. Break-arch dial and case top. Height 14in (36cm).

61 James Tregent, London. *c.*1770.
Ebonised eight-day striking bracket clock with two enamelled dials,
the subsidiary one for strike/silent. No quarter or half hour markers.
Break-arch dial with acanthus spandrels and break-arch case. Height
14in (36cm).

62 James Cowan, Edinburgh. *c*.1780.
Chippendale style mahogany eight-day striking and chiming three-train bracket clock
with pagoda top and reeded feet. The enamelled dial is behind a door with round glass.
No quarter hour or half hour indications. Fish scale frets in the sides of the case.

63 (general view)

63 Josiah Emery, London. *c.*1780.

Ebony eight-day striking and repeating bracket clock with its
original bracket. Signed between the two auxiliary dials, for
pendulum regulation and (right) for strike/silent. Date
aperture. Traditional silvered chapter ring on a brass dial plate.
No quarter or half hour markers. Acanthus spandrels. Break-
arch dial and an earlier style bell-top case with corner finials.
Height 22in (56cm) including bracket.

64 John Scott, London. *c.*1780.
Walnut three-train striking and chiming bracket clock with
enamelled dials, the subsidiary one for strike/silent. No quarter
or half hour markers. Signed under XII. Break-arch dial and
case with fish scale side frets and brass feet. Height 17in (43cm).

65 Kenneth Maclennan, London. *c.*1790.
Eight-day striking and repeating bracket clock in the
French style, but with Turkish style finials.
Enamelled dial with reversion to earlier beetle and
poker hands. No quarter or half hour markers. The
case is wooden with brass ornamentation, the front
opening as a door with a circular glass. The
movement has an anchor escapement with lenticular
bob pendulum. Height 12½in (31.5cm).

65 (detail)

66 John Marriott, London. *c.*1810.
Ebonised eight-day striking bracket clock with enamelled dials, the subsidiary one for strike/silent.
The main dial shows 24 hours in double XII indication. There are no winding holes; winding is
from the back. Early style hands with a tail to the hour hand. Symmetrical patterned spandrels.
(Most leaf designs were not.) The bell top case with arch top is generally in the continental style
with applied ornamentation, claw feet and side handles. Height 16in (41cm).

67 Joseph Thompson, London. *c.*1820.
Eight-day timepiece (non-striking) in a balloon
case veneered with banding and shell motif. Front
winding, matching pierced diamond hands, and
brass feet.

68 Dwerrihouse and Carter, London. *c.*1820.
Ebony eight-day striking bracket clock with earlier
style brass dial plate and silvered chapter ring.
Subsidiary dials for strike/silent and pendulum
regulation. Matching pierced hands with spade
ends (named after French, not English, spades).
The flat top case with side carrying handles, ball
feet and fish scale side frets, is in what is called
'Regency style', a term applied to certain designs
between about 1790 and 1840. Height 16in
(41cm). The styles are mixed and this could be a
rebuild of an earlier clock.

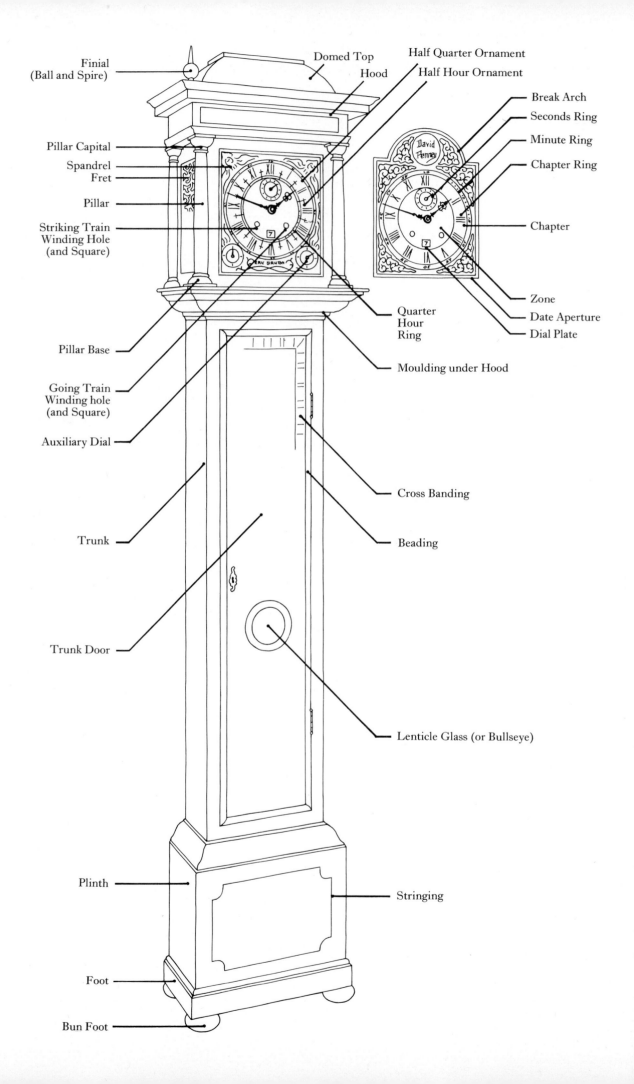

Finial
(Ball and Spire)

Domed Top

Hood

Half Quarter Ornament

Half Hour Ornament

Break Arch

Seconds Ring

Minute Ring

Chapter Ring

Pillar Capital

Spandrel

Fret

Pillar

Striking Train
Winding Hole
(and Square)

Chapter

Pillar Base

Going Train
Winding hole
(and Square)

Auxiliary Dial

Quarter
Hour
Ring

Zone

Date Aperture

Dial Plate

Moulding under Hood

Cross Banding

Beading

Trunk

Trunk Door

Lenticle Glass (or Bullseye)

Plinth

Stringing

Foot

Bun Foot

Longcase Clocks

69 Joseph Knibb, Oxon. *c.*1668.

Small ebony hour and quarter striking longcase clock in architectural style with corinthian pillars at the front and simpler quarter pillars and splats at the back of the hood. Narrow chapter ring with quarter divisions, half hour ornaments, and minute numerals within the minute ring. Dial plate engraved in the corners and centrally. Date aperture above VI. Simple pattern of hands. Convex moulding to the case trunk under the hood, three panel case door and bun feet. The movement has a short pendulum. The case is probably a reproduction, probably by Van Winsum. The side panels are wrong. Height 6ft 3in (1.91m) Dial 10in (25.5cm) square.

70 Joseph Knibb, London. *c.*1670

Laburnum and olive wood parquetry eight-day longcase clock striking on two bells, one for repeating the hour at the half hour (Dutch striking). Skeletonised chapter ring, including half hour markers. Winged cherub spandrels and simple hands, including a seconds hand below XII. Barley twist pillars of opposite directions and quarter pillars with splats at the back. Convex moulding under the hood and carved wooden cresting on the top of it. Round glass in the long case door. Scalloped foot to the case. Long pendulum. Height 7ft (2.13m) Dial 10in (25.5cm) square. The feet are wrong.

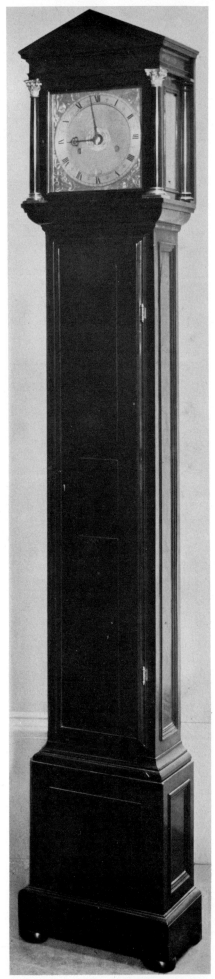

69

70 (detail)

70

71 Joseph Knibb, London. *c.*1670–1675.

Ebony, brass-mounted month longcase clock with
Roman striking on two bells, corresponding with
Roman numerals, a low pitched bell for V and a high
one for I. Chapter ring with IV instead of III, half
hour ornaments and minute numerals within the
minute ring. Simple hands, seconds pointer, date
aperture and winged cherub spandrels. Edge of dial
plate engraved and signed along the bottom edge.
Flat topped hood with convex moulding underneath
and corinthian capitals to the barley twist pillars,
turning in opposite direction, and quarter pillars
with splats at the back. Swag ornaments between the
capitals. The case had finely moulded panels for the
long door. The 'fielded' panels at the sides of the
plinth are probably not original. Long pendulum.
The ornament fixed above the door is a symbol of
Pan (owner's mark?) Height 6ft 9in (2.06m) Dial
10in (25.5cm) square. The foot is wrong and lenticle
may have been added.

72 Joseph Knibb, London. *c.*1670–1675.

Ebony month longcase clock striking on two bells.
Chapter ring and seconds ring in silver, with simple
hands. Dial plate with an engraved border, winged
cherub spandrels, matted centre with date aperture,
signed 'Joseph Knibb Londini Fecit' along the
bottom edge. Moulded panels to the case with an
oval glass in the door. Convex moulding under the
hood, which has a flat top and barley twist pillars
with opposite twists and quarter pillars with splats,
all having plain capitals. The hood slides forwards,
instead of being lifted (rising hood) as with most
early small longcase clocks. The 'fielded' panels at
the sides of the plinth are probably not original. The
ornament above the door is a Pan motif (owner's
symbol?). The foot is wrong. Height 6ft 8in (2.03m)
Dial 10in (25.5cm) square.

73 John Knibb, Oxon. Movement *c.*1670, case
*c.*1680 – a 'marriage'.

Laburnum and olive wood inlaid month striking
longcase clock with skeletonised silver chapter ring
on which every minute is numbered within the
minute ring divisions. Engraved border to the dial
plate, with winged cherub spandrels, date aperture
below XII, and signature along the bottom edge. No
seconds dial. Bolt and shutter maintaining power.
Flat topped hood with convex moulding underneath
and barley twist pillars and quarter pillars. Height 6ft
8in (2.03m) Dial 10in (25.5cm) square.

71

72

73

125

74 John Fromanteel, London. *c*.1675.

Walnut eight-day three-train hour and quarter striking longcase clock. The hours are struck on four bells simultaneously with ting-tang quarters. Movement with 1¼ seconds pendulum (about 61in or 1.55m) long. Chapter ring without quarter divisions, but with half hour ornaments and every minute numbered within the divisions. Seconds dial, calendar aperture, winged cherub spandrels, and signature along the bottom of the dial plate. Bolt and shutter maintaining power. Architectural style case with barley twist pillars and quarter pillars with splats. The case is made with small panels like a Dutch cabinet. Height 7ft 5in (2.26m) Dial 10½in (27cm) square.

75 Thomas Tompion, London. *c*.1675.

Eight-day striking longcase clock in star parquetry and burr veneer. Narrow chapter ring with minute numerals in the minute ring. Signed 'Thomas Tompion Londini' along the bottom of the dial plate, around which a thin line border is engraved. Date aperture and more elaborate hour hand than contemporary styles. Bolt and shutter maintaining power. Sliding hood with flat top and convex moulding underneath it. Bun feet. Height 6ft 8in (2.03m) Dial 10in (25.5cm) square.

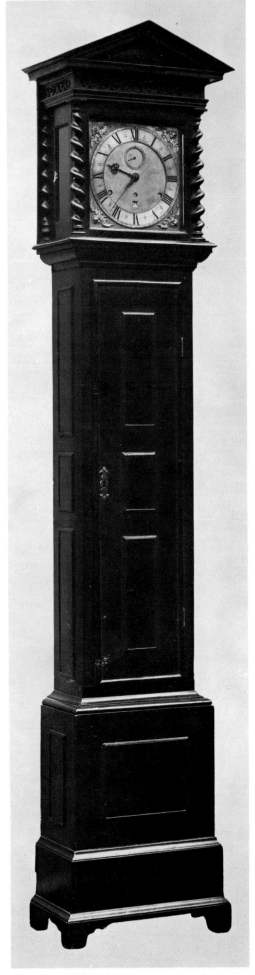

74

75 (detail)

75

76 (detail)

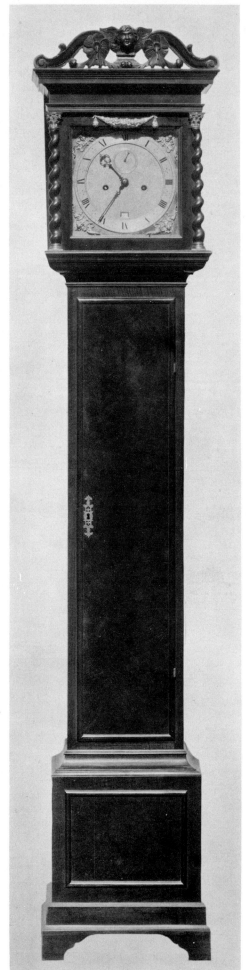

76

76 Thomas Tompion, London. *c*.1675.
Burr walnut eight-day striking longcase clock.
Narrow chapter ring, seconds dial and date
aperture. Signed Thomas Tompion Londini fecit'
along the bottom edge of the dial plate. Very fine
hands. Barley twist pillars and quarter pillars all
turning in the same direction and with corinthian
capitals. The hood has a central brass swag and
carved cresting or pediment. The case is not
original, the whole plinth having been renewed.
Height 6ft 9in (2.06m) Dial 9½in (24cm) square.

77 Robert Seignior, London. *c*.1675–1680.
Month striking longcase clock in parquetry and burr
veneer. Wider chapter ring with quarter hour
divisions, half hour ornaments and the minute ring
with half-quarter ornaments and minute numerals
within the divisions. Seconds dial with wider ring
numbered every ten seconds, and calendar aperture.
More elaborate hands, winged cherub spandrels,
and winding holes much lower than in
contemporary clocks. Hood with barley twist pillars
in the front only with the same direction of twist and
corinthian capitals; splats at the back. Hood with
domed top and ball finials. Apron to the foot of the
case. The hood top is probably an addition. Hood
and chapter ring 'brought up to date' and bun feet
removed around 1700, a common practice then.
Height 7ft 5in (2.26m) Dial 10in (24.5cm) square.

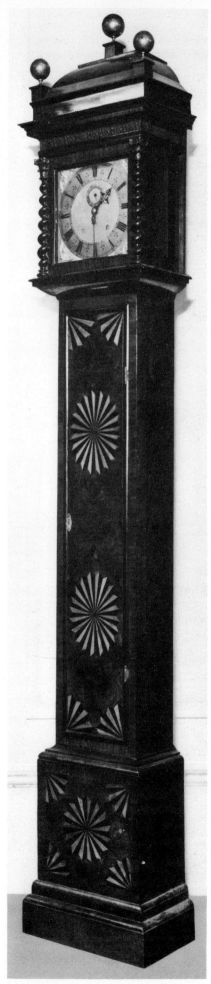

77

78 Nicholas Coxeter, London. *c.*1675–1680.
Eight-day striking longcase clock with parquetry
and floral marquetry panels and burr veneers.
Narrow chapter ring with minute numerals inside,
signature along the bottom, date aperture, winged
cherub spandrels, early style hands, and bolt and
shutter maintaining power. Sliding hood with a flat
top and barley twist pillars and splats. Oval bullseye
glass in the case door. Height 6ft 8in (1.96m) The
dial is small at 9in (23cm) square.

79 Thomas Tompion, London. *c.*1675–1680.
Burr walnut eight-day striking longcase clock.
Narrow chapter ring with minute numerals inside
and quarter hour divisions. Dial plate signed
'Thomas Tompion Londini fecit'. Silver seconds
ring. Bolt and shutter maintaining power. Sliding
hood with horned cresting (a style that became very
popular a century later but with concave moulding
underneath the hood unlike the convex moulding
here). Barley twist pillars in the same directions
and corinthian capitals. The foot looks wrong. Case
probably made by Knibb's casemaker. Height 6ft
9in (2.06m) Dial 10in (25.5cm) square.

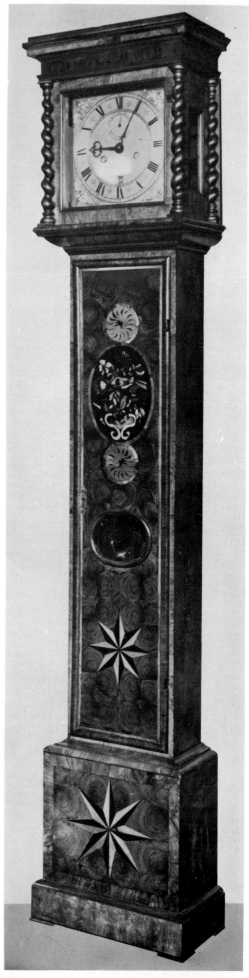

78

79 (detail)

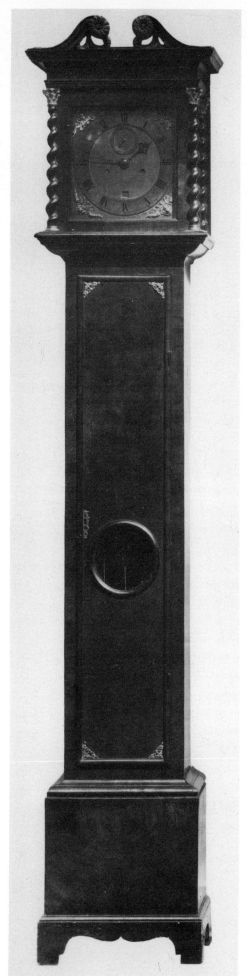

79

80 Thomas Tompion, London. *c*.1675–1680.

Parquetry and banded veneer striking longcase clock. Two illustrations, one in Britten's book on the collection (fig 20) and another in the sale album marked 59 – catalogue number – on the negative) and also in Hurcomb's book (page 17) appear similar superficially. Britten's description is 'marquetry longcase month clock. Height 6ft 10in; dial 10in square'. Grain in the veneer show the cases to be identical, but the foot is different in the catalogue version. Vernay said the case had been cut down by nearly two inches from these figures. The foot is, in fact, different in the three illustrations, by Britten, Vernay, and Hurcomb. Two different movements are described. Britten's version has ringed winding holes and a date aperture under the centre of the dial. That with the catalogue number has winding holes closed by bolt and shutter maintaining power and the date aperture over VI. Also, the engraving of the hour chapters on the 'Britten clock' is in a broad, more 'country' style, compared with the other dial. The bottom edge of the dial plate is engraved, but only the top of 'Th . . .' can be seen in the print. If Britten's figures are accepted the height is 2.08m and the dial 25.5cm square.

81 Edward East, London. *c*.1675–1680.

Eight-day striking longcase clock in a laburnum case with parquetry decoration and bullseye glass in the door. Narrow chapter ring with quarter hour divisions, half hour ornaments and minute numerals within the ring. Large narrow seconds ring, early winged cherub spandrels, date aperture, and bolt and shutter maintaining power. Flat topped hood with barley twist pillars. The plinth is not original; neither is the foot. This clock is not shown in the Hurcomb book. Height 6ft 10in (2.08m) Dial 10in (25.5cm) square.

82 Joseph Knibb, London. *c*.1675–1680.

Month striking longcase clock with floral marquetry and parquetry panels on a laburnum ground with olive wood borders. Fine skeleton dial with quarter divisions, half hour markers and every minute numbered inside the ring. Elaborate cherub mask spandrels, date aperture under XII and signature along the bottom of the dial plate. Stepped top to the hood and apron to the foot. Height 6ft 8in (2.03m) Dial 10in (25.5cm) square.

80

81   82

83 Joseph Windmills, London. *c.*1680.

Eight-day striking longcase clock in laburnum and olive wood parquetry. Chapter ring slightly wider than contemporary style. Wider and more elaborate hour hand. Signed 'Jos. Windmills Londini' along the bottom edge of the dial. Maintaining power. Flat topped sliding hood, although the case is short. Height 6ft 6in (1.98m) Dial 10in (25.5cm) square.

84 Joseph Knibb, Oxford. *c.*1680.

Floral marquetry eight-day striking longcase clock. Narrow chapter ring with wider than usual minute ring, having numerals engraved within it. Single line engraved border to the dial plate, which is signed along the bottom, 'Joseph Knibb Oxon fecit'. Hands of exact length to match dial engraving. Barley twist pillars of opposite directions with corinthian capitals. Flat topped hood. Height 6ft 5in (1.96m) The dial is very small at 9in (23cm) square.

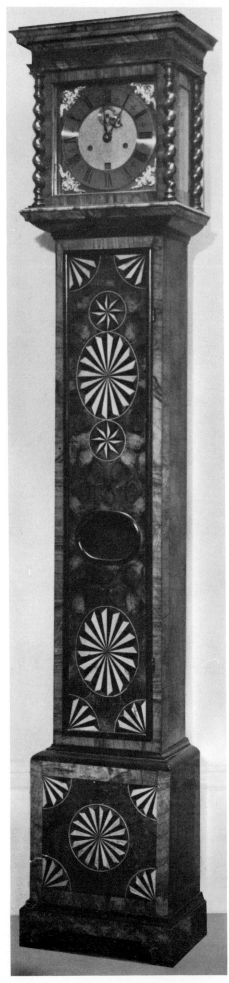

83

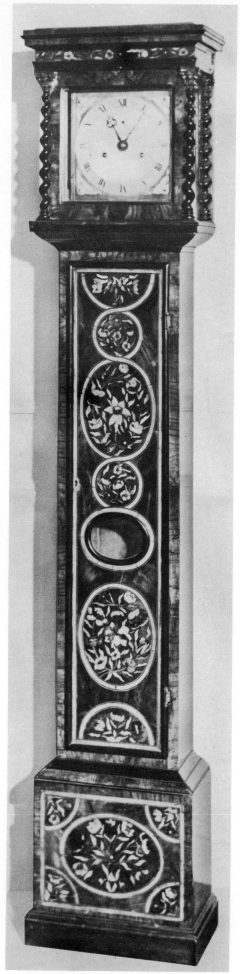

84 (detail)

84

135

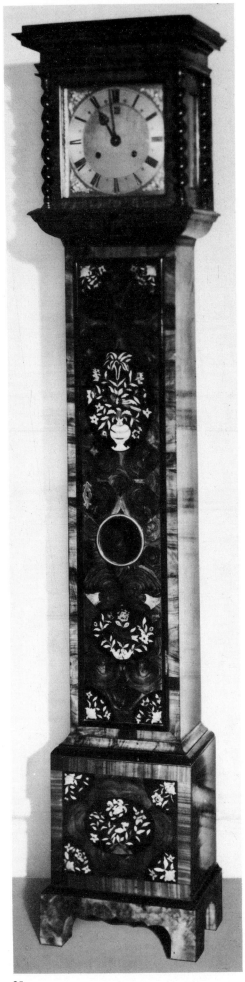

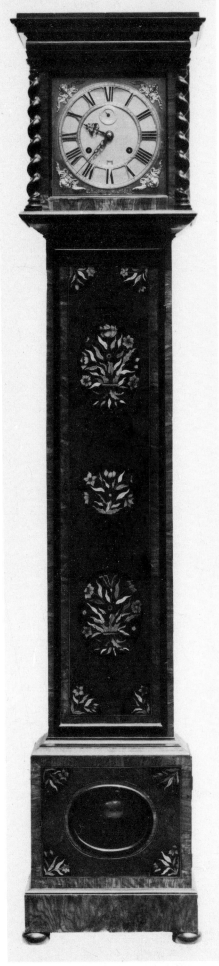

85

86

87 (detail)

85 Joseph Knibb, London. *c*.1680.
Month striking longcase clock with floral marquetry
panels on a ground laburnum with olive wood
borders. Date aperture below XII, winged cherub
spandrels, and narrow pattern hour hand. Barley
twist pillars and tall feet to the plinth. Height 6ft 9in
(2.06m) Dial 10in (25.5cm) square. The feet are
incongruous and wrong.

86 Daniel Parker, London. *c*.1680.
Month striking longcase clock with floral marquetry
panels and banding. The movement has a 1¼ seconds
pendulum, approximately 61in (1.55m) long, and
there is a window in the plinth to display the bob.
Skeleton chapter ring with quarter and half hour
markers inside the inner ring and minute numerals
within the outer ring. Seconds dial and date
aperture. Early winged cherub spandrels and dial
plate signed 'Daniel Parker Fleet Street London'
along the bottom. Flat topped hood with barley
twist pillars; bun feet. Height 6ft 8in (2.03m) Dial
10½in (27cm) square.

87 Thomas Tompion, London. *c*.1680.
Burr walnut month striking clock with carved
cresting to the hood, which has been restored. Dial
with winged cherub spandrels, seconds ring and
date aperture. Quarter hour, half hour and minute
divisions, but the minute numerals have been
moved outside the minute ring. The dial plate has
an engraved border and the words 'Tho=Tompion
Londini Fecit' along the bottom. The foot looks
wrong. Height 6ft 9in (2.06m) Dial 10in (25.5cm)
square.

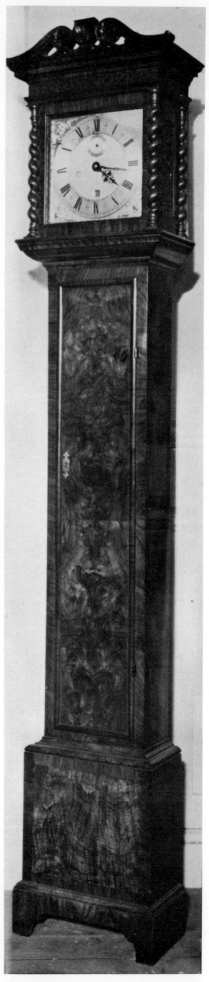

87

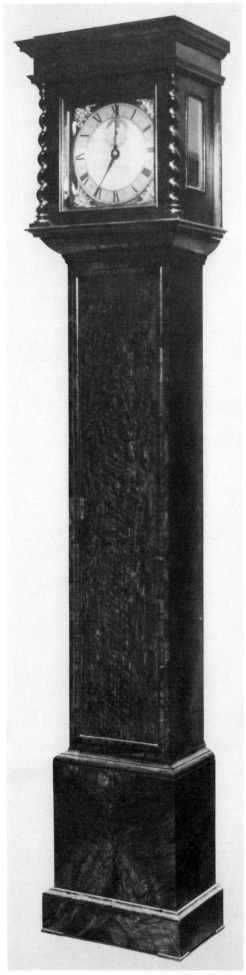

88 (detail)

88 (detail)

88

88 William Clement, London. *c*.1680.

Burr walnut month timepiece (i.e. without striking) with a 1¼ seconds pendulum (about 61in or 1.55m long) extending into the plinth, but no window in the plinth. Clement was credited by W. Derham with the invention of the anchor escapement, which made the long pendulum possible. The seconds pendulum resulted in a big gain in accuracy over the short one and it was thought that the 1¼ seconds pendulum would provide a further gain. Early style of dial with narrow chapter ring, simple winged cherub spandrels and early hands. Seconds ring and date aperture within it. Signed 'William Clement Londini' along the bottom of the dial plate. There is a pendulum regulation dial on the side of the movement, which can be seen through a side window of the sliding hood. Wrongly attributed by Hurcomb to Charles Goode. Height 6ft 6in (1.98m) Dial 10in (25.5cm) square.

89 Edward East, London. *c*.1680.

Small walnut month striking longcase clock with marquetry panels. The movement has a 61in (1.55m) pendulum swinging from one side to the other in 1¼ seconds and an oval glass in the plinth for the bob to be seen. Winged cherub spandrels, seconds ring and date aperture. Note the low position of the winding holes. Flat topped hood with barley twist pillars. Height 6ft 4in (1.93m) Dial 10in (25.5cm) square.

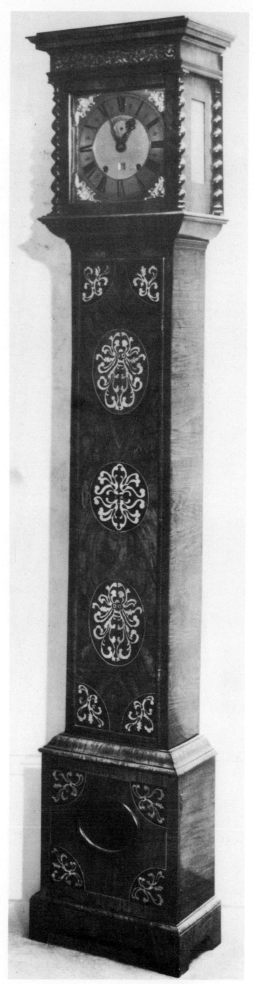

89

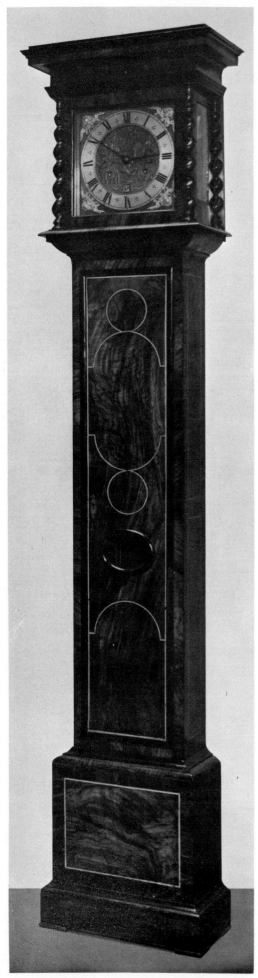

90 (detail)

90 Thomas Tompion, London. *c.*1680.

Described in the catalogue as 'thirty-hour', this striking longcase clock has a case of burr walnut with stringing. It has a sliding hood; most early clocks had rising hoods. The dial is of an early style with engraved centre and the signature 'Thomas Tompion Londini' on a panel. Winged cherub spandrels and date aperture. Platform topped hood with barley twist pillars. Thirty-hour clocks with key winding are very rare. Height 6ft 8in (2.03m) Dial 10in (25.5cm) square.

91 John Wise, London. *c.*1680.

Walnut eight-day striking longcase clock with marquetry panels. The dial has elaborate cherub spandrels and date aperture and the minute numerals are within the minute ring. Platform top and barley twist pillars to the front of the hood only. Bun feet.

92 Thomas Tompion, London. *c.*1680–1685.

Burr walnut eight-day striking longcase clock with banded edge veneered panels. The chapter ring has a very narrow minute circle with the numerals outside it. Winged cherub spandrels, seconds ring and date aperture. There is carved cresting with a cherub motif on three sides of the hood and pierced wooden side frets. Bun feet.

90

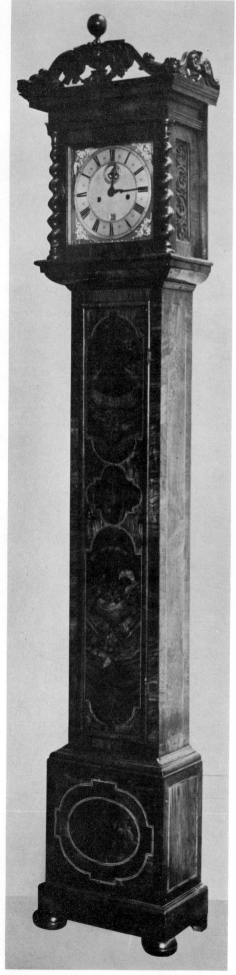

91

92

141

93 (detail)

93 Edward East, London. *c.*1680–1685.
Eight-day striking longcase clock in floral marquetry with an oval bullseye in the door. Narrow chapter ring and seconds ring with spandrels and hands of an earlier style. No date aperture. Domed top to the hood with ball and spire finials, probably not original. Height 7ft (2.13m) Dial 9½in (24cm) square.

94 Joseph Knibb, London. *c.*1680–1685.
Burr walnut month longcase clock striking on two bells that correspond to Roman numerals – a higher note for I and a lower one for V – to reduce the power reserve necessary. Note the IV instead of IIII on the chapter ring. Larger dial than on most contemporary clocks, but still with minute numerals within the minute ring. Elaborate cherub spandrels, narrow hour hand, date aperture and low winding holes. Domed top hood with three ball and spire finials. Height 7ft 2in (2.18m) Dial 11in (28cm) square.

95 Christopher Gould, London. *c.*1685.
Eight-day striking longcase clock in floral marquetry. Minute numerals and half-quarter ornaments within the minute ring, elaborate hour hand, seconds ring, ringed winding holes and engraving round the date aperture. Flat topped hood with same way barley twist pillars and quarter pillars. Marquetry on the hood door and banded veneered panels on the sides of the trunk.

93

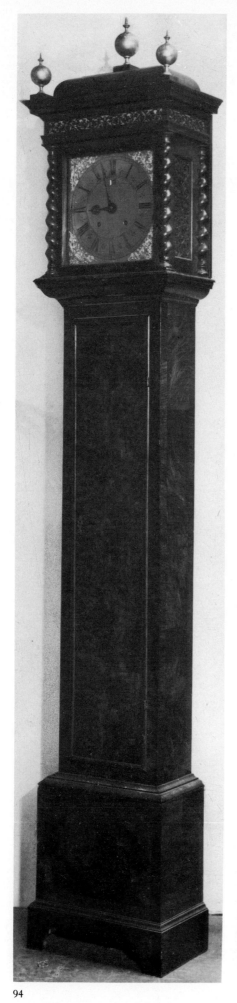

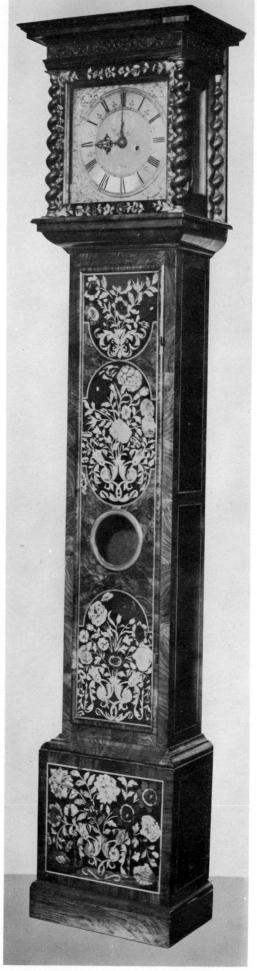

94

95

96 Joseph Knibb, London. *c.*1685.

Burr walnut month three-quarter train hour and quarter striking longcase clock with double banded veneered panels. Skeleton dial in earlier style with date aperture under the XII. Simple cherub spandrels and hands. Swag on the hood (another earlier feature), which has a shallow dome, three cup and spire finials and barley twist pillars. Late 18th century feet. Height 7ft 3in (2.21m) Dial 10in (25.5cm) square.

97 Thomas Tompion, London. *c.*1685.

Burr walnut month striking longcase clock. The dial is larger than contemporary style. The minute numerals have been moved outside the minute ring and have become larger and the quarter hour divisions on the inner ring remain. Elaborate cherub spandrels with engraving between them and 'Tho=Tompion Londini Fecit' engraved along the bottom of the dial plate. Minute ring and date aperture. Winged cherub carved cresting to the front of the hood only. Apron on the foot of the case, which is not original. The case does not belong to the movement (number 208), which is now in a more suitable, but not a Tompion or an original, case. Height 7ft 2in (2.18m) Dial 11in (28cm).

96

97 (detail)

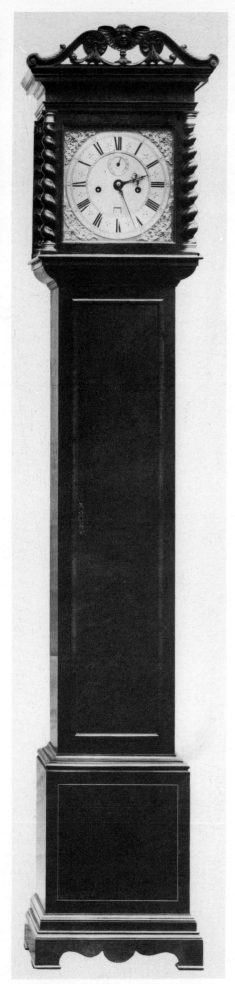

97

98 Daniel Quare, London. *c.*1685–1690.
Eight-day striking longcase clock with floral
marquetry panels and oval window in the door.
Minute numerals and half-quarter markers inside
the minute ring, quarter hour divisions, and smaller
than usual half hour ornaments. The seconds dial
has large numerals engraved outside the ring.
Elaborate cherub mask spandrels and date aperture.
The hood has carved shell motif cresting at the front
and varley twist pillars. The case is not original, as
the whole plinth has been renewed. Height 6ft 9in
(2.06m) Dial 10in (25.5cm) square.

99 Daniel Quare, London. *c.*1690.
Eight-day striking longcase clock in floral
marquetry. Minute numerals engraved outside the
narrow chapter ring. Elaborate cherub spandrels
and hour hand. Ringed winding holes and engraving
around the date aperture. Dial signed at the bottom.
The hood has a carved wooden pediment (cresting)
with a rosette in the centre and incongruous plain
pillars. (Most earlier pillars were twisted.) Height
7ft (2.13m) Dial 10in (25.5cm) square.

100 Christopher Gould, London. *c.*1690.
Eight-day striking longcase clock in floral
marquetry. The dial has elaborate cherub spandrels
and small minute numerals and half-quarter markers
engraved inside the minute ring. The winding holes
are ringed and there is engraving around the date
aperture and the centre of the dial. It has
particularly fine hour and minute hands with the
usual plain pointer for the seconds. Bolt and shutter
maintaining power. The hood has carved cresting
and is surmounted by a winged cherub finial, and
the hood door has marquetry decoration. Vernay's
illustration has a winged cherub central finial.
**The foot is wrong. (Also illustrated on the book
jacket.)** Height 7ft 2in (2.18m) Dial 10½in (27cm)
square.

98

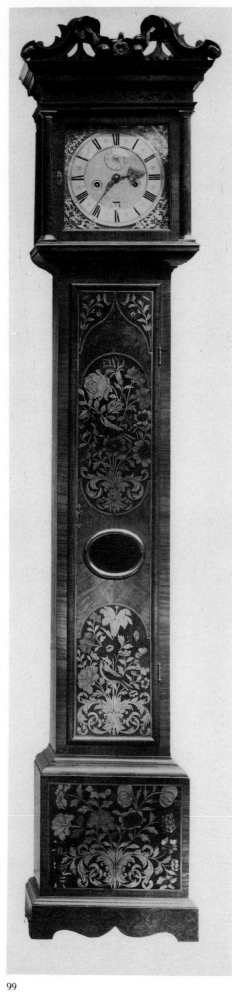

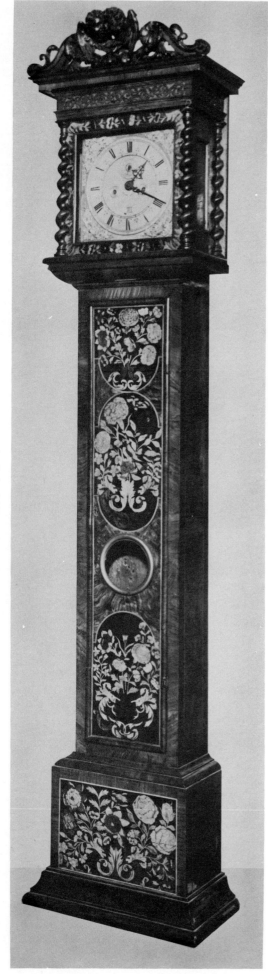

99   100

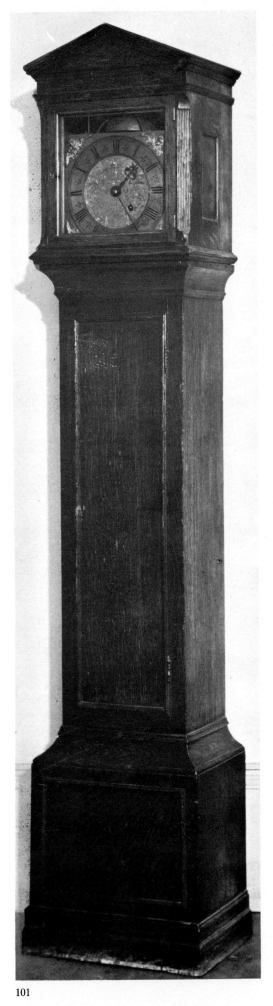

101

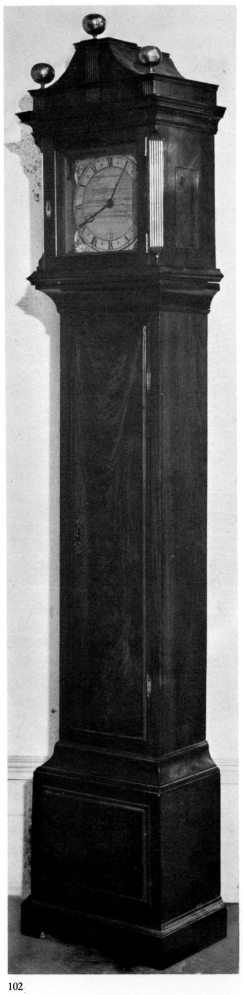

102

101 John Ebsworth, London. Movement *c.*1690. Case 18th century.

Striking clock in an oak case. Early style of dial with engraved centre and simple winged cherub spandrels. Name engraved in a panel in the dial zone. Early style hands. The case has an architectural top, but the moulding under the hood is concave.

102 No name. Movement *c.*1690. Case *c.*1780.

Listed in the catalogue as.'171. Mahogany long case strike clock', and similarly by Hurcomb. The case is similar in style to that of the previous clock illustrated, except for the pagoda top. The dial is of early style, with a narrow chapter ring, minute numerals within the minute ring, simple winged cherub spandrels, and plain hands, with bolt and shutter maintaining power. Very good movement with latched and unusually shaped plates. Square bolt heads as in lantern clocks. Crude pendulum regulation with a small regulator dial on the side. Height 6ft 9in (2.06m).

103 Charles Goode, London. *c.*1690.

Rare small striking longcase clock in floral marquetry, which is continued on the moulding and hood. Skeletonised chapter ring with minute numerals outside the minute ring and early style winged cherub spandrels. Same direction barley **twist** pillars and wrong domed top to the hood. **Wrongly attributed by Hurcomb to Clement.** Height 5ft 11in (1.83m) Dial 7½in (19cm) square.

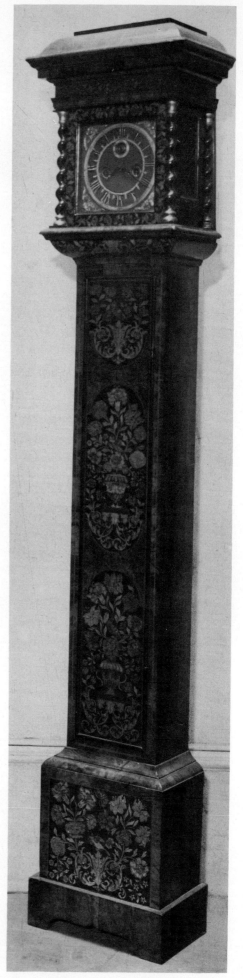

103

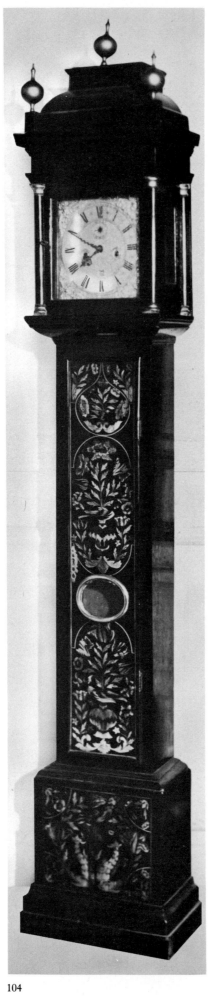

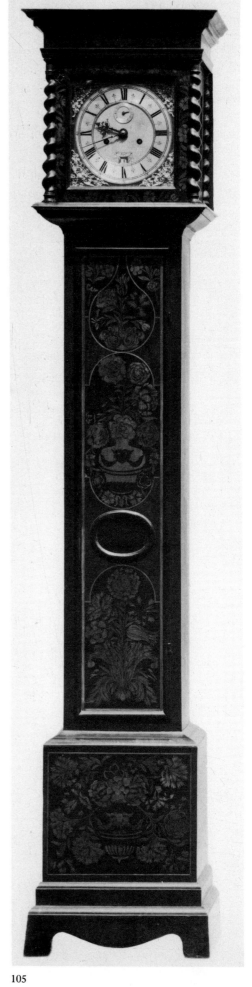

104

105

104 John Barnett, London. *c.*1690–1695.
Ebonised eight-day striking longcase clock in floral
and bird marquetry with an oval window in the case
door. Elaborate cherub spandrels, seconds ring,
date aperture, ringed winding holes, and wavy
minute hand. Hood with domed top, plain pillars
and three ball and spire finials. Height 7ft 1in
(2.16m) Dial 10in (25.5cm) square.

105 Charles Gretton, London. *c.*1690–1695.
Eight-day striking longcase clock in floral marquetry
on the hood as well as the case. Oval window in the
door. The minute numerals and half quarter
divisions are engraved outside the minute ring.
Elaborate spandrels, seconds ring and date aperture
with engraving around it. Flat topped hood with
barley twist pillars and concave moulding
underneath it. Added foot with an apron. Height
6ft 11in (2.11m) Dial 10in (25.5cm) square.

106 Thomas Wheeler, London. *c.*1690–1695.
Tall eight-day striking longcase clock in floral
marquetry. Minute numerals outside the minute
ring, elaborate cherub spandrels and hour hand.
Seconds dial and ringed winding holes. The tall
hood has an elaborate arch with pierced wooden fret
and inverted bell top, with three carved and gilded
urn finials, and marquetry on the hood door. Same
direction barley twist pillars. B. Hutchinson
remarked that the hood has 'suffered
aggrandisement'. Height 7ft 10in (2.39m) Dial 11in
(28cm) square.

106

107 Daniel Quare, London. *c.*1695.

Month striking longcase clock in floral and bird
marquetry. Fine dial and hands. The elaborate
cherub spandrels have engraving between them.
'Daniel Quare London' is engraved on the chapter
ring each side of VI. Small minute numerals outside
the minute ring. Ringed winding holes. Flat topped
hood with marquetry all over the front, and on the
convex moulding at the top of the case. Same
direction barley twist pillars. Height 7ft 2in (2.18m)
Dial 11in (38cm) square.

108 Joseph Knibb, London. *c.*1695.

Month striking longcase clock in floral and bird
marquetry with an oval glass in the door. It is short
for its time. Minute numerals within the minute
ring. Unusual winged cherub spandrels and
engraved border on the dial plate. Date aperture
under XII. Flat topped hood with opposite
direction barley twist pillars. The plinth does not
appear to match the case. Height 6ft 9in (2.06m)
Dial 10in (25.5cm) square.

109 Daniel Quare, London. *c.*1695.

Burr walnut month striking longcase clock. Minute
numerals inside the minute ring. Elaborate cherub
spandrels and hands. Serrated pattern engraving
around the centres of the hands, including the
seconds hand. Engraving between the spandrels and
'Daniel Quare London' at the sides of VI. Ringed
winding holes and engraving around the date
aperture. The movement has maintaining power.
Carved flower basket cresting on the hood and
convex moulding under it. Foot with an apron.
Height 7ft 5in (2.26m) Dial 11in (28cm) square.

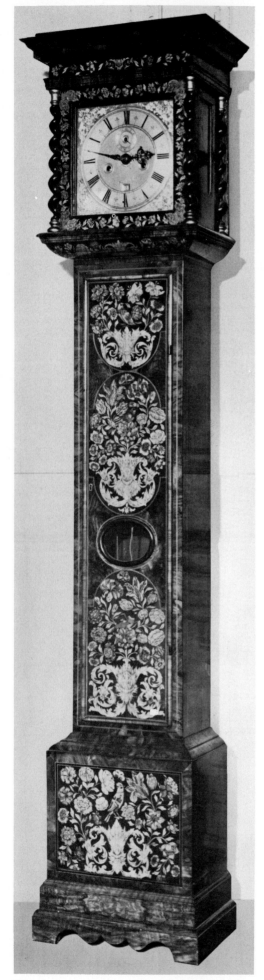

107

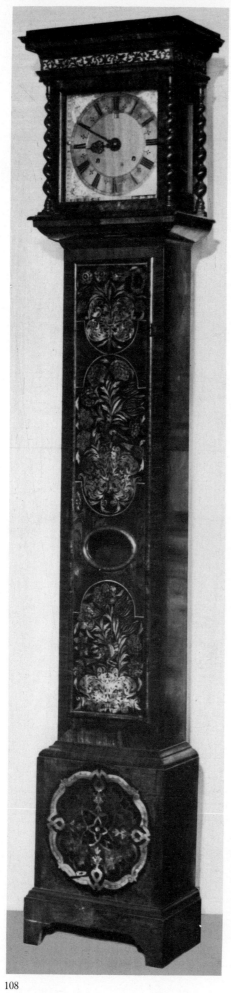

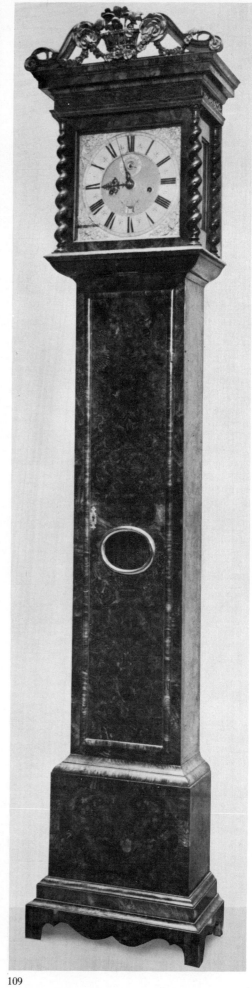

108

109

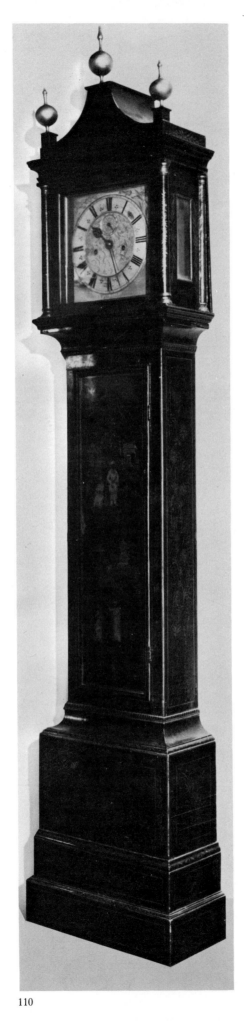

110 Joseph Knibb, London. *c*.1695. Case *c*.1740–50.

Eight-day two-train quarter and hour striking longcase clock in a black lacquered case showing Chinese scenes. The dial in the early style without spandrels, but is larger. It is engraved in the zone and corners of the dial plate with tulips and a rosette in the centre, but with a seconds ring and date aperture. The hour hand is not in the early style. 'Joseph Knibb Londini Fecit' is engraved along the bottom of the dial plate. The hood has a pagoda (or inverted bell) top hood with ball and spire finials and plain pillars. The moulding underneath the hood is concave, unlike clocks of the period where it was convex. Height 7ft 6in (2.29m) Dial 12in (30cm) square.

111 John Marshall, London. *c*.1695–1700.

Month-day striking longcase clock in floral marquetry with winged human figures. Minute numerals and half-quarter ornaments outside the minute ring. Elaborate cherub spandrels and hour hand. Wide seconds ring with large numerals. Ringed winding holes with engraved date aperture between them. Bolt and shutter maintaining power. The flat topped hood has flask finials, opposite twist pillars, and convex moulding underneath it. Height 6ft 10in (2.08m) Dial 11in (28cm) square.

112 James Clowes, London. *c*.1695–1700.

Month striking longcase clock with fine all-over floral marquetry case, the marquetry being also on the sides of the hood, trunk and plinth. Elaborate cherub spandrels and minutes engraved on the outside of the minute ring. Ringed winding holes and date aperture between them. The hood has a flat top with flask finials and plain pillars with gilded capitals. Moulding under the hood is convex. Height 7ft (2.13m) Dial 11in (28cm) square.

110

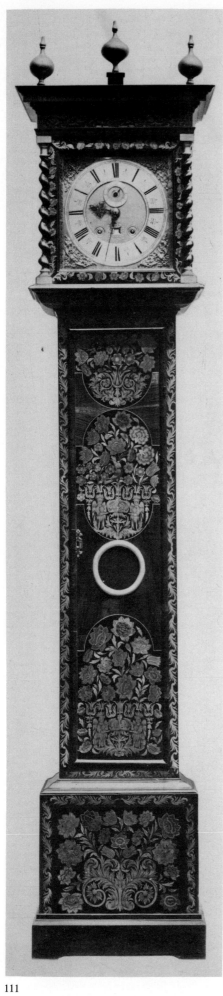

111

112

155

113 Charles Gretton, London. *c*.1695–1700.
Eight-day striking longcase clock in a floral marquetry case with a round bullseye in the door. Elaborate cherub mask and foliage spandrels. Small minute numerals outside the minute ring. Seconds ring, ringed winding holes and engraving around the centre of the zone. Domed top to the hood with skittle finials and marquetry on the front, plain pillars, and convex moulding underneath. Height 7ft 7in (2.31m) Dial 11in (28cm) square.

114 Jonathan Lowndes, London. *c*.1695–1700.
Described as an 'eight-day striking longcase' clock this could possibly be a long duration timepiece with two great wheels. Floral and bird marquetry panels on the case and marquetry on the front of the hood, including the domed top. Elaborate foliage spandrels, but minute numerals within the minute ring in the earlier style. Ringed winding holes in line with the centre of the hands. No seconds dial. Engraving round the date aperture. Convex moulding under the hood. Height 7ft 5in (2.26m) Dial 11in (28cm) square.

115 Elias Burges, London. *c*.1695–1700.
Eight-day striking longcase clock in floral marquetry with an oval bullseye in the door. Elaborate cherub mask and foliage spandrels. Minute numerals outside the minute ring. Seconds ring with numerals every five seconds and a ring of dots around the centre. Ringed winding holes with a ring of dots around each. Scrolling engraved around the date aperture. The hood has marquetry on the front, including the domed top, and same direction barley twist pillars. Height 7ft 3in (2.21m) Dial 11in (28cm) square.

113

114

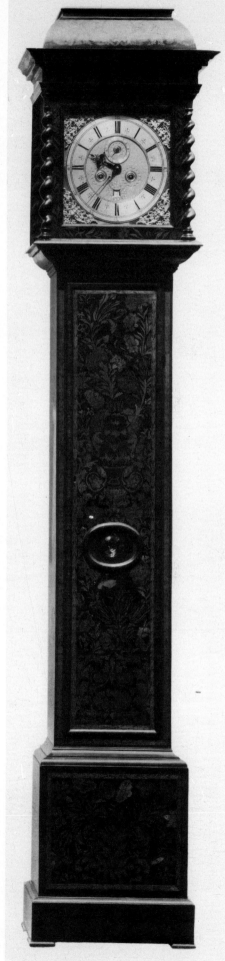

115

116

117

116 Thomas West, London. *c*.1695–1700.
Eight-day striking longcase clock in floral and bird marquetry. More elaborate cherub mask and foliage spandrels. Minute numerals and half-quarter ornaments outside the minute ring. Seconds ring with numerals every five seconds and a concentric ring of decorative dots inside it, repeated around the circular date aperture. Rings round the winding holes and centre of the dial. Elaborate hour hand. Marquetry over the front of the hood, which has a domed top with skittle finials. Plain foot. Height 7ft 3in (2.21m) Dial 10in (25.5cm).

117 Langley Bradley, London. *c*.1695–1700.
Eight-day three-train striking and 6-bell chiming longcase clock in floral and bird marquetry. More elaborate cherub mask and foliage spandrels and numerals outside the minute ring. Every five seconds numbered on the seconds ring. Ringed winding holes and a date aperture under the going train winding hole. Large and elaborate hour hand. Same direction barley twist pillars to the domed hood, which has ball and spire finials. Bullseye in the door, convex moulding under the hood and an apron to the high foot, which does not look right. Height 7ft 10in (2.39m) Dial 11in (28cm) square.

118 Charles Gretton, London. *c*.1695–1700.
Eight-day striking longcase clock in floral and bird marquetry with a round bullseye in the door. Deep convex moulding under the hood, which has a high domed marquetry top. More elaborate cherub and foliage spandrels. Ringed winding holes. Circular date aperture with rings and scrolled carving around it. Minute numerals and half-quarter ornaments outside the minute ring. Particularly fine hands. Height 7ft 6in (2.29m) Dial 11in (28cm) square.

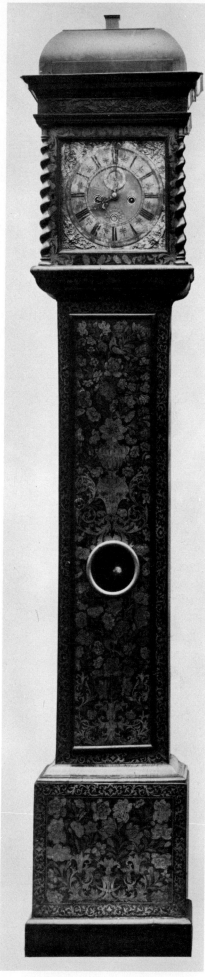

118

159

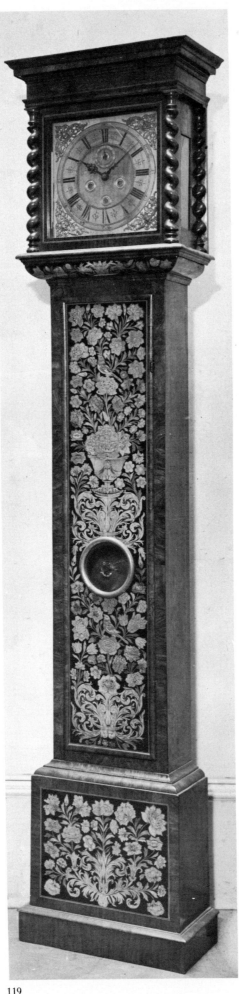

119

119 Thomas Taylor, London. *c.*1695–1700.
Eight-day striking longcase clock in floral and bird
marquetry with a bullseye in the door. More
elaborate cherub and foliage spandrels. Slightly
larger minute numerals with half-quarter ornaments
outside the minute ring. Seconds dial numbered
every five seconds. Ringed winding holes with
maintaining power and a ringed date aperture
between them. The bottom of the dial plate is signed
'Tho Taylor in Holborn London'. Flat topped hood
with opposite twist barley twist pillars and convex
moulding under it. Height 6ft 10in (2.08m) Dial
11in (28cm) square.

120 Thomas Tompion, London. *c.*1700.
Month striking longcase clock in fine figured walnut
case. More elaborate mask and foliage spandrels
with engraving between them and 'Tho: Tompion
Londini Fecit' engraved along the bottom edge.
Larger minute numerals, and half-quarter markers
outside the minute ring. 'Tho Tompion London'
also signed on a cartouche on the dial. The
movement has bolt and shutter maintaining power.
High domed hood with three ball finials, pierced
wooden side frets and plain pillars. The moulding
under the hood is concave, instead of convex in the
style of earlier longcase clocks. Movement
numbered 338. Original bun feet — very rare.
Height 7ft 10in (2.39m) Dial 11in (28cm) square.

120

120 (detail)

161

121

121 Thomas Tompion, London. *c*.1700.
Month striking longcase clock in finely figured
walnut case. More elaborate mask and foliage
spandrels, larger minute numerals with half-quarter
markers outside the minute ring, seconds dial and
date aperture. 'Tho: Tompion Londini Fecit;
engraved along the bottom edge of the dial plate.
Bolt and shutter maintaining power. High domed
hood with three ball finials, the centre one on
cresting, ball feet and concave moulding under the
hood. The clock is similar to the previous one by the
same maker, except for the cresting, side frets to the
top of the hood (absent on the other), more
elaborate piercing of the side frets and the absence of
the maker's name in the dial zone. Height 7ft 11in
(2.41m) Dial 11in (28cm) square.

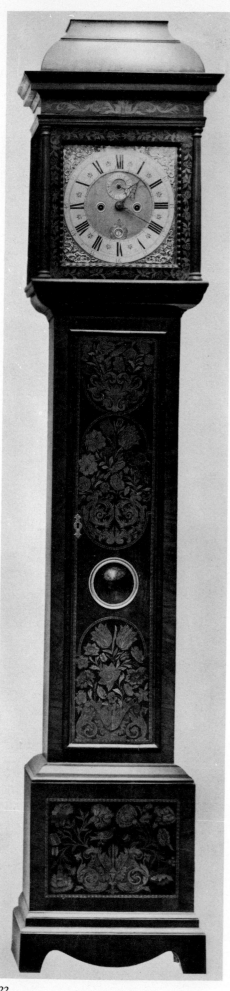

122 Isaac Lowndes, London. *c.*1700.
Eight-day striking longcase clock with floral and
bird marquetry panels with a bullseye in the door
and marquetry on the front of the hood, including
the domed top. Twin cherubs and crown spandrels.
Dial larger than formerly and with half-quarter
ornaments and larger minute numerals. Wide
seconds ring with every five seconds numbered.
Ringed winding holes and date aperture, with
foliage engraving around it and above VI. The plain
pillared hood has a beaded inside edge to the door
and convex moulding under it. The case foot is
tapered with an apron and looks wrong. Height
7ft 10in (2.93m) Dial 12in (30cm) square.

122

123 (detail)

123

123 Jonathan Puller, London. *c*.1700.

Tall (for the time) month three-train longcase clock, striking and chiming on six bells, in floral and human figure marquetry case, the marquetry covering all the front of the case including the frame around the door. (Often the door only was marquetry.) More elaborate cherub and foliage spandrels. Numerals outside the minute ring. Balloon-shaped panel around the hands engraved 'Jona. Puller Londini Fecit'. Date aperture and seconds hand. Auxiliary dials at the top corners for (left) pendulum regulation, and (right) for silent/strike/no strike. High domed top with relief cast acanthus finials. Claw and ball feet. Height 8ft 1in (2.46m) Dial 12in (30cm).

124 Joseph Windmills, London. *c*.1700.

Month striking longcase clock in seaweed marquetry all over the front of the case. Twin cherub and crown spandrels. The quarter divisions, half hour and half-quarter ornaments are retained, with outside minute numerals. Elaborately pierced hour hand. Herringbone engraving on the edge of the dial plate, round date aperture and the maker's name and place engraved at the side of VI. Domed top, plain pillars, oval glass in the door, and convex moulding still retained under the hood. Height above average at 8ft (2.44m) Dial 12in (30cm).

124

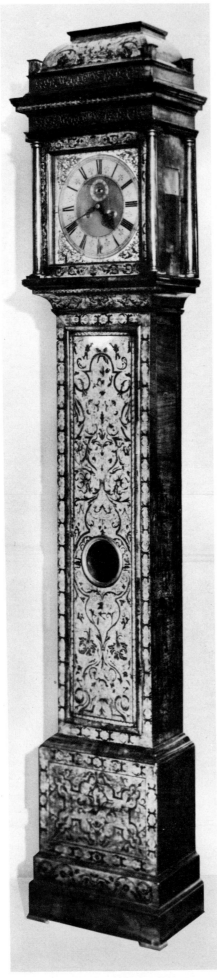

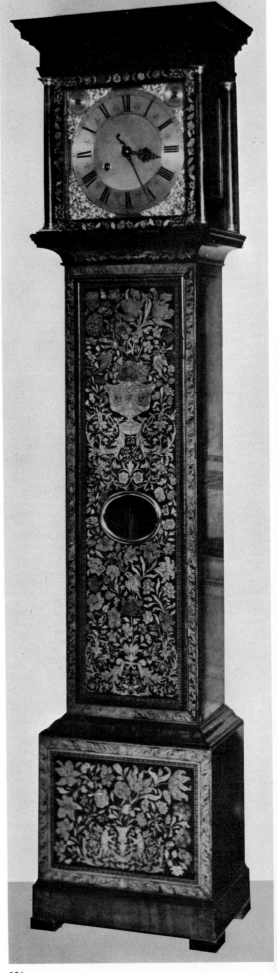

125

126

125 Benjamin Collyer, London. *c.*1700.

Month striking longcase clock in an elaborate foliage and bird all-over marquetry case. Cherub and foliage spandrels. Small minute numerals outside the ring and quarter divisions and half hour ornaments retained, but no half-quarter markers. Herring bone engraving around the dial plate edge and the maker's name and place at the sides of VI on the chapter ring. Date aperture with engraved ornamentation and ringed winding holes. Elaborately pierced hour hand. Marked concave moulding under the hood. High domed hood, glass side panels and plain pillars.

126 Daniel Quare, London. *c.*1700.

Fine equation timepiece (i.e. not striking), that runs for a year at a winding, in floral and urn marquetry case with an oval door window. Note the counterpoised minute hand. The single 69lb (31.3kg) weight hangs centrally behind the pendulum. The subsidiary dials are an annual calendar (top right) and an equation dial showing the difference between mean and apparent time (top left) for setting the clock by the sundial. The minute numerals are within the minute ring in the earlier style and the spandrels are of elaborate foliage pattern without cherubs, a style popular later. Wetherfield purchased this clock in Spain, which was a good market for English clocks in the 18th century. Height 7ft 10in (2.39m). The dial is larger than earlier clocks in the collection at 14in (36cm) square.

127 Fromanteel and Clarke, Amsterdam. *c.*1700.

Month longcase clock striking hours and quarters and with an alarm (according to Britten), but it seems to have only two trains and the central ring is ornamentation, not an alarm dial. The marquetry case has a number of human faces depicted in the pattern. The dial plate has an engraved border and cherub and foliage spandrels. There are two auxiliary dials above the ringed winding holes, that on the right giving the Moon's phase and age, and that on the left (not determined). There are two apertures for calendar information, above VI. The hood has a tall domed hood with elaborate finials of Atlas with two heralds, and the case stands on tall feet, which appear to have been added. The moulding under the hood is concave. Height 7ft 7in (2.31m) Dial 11in (28cm) square.

127

128 Henry Elliott, London. *c*.1700.

Eight-day hour and quarter striking longcase clock in floral marquetry, which also depicts birds and mermaids. Cherub and foliage spandrels. Half-quarter markers, ringed winding holes and engraving around the date aperture. The three subsidiary dial rings are for (not determined) (left), seconds (centre), and silencing the chiming (right). The case has a domed top and retains the convex moulding under the hood, which has plain pillars.

129 Christopher Gould, London. *c*.1700.

Fine small eight-day striking longcase clock that will repeat the hours, in walnut case. Britten says it repeats on six bells (implying quarter striking), but no evidence of winding for a third train can be seen on the dial. The dial plate has an engraved border and older style winged cherub spandrels, but the minute numerals are outside the minute ring. Quarter hour divisions and half ornaments are retained and there is a date aperture. The case has a deep plinth and concave moulding under the hood, which has a high domed hood with three urn finials. Height 6ft 2in (1.88m) The dial is very small at 7⅝in (19cm) square. Five or six miniature Goulds are known.

130 Thomas Tompion, London. *c*.1700.

The so-called 'Record Tompion' (see Introduction) made for King William III and probably used in Hampton Court Palace. It was one of the clocks sold to the USA at the Wetherfield sale in 1928, but was resold in the 1930s to J. S. Sykes in England. However, he sold it in 1956 to Williamsburg (the restored town) in Virginia, USA. It is a three-month striking longcase clock in a burr walnut case with silver and gilded mounts. The dial has a perpetual calendar giving the month, number of days in the month, and date, and corrects for leap years. It is one of two by the same maker with such a dial, the other being on a longcase equation clock by Tompion and Banger for Prince George of Denmark. The half-quarters, marked by crosses, are the first Tompion used. The movement, like those of Tompion's three equation clocks, is not numbered like his other clocks. The case has a gilt metal base showing cherubs, swags and scroll feet. (The only other with a similar metal foot is an equation clock by Tompion and Banger in Buckingham Palace.) Beneath the hood are four open-work metal corner brackets, and on top, four silvered urn finials and a central figure of Minerva with her shield, below which is the cypher of William III. The authenticity of the Minerva figure has been questioned, but it has been judged genuine. The hood also has fine pierced and fire gilded freize panels and side panels of arabesque design. The clock stands on an ebonised base that is not contemporary. Height without the base 10ft 2in (3.1m) Dial 12in (30cm).

128

168

129

130

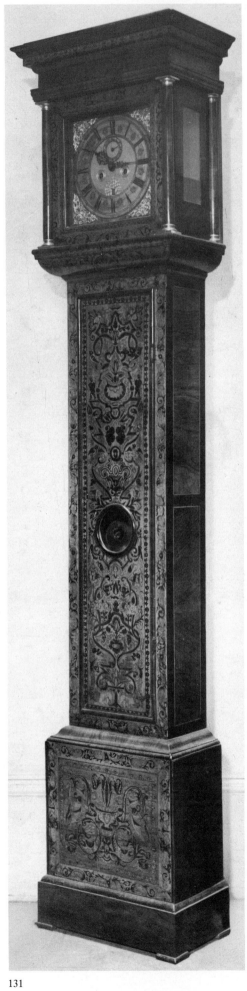

131

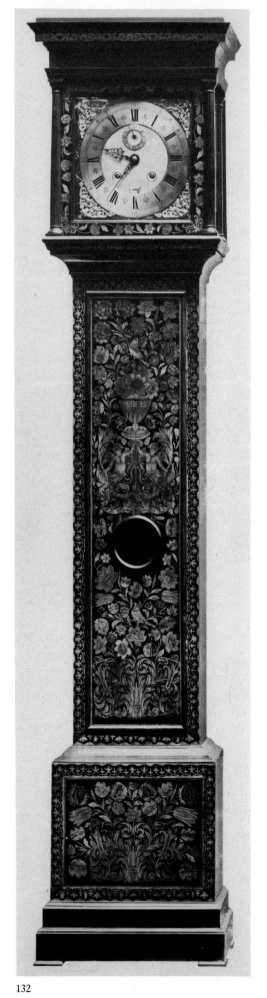

132

131 John Paulet, London. *c*.1700.

Eight-day striking longcase clock in a fine floral marquetry case that also shows birds and human faces and has banded veneered panels on the sides and a bullseye in the door. Cherub and foliage spandrels, half-quarter indications, ringed winding holes, and a date aperture with engraved decoration. The hood is flat topped with plain pillars and the case moulding under it is convex.

132 Isaac Lowndes, London. *c*.1700.

Month striking longcase clock in a floral marquetry case with birds and human figures. Flat topped hood with concave moulding under it. The plinth top moulding is also basically concave. Twin cherub and crown spandrels. The minute numerals have become larger, as have the seconds numerals. The half-quarter ornaments are particularly prominent. The chapter ring is signed 'Isaac Lownds in ye Pall Mall'. Engraved border to the dial plate, ringed winding holes, and date aperture decorated by engraving. Height 7ft 5in (2.26m) Dial 12in (30cm).

133 Joshua Willson, London. *c*.1700.

Eight-day striking longcase clock in fine floral marquetry with birds and human figures and banded veneered panels on the sides. Bullseye in the door and concave moulding under the flat topped hood. Cherub and foliage spandrels, ringed winding holes, dotted decoration around the date aperture and dial centres, and an elaborately pierced hour hand. Height 7ft 2in (2.18m) Dial 11in (28cm) square.

133

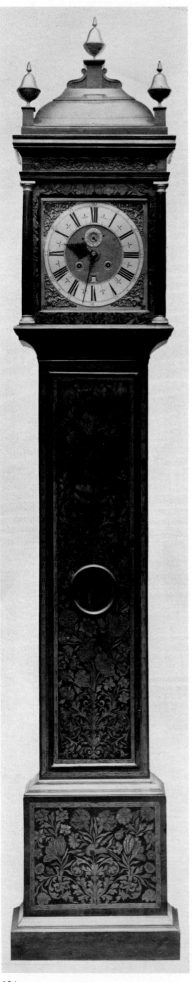

134

134 No name. *c.*1700.

Month striking longcase clock with an alarm in a floral marquetry case. Inverted bell top with three acorn style finials and concave moulding under the hood. Twin cherub and crown spandrels, half-quarter markers, no border engraving on the dial plate, ringed winding holes, and engraving around the date aperture. The hour hand is particularly elaborate. Height 8ft (2.44m) Dial 12in (30cm) square.

135 Isaac Papavoine, London. *c.*1700.

Eight-day longcase clock striking the hours and a single blow at the half hours, continental style. The floral marquetry of the case is rather French in style, as is the mount around the bullseye. The hood is flat topped and the moulding underneath it concave and shallow in an earlier style. The cherub spandrels are less elaborate than others of the time and the minute numerals not so large. There is engraving on the dial plate around the chapter ring, and the hour hand has a pierced stem. Height 7ft 2in (2.18m) Dial 12in (30cm).

136 Jonathan Puller, London. *c.*1700.

Eight-day striking longcase clock in floral marquetry with birds and human figures. Cherub and foliage spandrels. Small minute numerals and no half-quarter markers. Plain winding holes and date aperture. Concave moulding under the hood and ogee (concave-convex) moulding on the plinth. The hood had a deep domed top with pineapple finials and reversion to barley twist pillars with opposite twists. Added foot. Height 7ft 7in (2.31m) Dial 11in (28cm) square.

135

136

137

138

137 Daniel Quare, London. *c.*1700.

Month striking longcase clock in a case with marquetry panels (in an earlier fashion) on a ground of amboyna wood. The flat topped hood with barley twist pillars in opposite direction, convex moulding under it, and bun feet are traditional, but the dial with large minute numerals and half-quarter ornaments with twin cherub and crown spandrels are contemporary. The hour hand is slender and the chapter ring is signed 'Dan Quare London'. The plinth is not original; the marquetry is less detailed. Height 7ft 4in (2.24m) Dial 12in (30cm) square.

138 Cornelius Herbert, London. *c.*1700.

Eight-day striking longcase clock in a case with floral marquetry panels in an earlier style, and banded veneered panels on the sides. The domed hood has ball and spire finials and small side windows. The moulding under it is convex and the case has bun feet. Twin cherub and crown spandrels, ringed winding holes and engraving around the date aperture. The minute numerals are fairly large and accompanied by half-quarter markers. Signed on the chapter ring and wrongly ascribed by Hurcomb to Edmund Day.

139 John Pepys, London. *c.*1700.

Burr elm month striking longcase clock, with banded edges to the plinth, platform foot, and oval glass in the door. The hood top is flat with plain pillars and convex moulding under it. Winged cherub and foliage spandrels with engraving on the dial plate between them, and minute numerals within the minute ring in an earlier style. Ringed winding holes and the calendar aperture within the seconds ring. Height 7ft 1in (2.16m) Dial 11in (23cm) square.

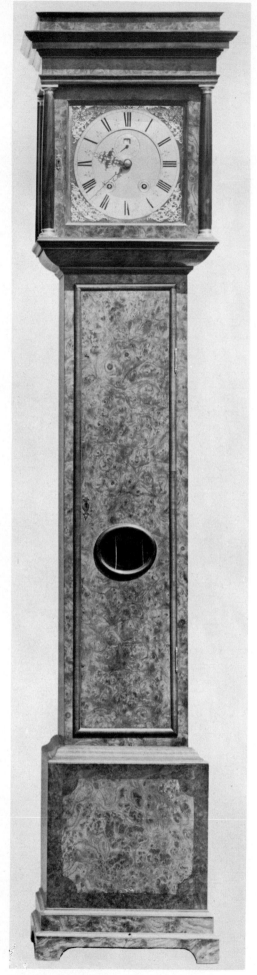

139

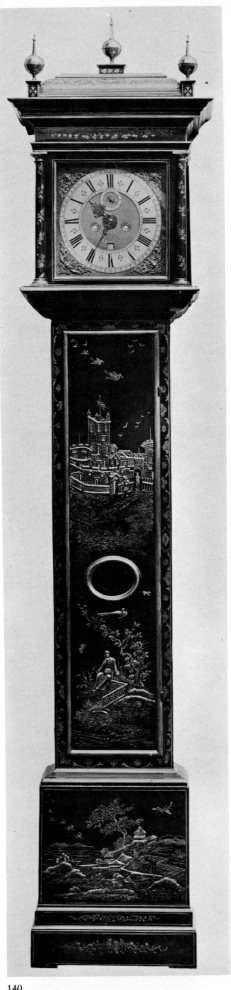

140

140 Christopher Gould, London. *c*.1700.

Fine eight-day striking longcase clock in a lacquered case showing Chinese scenes. Winged cherub and foliage spandrels, border engraved on the dial plate, and 'Christopher Gould Londini fecit' engraved along the bottom edge. Every minute is numbered in the very early style, but outside instead of inside the minute ring. Exceptionally fine hands with a large pierced boss to the hour hand. Seconds dial, ringed winding holes and engraving around the date aperture. Bolt and shutter maintaining power. Shallow domed hood with ball and spire finials and convex moulding underneath. Height 7ft 6in (2.29m) Dial 12in (30cm) square.

141 John Knottesford, London. *c*.1700.

Month three-train striking and chiming clock in a floral marquetry case with birds, dragons and winged human figures. The third winding square is in the III chapter. The dial has winged cherub and foliage spandrels and an elaborate cross-over patterned hour hand. Deep domed hood with no pillars. The trunk has convex moulding at the top and a foot that looks wrong. Height 7ft 7in (2.31m) Dial 12in (30cm) square.

142 John Finch, London. *c*.1700.

Eight-day striking clock in a floral marquetry case with birds and human figures and a shell below the marquetry circle around the window in the case door. Flat topped hood with concave moulding underneath it in the new style. Height 7ft 3in (2.21m) Dial 12in (30cm) square.

141

142

143 (detail)

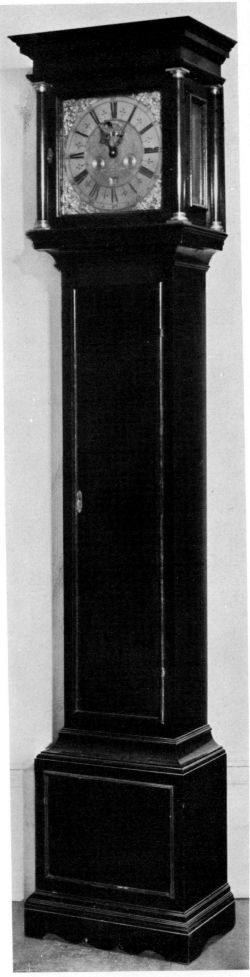

143 Thomas Tompion, London. *c.*1700.
Eight-day striking longcase clock in (according to
the catalogue) a stained oak case. Fairly large minute
numerals with half-quarter ornaments. Ringed
winding holes with bolt and shutter maintaining
power. Winged cherub and foliage spandrels with
engraving between them. Date indicator with
indentations by the numerals to allow them to be
changed with a pin. Engraved 'Tho Tompion
Londini fecit' on a cartouche on the matted zone.
Flat topped case with plain pillars and concave
moulding under it. Aproned foot. Height 6ft 10in
(2.08m) Dial 11in (28cm) square.

144 Jonathan Lowndes, London. *c.*1705.
Eight-day striking longcase clock in arabesque and
foliage marquetry. Twin cherub and crown
spandrels, large minute numerals with diamond
half-quarter and half-hour markers. Narrow hour
hand. High ringed winding holes, date aperture.
The hood has a very high domed top with ball and
spire finials, plain pillars and concave moulding
underneath. Height 8ft (2.44m) Dial 12in (30cm)
square.

145 Thomas Bridge, London. *c.*1705.
Eight-day striking longcase clock in arabesque
marquetry case with a very high domed top with ball
and spire finials. Convex moulding is retained under
the hood and barley twist pillars, in opposite
directions. Winged cherub and foliage spandrels
with engraving between them. The minute
numerals are small, with half-quarter ornaments.
Winding holes are ringed and there is engraving
round the date aperture and centre of the zone. The
seconds hand is a loop instead of the usual pointer.
Height 7ft 11in (2.41m) Dial 11in (28cm) square.

143

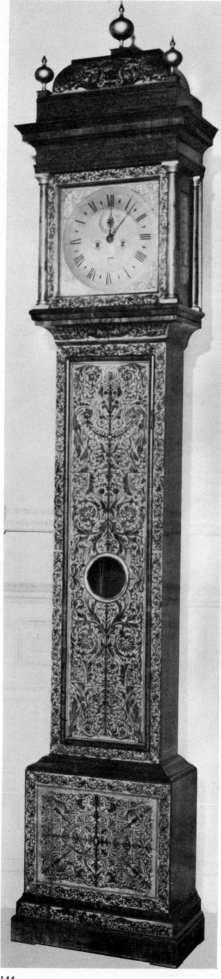

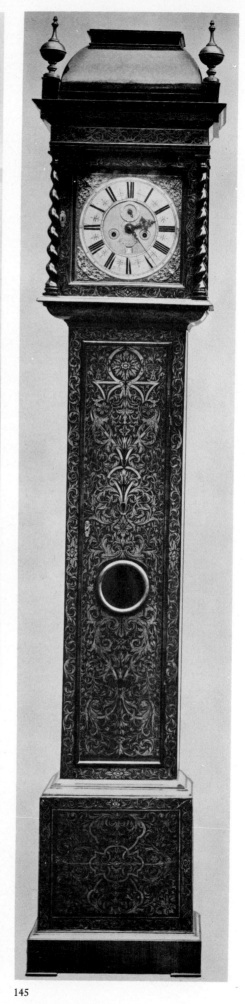

144

145

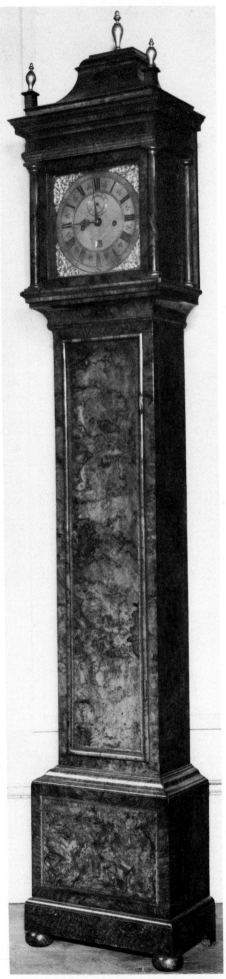

146 (detail)

146

146 Daniel Quare, London. *c*.1705.

Burr walnut month striking longcase clock with a bell top and skittle finials. Contemporarily fashionable concave moulding under the hood, but bun feet to the case. Twin cupid and crown spandrels. Fairly large minute numerals, half-quarter ornaments, and cross-over pattern hour hand. Chapter ring signed 'Dan Quare London'. Note similarity with the case of the Quare clock number 148, except that this has bun feet. Height 7ft 6in (2.29m) Dial 11in (28cm) square.

147 Thomas Andrews, London. *c*.1705.

Month striking longcase clock in an arabesque marquetry case, the small panel in the plinth showing a contemporary walking figure with a sword. Twin cherub and crown spandrels, half-quarter ornaments, ringed winding holes, and squared-off engraving round the date aperture. Signature and location engraved on the chapter ring at the sides of VI. Flat topped hood, plain pillars and concave moulding under it.

147

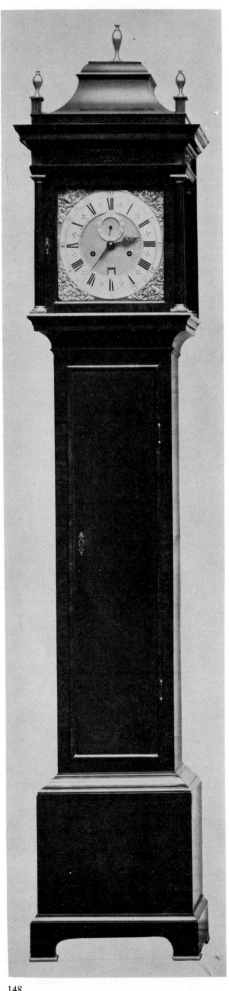

148

148 Daniel Quare, London. *c*.1705.
Burr walnut month striking longcase clock with a
bell top and skittle finials. Concave moulding under
the hood, and feet to the case. Winged cherub
spandrels. Fairly large minute numerals with half-
quarter ornaments, and cross-over pattern hour
hand. Chapter ring signed 'Dan Quare London'.
Note the similarity with the Quare clock numbered
146, except for the slightly lower winding holes and
feet that look wrong. Height 7ft 3in (2.21m) Dial
11in (28cm) square.

149 Daniel Quare, London. *c*.1705.
Month striking longcase clock in the earlier style of
panelled floral marquetry with birds and shells. The
marquetry is continued on the pillars. High inverted
bell top with urn and flame finials and concave
moulding under it. Mask and foliage spandrels,
fairly large minute numerals with half-quarter
markers, and cross-over pattern hour hand. Signed
'Dan Quare London' on the chapter ring at the sides
of VI. The foot does not look right. Height 7ft 9in
(2.36m) Dial of the larger, 12in (30cm) square, size.

150 Joseph Knibb, Hanslop. *c*.1705.
Month striking longcase clock in a plain ebonised
case with concave moulding under the hood and
bun feet, in the earlier style. The high domed hood
has ball finials and plain pillars. Foliage spandrels
with decorative engraving between them and
'Joseph Knibb at Hanslop' engraved along the
bottom of the dial plate. Reversion to the earlier
style of minute numerals engraved within the
minute ring. The divisions are short lines with pin
heads, following the pattern of the half hour
ornaments, instead of normal scale divisions. The
hands are also of the simpler earlier style. There is a
date aperture under XII. The clock has Roman
striking; note the IV on the dial. Height 8ft 1in
(2.47m) Dial 12in (30cm) square.

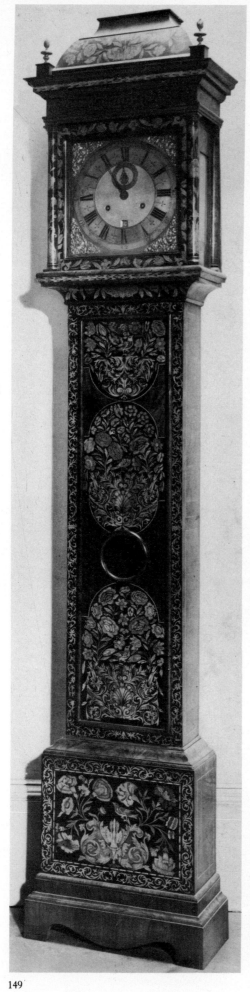

149

150

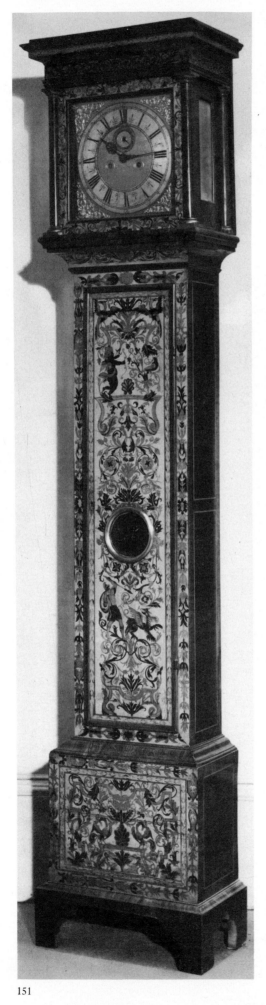

151

151 Charles Bonner, London. *c.*1705.

Eight-day striking longcase clock in an arabesque marquetry case also showing a warrior killing a dragon with a spear and a cherub shooting a bird with a bow and arrow. The flat topped hood has concave moulding under it, and the case is on a high foot which looks false. Twin cherub and crown spandrels, small minute numerals, half-quarter markers, ringed winding holes, engraving around the date aperture, and an hour hand with an oval pierced end.

152 Thomas Tompion and Edward Banger, London. *c.*1705.

Burr walnut eight-day striking longcase clock with tall domed and crested top with three ball finials. The case has concave moulding under the hood and above the plinth, and ball feet. Winged cherub and rosette spandrels, with engraved patterns between them, the makers' names being in an oval cartouche on the lower part of the zone above the date aperture. Half-quarter ornaments retained. The movement has bolt and shutter maintaining power and is numbered 352. The case looks very correct, but is a reproduction according to one authority. Height 7ft 11in (2.41m) Dial 11in (28cm) square.

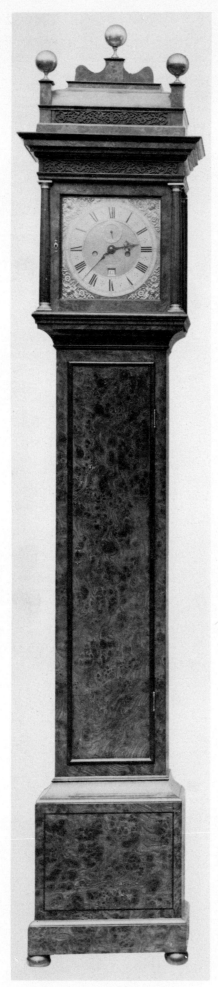

152 (detail)

152

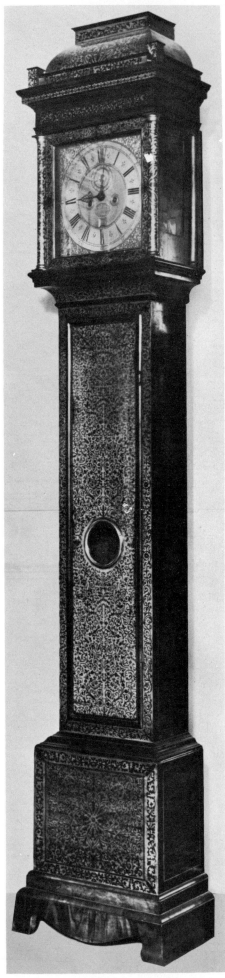

153

154

153 Thomas Smith, London. *c.*1710.

Eight-day striking longcase clock in a very finely detailed scroll marquetry case, the pattern covering the whole front, including the pillars. Concave moulding under the hood, that has a high domed top, and an apron to the high tapered foot. Elaborate spandrels, ringed winding holes, half-quarter ornaments, and triangular-shaped hour hand. Above the date aperture is an oval cartouche engraved with the maker's name and place. Britten shows this clock with urn finials. The foot is wrong. . Height 8ft (2.44m) Dial of the larger size, 12in (30cm) square.

154 'George Graham, London'. *c.*1710.

Month striking longcase clock in a floral marquetry case with bird and cherub motifs. Flat topped hood with plain pillars and a decorative banding around the bottom, above the concave moulding of the case. The chapter ring has small numerals with half-quarter decorations, in an earlier style, and the hour hand is elaborately pierced. The seconds hand has a tail. The clock does not appear to be in Graham's style.

155 Daniel Quare, London. *c.*1710.

Month three-train hour and quarter striking longcase clock in a burr walnut case with a high inverted bell top, concave moulding under the hood and at the top of the plinth. Mask and foliage spandrels with engraving between them, large minute numerals with half-quarter ornaments repeating the half hour ornament pattern, and ringed winding holes. Slender, delicately engraved hour hand and minute pointer. Date aperture over VI. Height 8ft (2.44m) Dial 12in (30cm) square.

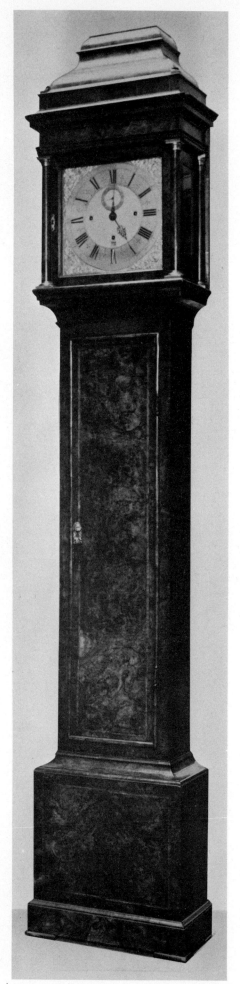

155

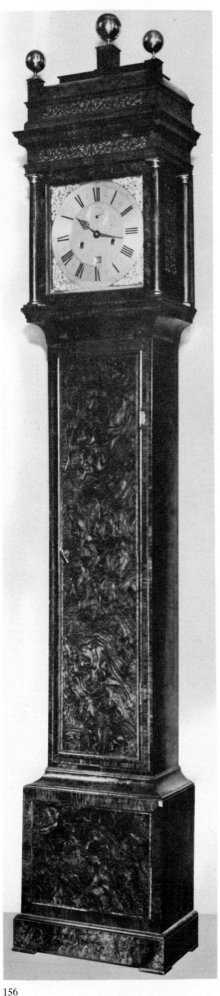

156 Daniel Quare, London. *c*.1710.
Month striking longcase clock in a burr walnut case with tall domed hood surmounted by three ball finials. Concave moulding under it and above the plinth. Note the similarity with the case of the Quare clock number 155. Large minute numerals with half-quarter markers of the same pattern as the half hour ornaments. Fine slender hands. In Hurcomb's book, the same illustration is used correctly on page 20 and repeated incorrectly for an East clock on page 19. The case could be by Tompion's casemaker. Quare and Tompion were friends. Height 8ft 1in (2.46cm) Larger sized dial at 12in (30cm) square.

157 Edmund Day, London. *c*.1710.
Month striking longcase clock in an arabesque marquetry case with bird motifs. Flat topped hood, plain pillars, concave moulding, and bun feet. Cherub and foliage spandrels, engraved edge to the dial plate, half-quarter indications and delicate half hour decorations. Finely pierced hands and ringing round winding holes and date aperture. Height 7ft 3in (2.21m) Large sized dial at 12in (30cm) square.

158 Abraham Oosterwyk, Middelburg, Holland. *c*.1710.
Month longcase clock striking on two bells, in a fine arabesque marquetry case. Tall domed hood with cone finials. Concave moulding under the hood and above the plinth. Foot with apron. Foliage spandrels, large minute numerals with half-quarter ornaments and butterfly half hour ornaments. Ringed winding holes and elaborate engraving around the date aperture. Height 8ft 2in (2.49m) Dial 12in (30cm).

156

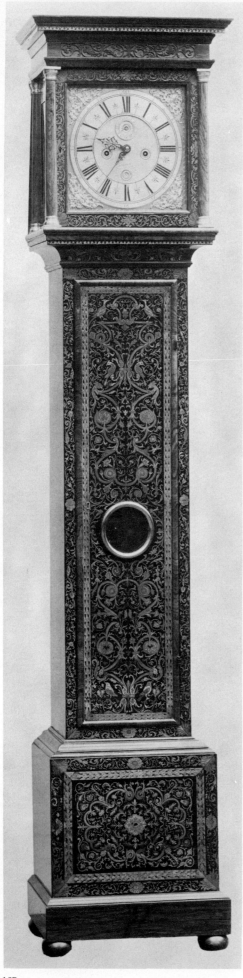

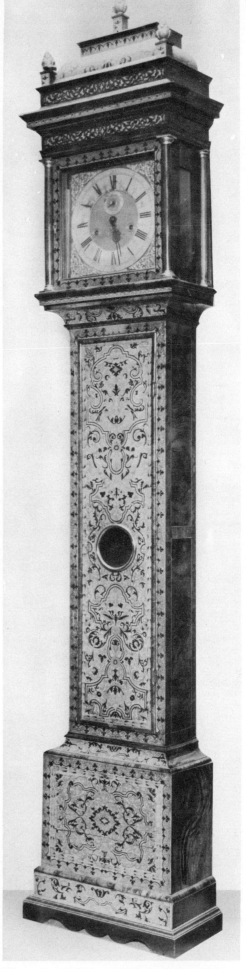

157.

158

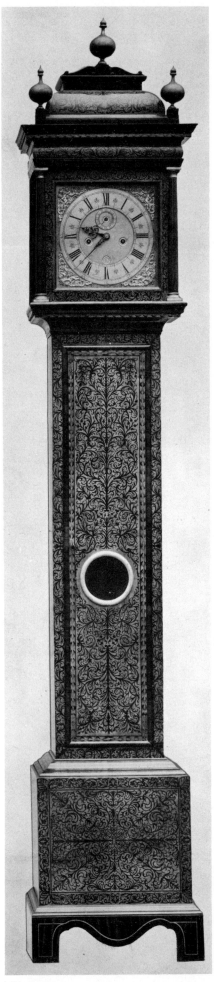

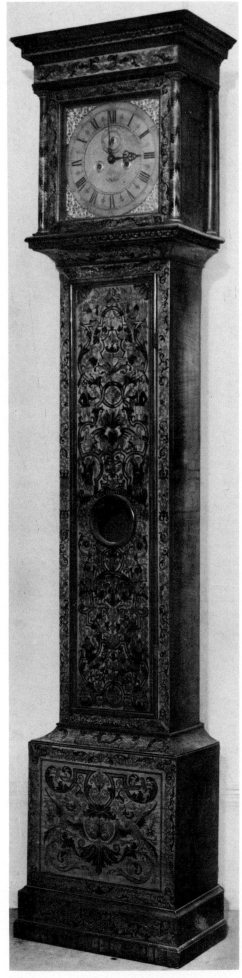

159   160

159 Joseph Windmills, London. *c.*1710.
Eight-day striking longcase clock in a seaweed
marquetry case, with banding on the sides and the
foot. The domed hood has cresting and three ball
and spire finials. Twin cherubs and crown spandrels
with engraving between them, half-hour markers,
and butterfly pattern half hour ornaments. Ringed
date aperture and winding holes. Signed on the
bottom of the chapter ring. The foot is ridiculous!
Height 7ft 10in (2.39m) Dial 11in (28cm) square.

160 Esaye Fleureau, London. *c.*1710.
Eight-day striking longcase clock in fine arabesque
marquetry with birds and figures, including
falconers and Father Time. Britten (Fig. 98 in his
book) says the marquetry is continued on the sides
of the case, but in the photograph in the catalogue
album it is continued only on the sides of the
concave moulding under the hood and on the sides
of the foot. Twin cherubs and crown spandrels, half
quarter ornaments and butterfly half hour
ornaments. Height 7ft 6in (2.29m) Dial 12in (30cm)
square.

161 John Eagle, London. *c.*1710.
Eight-day striking longcase clock with unusual floral
marquetry showing four scenes involving warriors.
Flat topped hood with reversion to convex moulding
under it. Plinth with a foot. Twin cherub and crown
spandrels. Ringed winding holes and three dot half
hour ornaments. Date aperture. Height 7ft 3in
(2.21m) Dial 11in (28cm) square.

161

162 Richard Colston, London. *c.1710.*
Eight-day striking longcase clock in an intricate marquetry case. Flat topped hood with concave moulding under the hood and above the plinth, which has a foot. Twin cherub and crown spandrels and engraved band around the dial plate. Prince of Wales feathers half hour ornaments. Half-quarter markers and minute numerals outside the minute ring but enclosed by an engraved circle. Narrow hour hand and elaborate engraving around the date aperture. Height 7ft 5in (2.26m) Dial 12in (30cm) square.

163 Nicholas Lambert, London. *c.1710.*
Month striking longcase clock in floral marquetry which also features cherubs. Concave moulding under the hood and above the plinth. Prominent dot half-quarter markers, narrow hour hand, seconds dial and date aperture with engraving around it.

164 Benjamin Collyer, London. *c.1710.*
Burr walnut eight-day striking longcase clock. The hood has a platform top and free standing pillars. (Pillars incorporated in the hood were almost universal in London clocks.) The moulding under the hood is convex, in the general style before 1700. Winged cherub and foliage spandrels, small minute numerals in an earlier style, but with an outer engraved circle and no half-quarter markers. Ringed winding holes and engraving around the date aperture. Height 7ft 2in (2.18m) Dial 11in (28cm) square.

162

163

164

165 'Thomas Tompion, London'. *c.*1715.
Burr walnut month three-train hour striking
longcase clock that chimes the quarters on six bells.
The case has a shaped and bevelled mirror door on
Vauxhall glass. Concave moulding under the hood
and on the plinth. The break arch dial and break
arch top to the hood represent a new style. In the
arch is a dial for hours and quarters/hours/silent all
(left) and another for regulation. In the centre is an
engraving (of a cheerful bird on a pillar), which is
out of character. The maker's name and place, on
the lower part of the chapter ring. An authentic
Tompion signature on a chapter ring has yet to be
found. Large minute numerals, prominent diamond
ornaments to indicate half-quarters, and *fleur-de-lys*
half hour ornaments. Twin cherub and crown
spandrels. Britten dates this clock at 1710–1725 and
suggested that it was made by Tompion's nephew of
the same name, who was apprenticed in 1694 and
became Free of the Clockmakers Company in 1702,
but there is no record of a clock or watch by him,
and Baillie said he probably retired in 1713. In 1720,
he and his wife were committed to Newgate for
picking eleven guineas from a woman's pocket.
B.Hutchinson suggests that the clock may have been
made originally by W.Webster (died 1734).

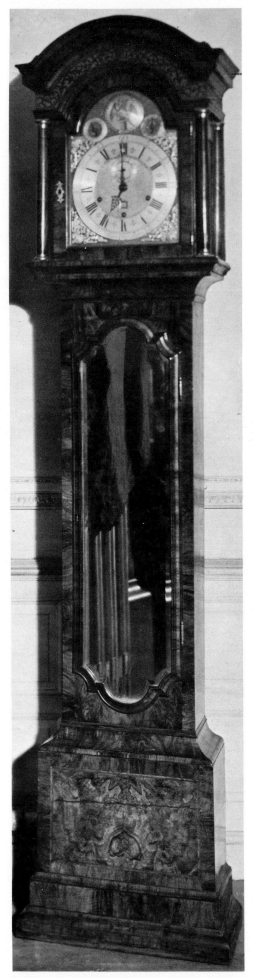

165

166 Charles Clay, London. *c*.1715.

Impressive month striking longcase clock in an arabesque marquetry case, including the pillars, with bird motifs. The inverted bell top has three urn and tulip finials (two broken) and the hood is supported by elaborate corner brackets. Mask and floral spandrels and large minute numerals, without half-quarter markers, but with an outer engraved circle. Quarter divisions and *fleur-de-lys* half hour markers. Signed in an oval cartouche above two calendar apertures. According to Hurcomb the calendar is perpetual, but he probably meant annual, i.e. accurate over a year, but not correcting for leap years. (Clock with two calendar apertures usual indicate the old style date and new style, after 1752).

166

167 (detail)

167 Christopher Gould, London. *c*.1715.
Eight-day striking longcase clock chiming on eight
bells, in a marquetry case with birds and human
figures, the marquetry being continued on panels on
the sides, including the plinth, and on the pillars
and quarter pillars at the rear. Inverted bell top with
ball and spire corner finials. Concave moulding
under the hood and above the plinth. Winged
cherub and floral spandrels of conventional style
surrounded by engraving, and with engraving round
the dial centre in a very early fashion. Half-quarter
markers and *fleur-de-lys* half hour ornaments.
Ringed winding holes and date aperture. Above the
chapter XII is a lever in a slot marked Silent-Strike.
The bottom of the dial plate is signed CHR GOULD
LONDINI FECIT in the early style.

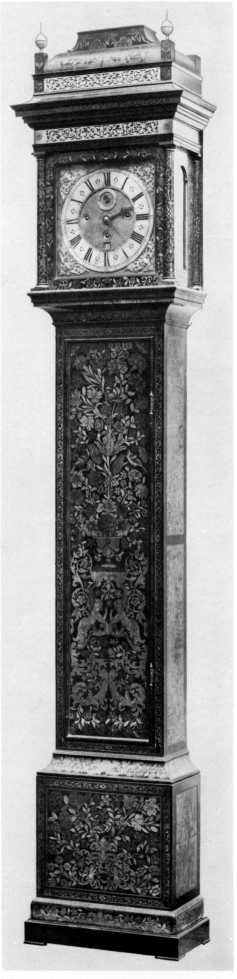

167

168

168 Francis Gregg, London. *c*.1720.

Break arch dial and movement of an eight-day striking longcase clock with calendar and equation of time dial. In the arch is a seconds dial with very large numerals inside the divisions. A regulator is on the left of it and a strike/Silent control on the right. There are very large minute numerals and prominent diamond-shaped half-quarter markers with *fleur-de-lys* half hour ornaments and a small hour hand. The winding holes are high and there is another square in a hole by the chapter I, probably for setting the annual calendar and equation dial, which revolves once a year and shows the month, number of days in it in Roman numerals, actual date at the bottom edge, and amount by which the sundial is fast or slow at the top. Signed in a sector over the centre. Dial 12 by 18in (30 by 46cm).

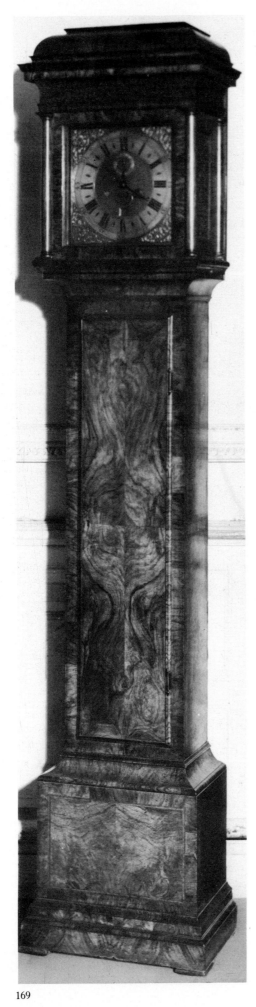

169

169 George Graham, London. *c.*1720.

Eight-day striking longcase clock in a book-matched walnut case with domed top and concave moulding under the hood and at the top of the plinth. Diamond half hour ornaments. Signed on an oval cartouche in the zone. The movement has maintaining power. Height 7ft 1in (2.16m) Dial 11in (28cm) square.

170 George Graham, London. Movement *c.*1720.

Month regulator (non-striking) in a mahogany case with a glass door, the style of which is not Graham's. Circular silvered dial in a break arch hood. The dial was said to show solar time and mean solar time, by two concentric minute hands, the difference between them being the equation of time, but could have shown mean solar and sidereal time. Hours are shown in a sector and the seconds hand is at the top. The sector above it indicates (not identified). The single winding hole is under the hour sector and the signature under that. Height 6ft 4in (1.93m) Dial 12in (30cm) diameter.

171 Joseph Williamson, London. Movement *c.*1720.

Eight-day striking longcase clock in an oak case with a break arch dial. The case, with its break arch hood, cresting and ball finials, is later than the movement. Elaborate mask and foliage spandrels. Signed on a central boss in the arch. Ringed winding holes with bolt and shutter maintaining power. *Fleur-de-lys* style half hour ornaments and diamond half quarter markers.

170

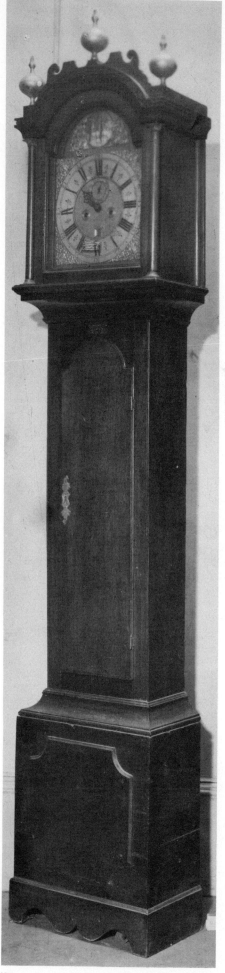

171

199

172 Daniel Quare, London. *c*.1720.
Month striking longcase **clock** in a burr walnut case
with concave mouldings. The dial is unusual, with
its small break arch on a tall dial, matched by a small
break arch under the flat topped hood. In the arch is
an annual calendar, which also shows the equation
of time. Half-quarter markers and an elaborately
engraved cartouche with the maker's name and place
over VI. Ringed winding holes with bolt and shutter
maintaining power. Height 7ft 6in (2.29m) Dial 12
by 17in (30 by 43cm).

173 Joseph Williamson, London. *c*.1725.
Eight-day striking longcase clock with calendar and
equation of time dial in a scroll marquetry case with
break arch dial and domed top with three ball finials.
The case is not original. Britten shows only the dial.
Elaborate mask and foliage spandrels and narrow
hour hand. No half-quarter ornaments. The hand in
the arch carries a Sun effigy and shows month, date,
and Sun slow or fast in relation to the mean time
shown by the clock dial. There is an applied
cartouche under the ringed winding holes engraved
'JOSEPHUS WILLIAMSON LONDINI FECIT', and, in the
centre, the Latin motto, 'Horae indicantur apparetes
involutis Equationibus'. Height 8ft 2in (2.49m) Dial
12 by 17 in (30 by 43 cm).

174 Thomas Bennett, London. *c*.1725.
Book-matched burr walnut eight-day striking
longcase clock with a high inverted bell top
surmounted by bird of prey finials. In the break arch
dial, a hand shows the date. Mask and foliage
spandrels. No half-quarter markers. Diamond half
hour ornaments, high winding holes and a narrow
hour hand. Signed at the bottom of the chapter ring.
Height 8ft 4in (2.54m) Dial 12 by 16in (30 by
41cm).

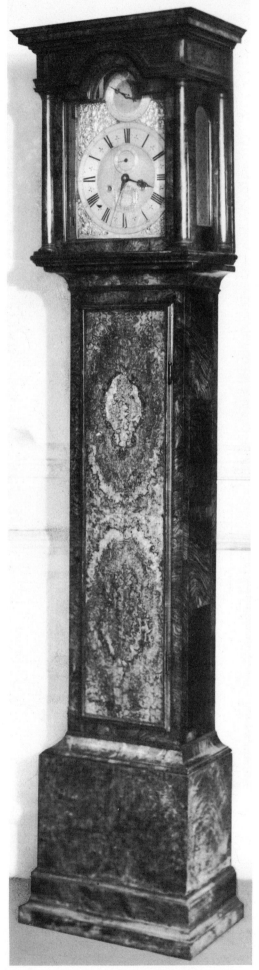

172

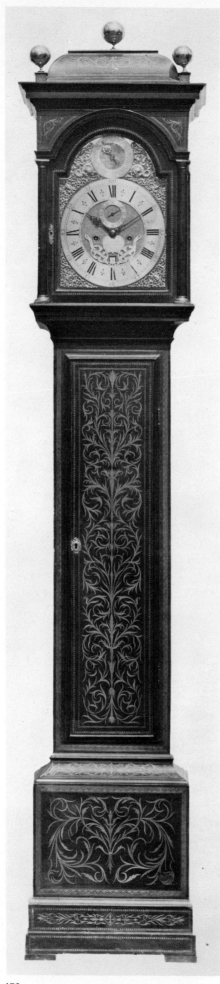

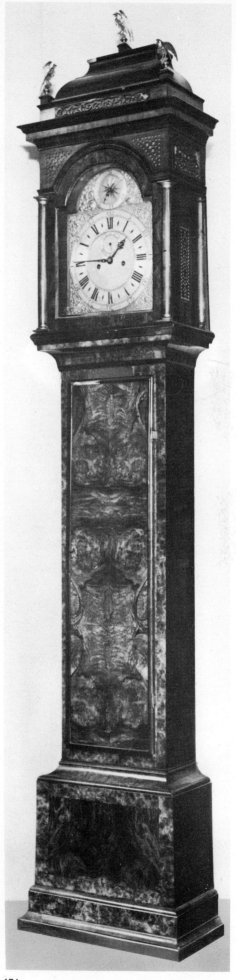

173

174

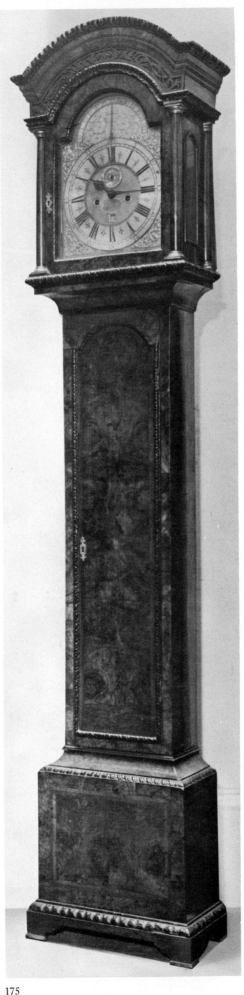

175 Samuel Lee, London. *c*.1725.

Eight-day striking longcase clock in a burr walnut case with carved mouldings around the break arch hood, under the pillars at the top and bottom of the plinth, and around the door, which has a break arch top, a departure in style. Mask and foliage spandrels, seconds dial, calendar aperture, and an oval cartouche with the maker's signature. There are no half-quarter markers and the half hours are indicated by *fleur-de-lys*. The hand in the arch, reading over a semi-circle marked 0 to 60, with an engraved zone, is probably a regulator. Height 7ft 8in (2.34m) Dial 12 by 16in (30 by 41cm).

176 Andrew Davis, London. *c*.1725.

Eight-day striking longcase clock in a floral marquetry case with birds. The date is late for marquetry (which is all over the front, including the pillars) as indicated by the mouldings, which are concave, and break arch dial. Mask and foliage spandrels and an engraved border to the dial plate. Half-quarter markers and *fleur-de-lys* half hour ornaments. Narrow hour hand. The dial in the arch is marked Strike/Not strike. Probably a 'marriage', the hood having been rebuilt to accommodate the break arch dial. Height 7ft 5in (2.26m) Dial 12 by 16in (30 by 41cm).

177 George Graham, London. *c*.1725.

Eight-day striking longcase clock in a burr walnut case with banding and high domed hood with concave moulding under it. The moulding on top of the plinth is ogee (double curved). Mask and foliage spandrels, no half-quarter markers. This is the earliest clock in the collection without half hour ornaments between the chapters. The inner quarter hour divisions are retained. Bolt and shutter maintaining power, date aperture and seconds ring. Height 7ft 6in (2.29m) Dial 12in (30cm) square.

175

176

177

178

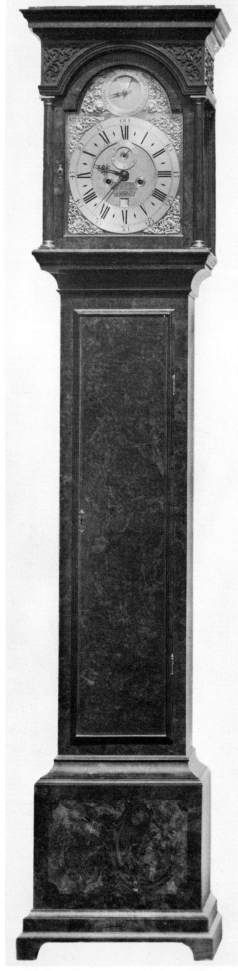

179

178 Daniel Delander, London. *c*.1725.
Month striking longcase clock in a burr walnut case with high inverted bell top with three ball finials. Break arch dial with mask and foliage spandrels, and a regulator in the arch, with human figures engraved on each side of it. Large minute numerals with diamond half-quarter markers and *fleur-de-lys* half hour ornaments. Signed cartouche on the zone. Narrow hour hand. Height 8ft 11in (2.72m) Dial 12 by 17in (30 by 43cm).

179 Joseph Williamson, London. *c*.1725.
Burr walnut eight-day striking longcase clock with break arch dial, flat topped hood, and cut away foot. In the arch is a hand indicating the day of the week, and a sector on which (presumably) an annual calendar is provided, as there is a square for setting it. There is an aperture for the date over VI. The winding holes are ringed and the clock is signed on a cartouche on the zone. All chapters are the right way up, i.e. the lower ones are reversed. Height 7ft 7in (2.31m) Dial 12 by 16in (30 by 41cm).

180 Thomas Clift, Hull. *c*.1730.
Eight-day striking longcase clock in a black lacquered case with a Chinese scene on the door only. The door had a break arch top. The dial is signed on a circular plaque in the arch. Very large minute numerals, no half-quarter marks and no half hour ornaments. Also, for the first time in the collection, no quarter hour divisions. Minute hand with a pierced stem. Height 7ft 8in (2.34m) Dial 12 by 16in (30 by 41cm).

180

205

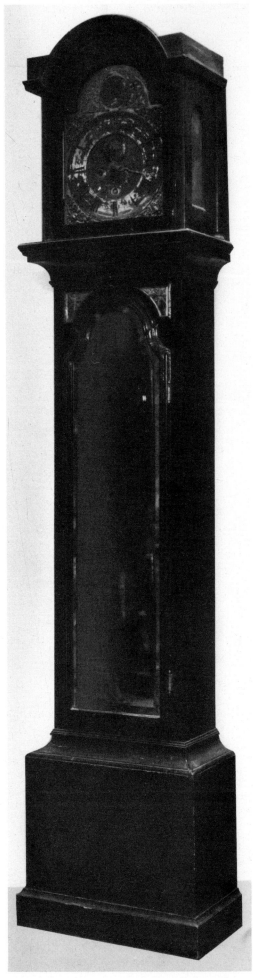

181

182

181 Philip Abbott, London. *c.*1730.

Eight-day striking longcase clock in a red lacquer case. Pagoda top with three ball and spire finials. Break arch dial with mask and foliage spandrels, a domed plaque in the arch bearing the maker's name and place. The chapter ring has minute numerals with half-quarter markers, and *fleur-de-lys* half hour ornaments. Vernay illustrated it without the finials. Height 7ft 8in (2.34m) Dial 12 by 16in (30 by 41cm).

182 James Jenkins, London. *c.*1730–1735.

Eight-day striking longcase clock with a (damaged) break arch dial and case with a mirror door having an arched top. The front pillars of the break arch hood are missing. Ringed date aperture and winding holes. The clock is attributed to an unknown maker in the catalogue.

183 William Kipling, London. *c.*1735.

Eight-day three-train striking and musical longcase clock in a black lacquered case with a break arch dial, flat top, and aproned foot. The third train is wound by a square by the chapter II, and from its position likely to be spring-driven, which makes the clock highly suspect. The four-tune indicator is in the dial arch. There are two auxiliary dials in the top corners, one for silencing. (The print is out of focus and it is impossible to see what the other is for). There are large minute numerals, diamond half hour ornaments, and quarter hour divisions.

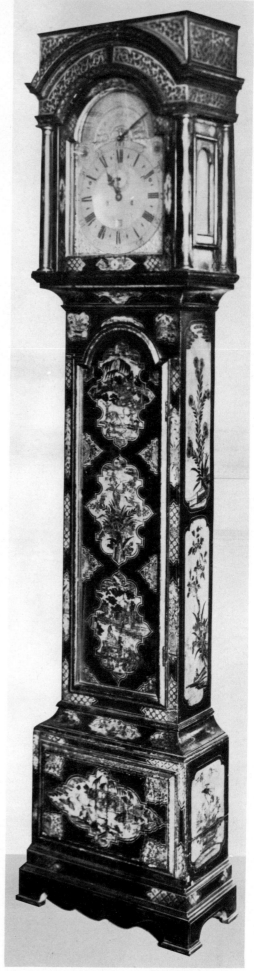

183

184 (detail)

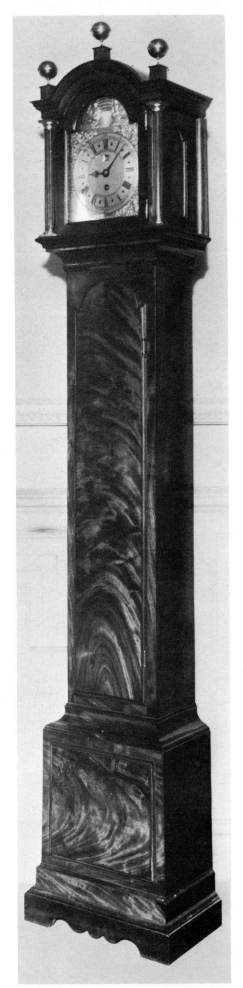

184

184 Daniel Delander, London. Movement *c*.1735. Case 19th C.

Small longcase timepiece (non-striking), that runs for a year at a winding. It had a calendar and equation dial and is in a 19th century mahogany case with a break arch top and door with three ball finials and an aproned foot. The pillars are fluted. The dial in the arch shows the equation of time difference between Sun and clock, whether fast or slow, the month and the date, corrected for the length of the month. There is also a date aperture over XII that has to be corrected monthly . Half-quarter markers bisect the outer minute ring circle and half hours are shown by diamonds. Quarter hour divisions are retained. Height 6ft 5in (1.96m) Dial 7¼ by 10¼in (19 by 27cm).

185 George Graham, London. *c*.1735.

Ebonised eight-day striking clock. (Named John Graham in the catalogue and John Gordon by Hurcomb. There were London makers of both names and the name on the cartouche on the zone is indistinct on the print.) There is a calendar showing the date by a hand and a dial – a feature that Quare adopted and that became popular with some provincial makers later – in the break arch of the dial. Two auxiliary dials are situated in the corners of the main dial. The chapter ring has half-quarter diamond markers. The case has a panelled door and door panels in a earlier style, except that the door panels are shaped.

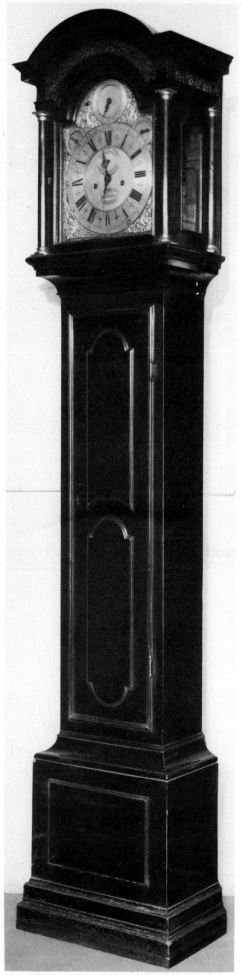

185

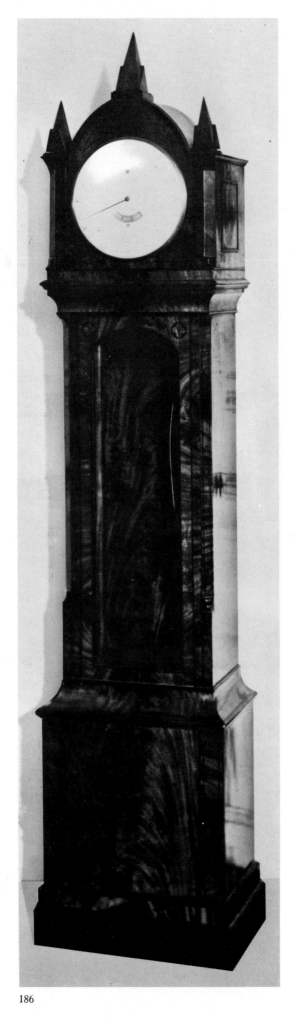

186

186 George Graham, London. *c.*1740. Case *c.*1790.

Month regulator in a mahogany case with a glass door and Gothic arched top. The movement has jewelled pallets, dead-beat escapement, bolt and shutter maintaining power and a Harrison grid-iron compensated pendulum. Hours are shown by a moving dial behind the sector, under which is the winding hole. The large central hand shows minutes and the upper one, seconds. Height 6ft 5in (1.96m).

187 Isaac Nickals, Wells, Norfolk. *c.*1740.

Eight-day three-train striking and chiming longcase clock with a central seconds hand, repeating work and an annual calendar, in a coloured and gold lacquered case showing four scenes in panels. In the arch is a phase of the Moon dial with a tidal dial in a semi-circle round it. Above this is a slot marked Strike/Silent. The age of the Moon is shown in the aperture below XII. The auxiliary dials are (top) Repeat/Not repeat, and Strike quarters/No strike quarters, and (bottom) day of the week, and month of the year, giving the number of days in the month. The chapter ring has all the traditional indications except half-quarters and is signed in large script at the bottom. Under the Moon is the inscription 'Tempus Rerum Imperator' (Time is sovereign over all things). The hood has a break arch, like the dial, and is surmounted by 'whales' tails' cresting, a style that became popular later in America.

188 John Rainsford, London. *c.*1750.

Mahogany one-train timepiece (non-striking) in a longcase. The hood is in pagoda style with a wooden fret in the front. (Why, if it does not strike?) It has orthodox concentric hands with a seconds ring (instead of what became the regulator lay-out) but without hour divisions or spandrels. Bevels replace the usual hood pillars. Perhaps the result of mixed 'marriages.' Height 6ft 8in (2.03m) Dial 10in (25.5cm) square.

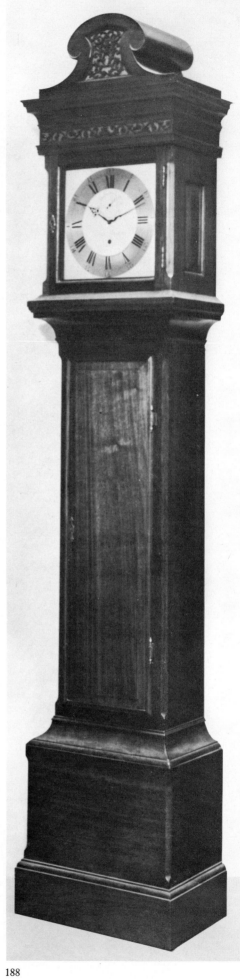

187

188

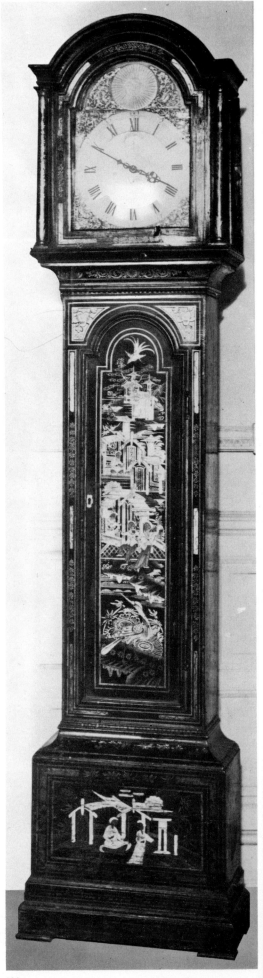

189

190

189 Justin Vulliamy, London. Movement *c*.1750.
Eight-day striking longcase clock in a provincially made mahogany case with inlaid ornaments. The flat topped hood has free standing pillars. In the dial arch is a plaque engraved with an eagle and 'Tempus fugit'. The dial zone bears a cartouche with the maker's name and place. Foliage spandrels and date aperture. Both quarter divisions and half hour ornaments have disappeared from the chapter ring. Shaped top to the door, copied on the plinth panel. The case looks provincial and does not belong to the movement. Height 6ft 9in (2.06m) Dial 12 by 17in (30 by 43cm).

190 Justin Vulliamy, London. Movement *c*.1750.
Eight-day striking longcase clock in a lacquered case with break arch hood. In the arch is a rayed Sun face. There are acanthus spandrels and the maker's name and place appear on a cartouche on the zone. There are no quarter divisions or half hour ornaments on the chapter ring. Height 7ft (2.13m) Dial 11 by 16in (28 by 41cm). This must be a marriage or fake. Case and movement are out of periods.

191 William Hawkins, Bury St. Edmunds.
c.1750–1700.
Large eight-day striking longcase clock in a black lacquered case with a break arch and pagoda top surmounted by three urn and knop finials. There are urn pattern spandrels and the chapter ring, except for the large minute numerals outside the minute ring, returns to the older style with quarter divisions and *fleur-de-lys* half hour ornaments. In the arch is a Moon dial on a star-studded firmament, and, in the semi-circle above it, the Moon's age. The auxiliary dials are for regulation and for silencing the striking. Signed on a cartouche with a date aperture below it. The clock is very tall at 9ft (2.75m).

191

192 (detail)

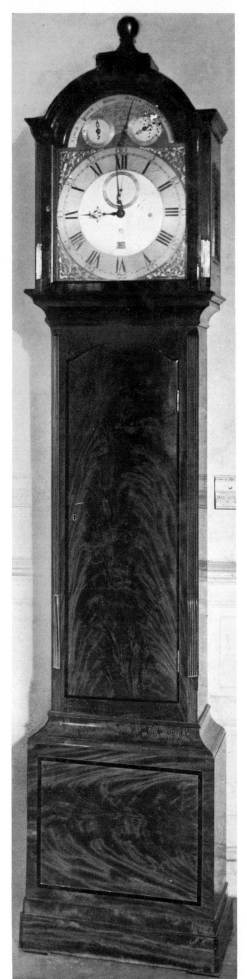

192

192 George Lindsay, London. *c.*1755.

Eight-day three-train striking and musical clock in a slightly wider than usual mahogany case (they became wider and wider in provincial clocks) with break arch hood surmounted by a ball finial. The hood has reeded bevels, instead of pillars, as has the case, the lower parts of the reeding being inlaid with metal. The dial has acanthus spandrels and cross-over pattern hour hand. Unusually, the inner ring of the zone has half hour instead of quarter hour divisions. Large seconds ring. In the arch is a tune selector marked March/Dance/Song/Dance/Allemand/Hornpipe, with a central inscription 'Geo. Lindsay Sev^t to the Prince of Wales LONDON'. (The Prince became King George III). The other auxiliary dials are Forte/Piano (loud/soft) on the left and Both strike/Both silent/Chimes silent on the right. Height 8ft (2.14m).

193 Benjamin Gray and Justin Vulliamy, London. *c.*1760.

Eight-day striking longcase clock in a walnut case with vertical book-matched door and horizontally book-matched plinth. The hood has a flat top and there is a square dial. The makers' names and place are on a cartouche on the zone. Foliage spandrels, no quarter hour divisions or half hour ornaments. Height 6ft 10in (2.08m) Dial 12in (30cm) square.

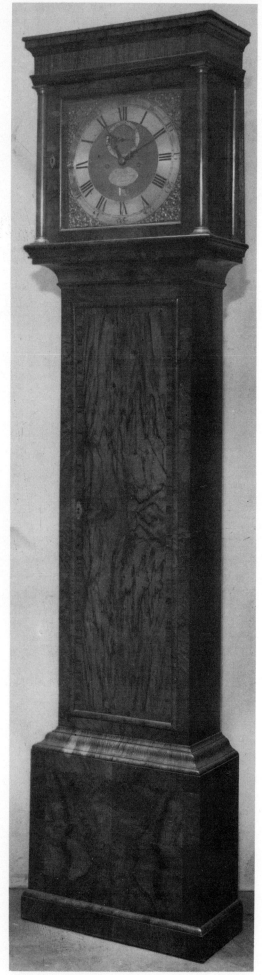

193

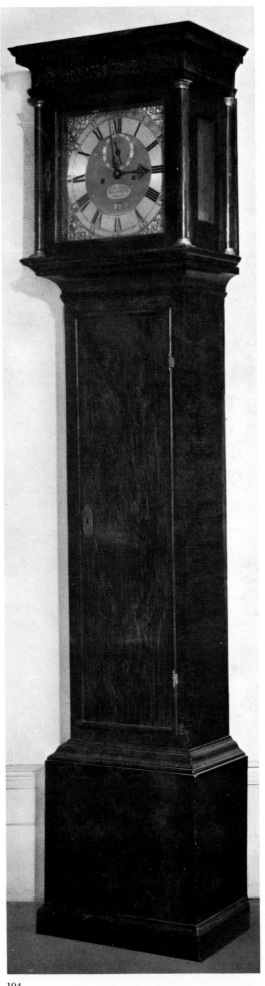

194 Benjamin Gray and Justin Vulliamy, London. *c.*1760.

Eight-day striking longcase clock in a plain walnut case similar to that by the same makers on page 215, except that the wooden fret at the top of the hood is omitted. The dials are almost identical.

195 John Shelton, London. *c.*1765.

'Journeyman clock' in a mahogany violin shaped case with level-adjusting feet. Arched dial and break arch hood. There is no central hand, but separate ones at top and bottom for minutes and seconds, and an aperture for the hour between them. The winding square is on the left. A similar clock is in the Museum of the History of Science, Oxford. Height 5ft 6½in (1.65m) Dial 5½ by 8½in (14 by 21.5cm).

196 James Hodges, London. *c.*1770. Case, which has been 'doctored', *c.*1900.

Eight-day striking longcase clock in a walnut case with floral marquetry decoration. The pagoda topped hood has finials and free standing pillars with corinthian capitals. Break arch dial with acanthus pattern spandrels and Strike/Silent control in the arch. The zone has a sunken seconds dial and semi-circular strap with the signature. No inner circle to the chapter ring. Height 8ft 2in (2.49m) Dial 12 by 17in (30 by 43cm).

194

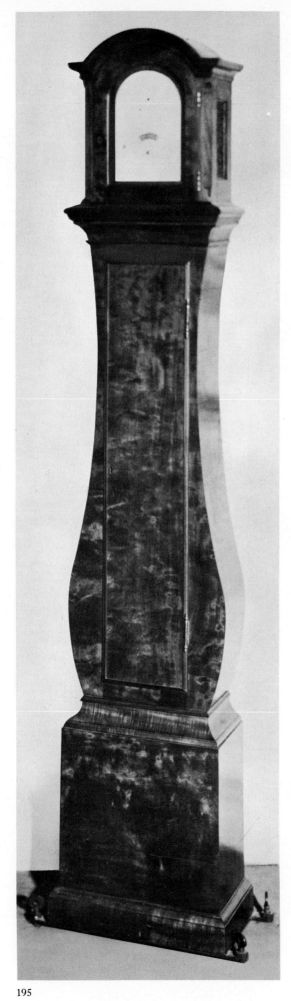

195

196

217

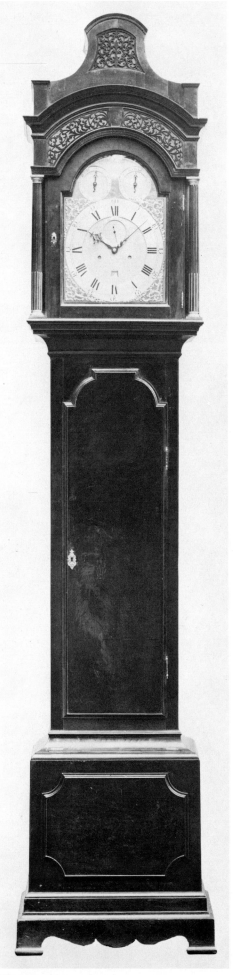

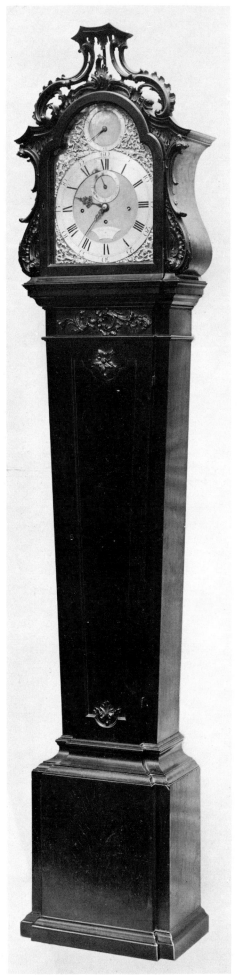

197

198

197 John Ellicott, London. *c*.1770.

Mahogany eight-day longcase clock with pagoda style hood and break arch dial. The movement has a dead beat escapement, bolt and shutter maintaining power, and, according to Britten, a 'peculiar compensation arrangement' – probably what is now called 'Ellicott's compensation', in which the pendulum rod is made of brass and steel. The differential expansion moves levers which raise or lower the pendulum bob to maintain its position. In the arch are regulation and strike silencing adjuster dials, with 'Ellicott London' engraved between them. Acanthus pattern spandrels, seconds ring, and date aperture. Height 8ft 7in (2.62m) Dial 12 by 16in (30 by 41cm).

198 John Holmes, London. *c*.1775.

Eight-day three-train striking longcase (or coffin) clock with ting-tang quarters in a carved mahogany Chippendale pattern case. The regulating dial in the arch is marked from 1 to 30. The seconds dial is in the zone, as is a cartouche with maker's signature. Acanthus spandrels and no quarter or half hour indications on the chapter ring.

199 Richard Comber, Lewes. Date 1778.

Eight-day three-train striking and chiming longcase clock in a mahogany case with tall feet and break arch hood with ball and spire finials. It chimes on eight bells. The main dial and seconds dial in the arch are in white enamel, and there are unusual spandrels in a style almost anticipating the art nouveau style introduced in the 1880s. There is a serpentine minute hand, and the hour hand has an unusual pierced form. The seconds hand is in regulator style and the slim concentric pointer indicates the date on a 1 to 31 scale inside the chapter ring in a manner fashionable in France. The dial bears the maker's name and place and there is also an inscription on the back plate 'Made by Richd Comber Lewes 1778'. The seatboard for the movement is of metal instead of the usual wood. To avoid chipping of the enamel dials, the winding squares are below the dial and are accessible when the door is opened. Nine extra spur wheels are needed for this arrangement. There is a slot with a lever in the bottom of the dial plate, presumably for silencing the chimes. Height 7ft 3in (2.21m) Dial 12 by 17in (30 by 43cm).

199

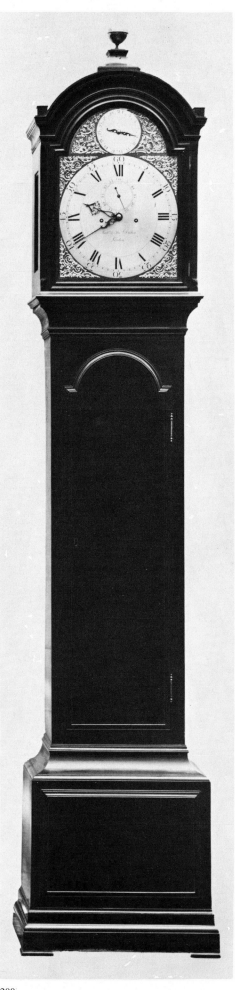

200 Matthew and Thomas Dutton, London.
*c.*1780 (could be later).

Eight-day striking longcase clock in a mahogany case with break arch hood and matching top to the door. The dial is a brass disk, instead of the usual ring, silvered all over and fastened to the dial plate. (Originally there may have been an enamelled dial). The seconds ring is engraved on the zone and there is a separate dial for the date in the arch. Acanthus pattern spandrels and cross-over pattern hour hand. Fine movement. Hurcomb shows the clock with a similar but different hood. Height 7ft 1in (2.16m) Dial 12 by 16in (30 by 41cm).

200

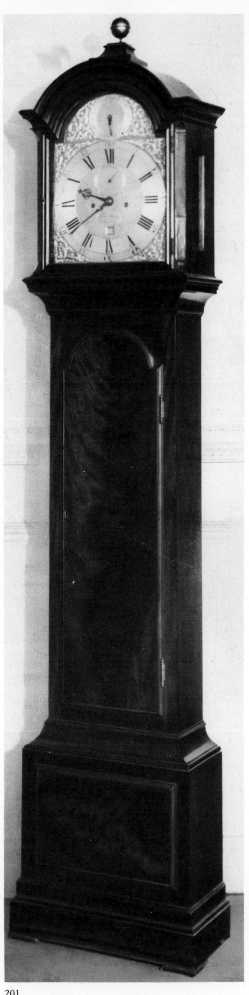

201 Thomas Mudge, London. *c.*1780.
Eight-day striking longcase clock in a mahogany case
with break arch dial and hood and single ball finial.
Signed on a cartouche on the zone. Strike/Silent
indicator in the arch, acanthus style spandrels, and
chapter ring with large minute numerals and no
quarter hour divisions or half hour ornaments. Rich
was casemaker to Mudge and also worked for
Vulliamy.

201

202 Thomas Colley, London. *c.*1780

Eight-day striking longcase clock in a mahogany case with break arch and pagoda top, with decorative inlay and ball and spire finials. The reeded pillars are inlaid in the lower parts with metal strips. The dial has a cartouche reading 'Graham's succ' Tho Colley LONDON'. Acanthus pattern spandrels, large seconds ring, date aperture, bolt and shutter maintaining power and a Strike/Silent hand in the dial arch. The chapter ring has no half hour ornaments; instead, there are half hour divisions where the quarter hour divisions normally appear.

203 John Ellicott, London. *c.*1780.
(Could be earlier.)

Eight-day striking longcase clock in a mahogany case with a pagoda top that has carving on the front and finials. The pillars are reeded, as are the quarter pillars on the trunk, to which there are capitals, like the pillars. The movement has a dead beat escapement. Mask and foliage spandrels, no quarter of half hour indications, and a cross-over pattern hour hand. The seconds ring is slightly wider than on some previous clocks and it is numbered every ten seconds. Strike/Silent in the arch with a dolphin emblem each side. Height 7ft 10in (2.39m) Dial 12 by 16in (30 by 41cm).

202

203 (detail)

203

223

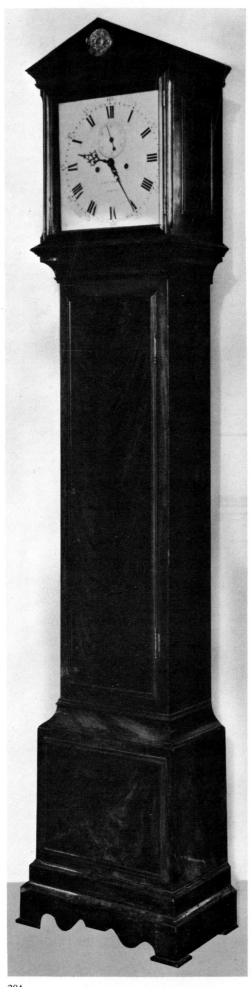

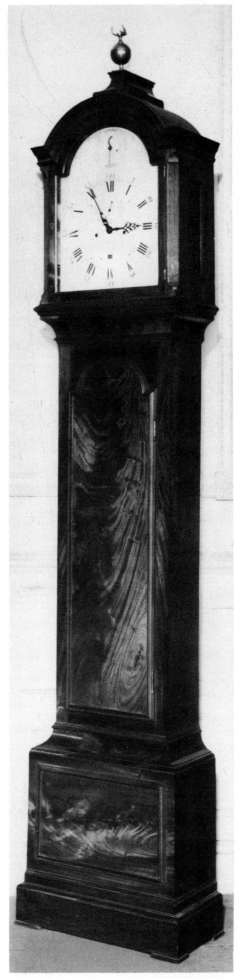

204

205

204 Charles Haley, London. The white painted dial was introduced *c.*1770 and this clock is dated *c.*1780.

Eight-day striking longcase clock in a mahogany case that has reverted to the style of the previous century, but with concave instead of convex moulding under the hood. It has carving in the centre of the top and an aproned foot. The biggest difference from other clocks in the collection is that it has an all-over painted iron dial that is plain, without the corner ornaments painted in gold to represent spandrels, or the coloured flower sprays or fruit that were fashionable at the time with provincial makers.

205 John Holmes, London. *c.*1780.

Eight-day striking longcase clock in a mahogany case with break arch top and finial. It has an all-over silvered brass dial instead of the traditional brass dial plate and separate chapter ring. The dial is break arch in shape, with a seconds hand, date aperture, and a Strike/Silent control in the arch.

206 Thomas Clare, Warrington. *c.*1790.

Carved mahogany striking longcase clock, which is unusual in having a dial in Battersea enamel. The enamelled square portion and the break arch portion of the dial are separate and held on to the dial plate by corner and side screws. Acanthus style corner and dial decorations in coloured enamel. The chapter ring and boss with the maker's name are convex in form. The hood had horned cresting, an urn finial, free standing pillars with corinthian capitals, and oval side frets. The quarter pillars of the trunk are reeded and the feet are tall. Height 7ft 7in (2.31m) Dial 12 by 17in (30 by 43 cm).

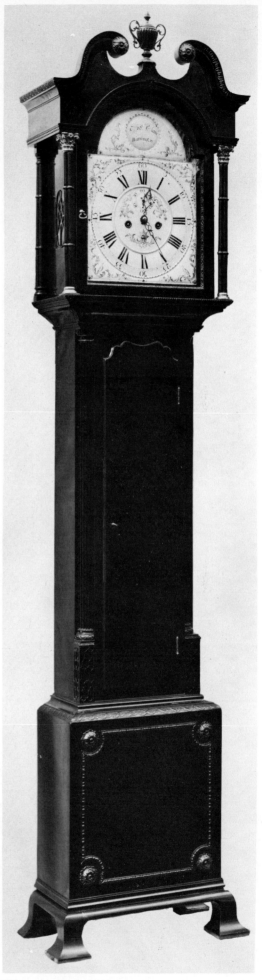

206

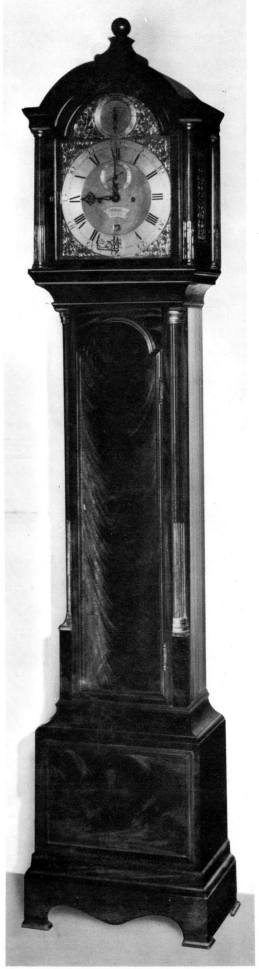

207

208

207 John Holmes, London. *c.*1790.

Mahogany striking longcase clock. Acanthus style spandrels, no inner circle engraved on the chapter ring, maker's name and place on a sector shaped cartouche on the zone, seconds and date aperture, and Strike/Silent control in the arch. Break arch hood with reeded bevels at the sides and three ball and spire finials. Height 7ft 4in (2.24m) Dial 12 by 16in (30 by 41cm).

208 Thomas Iles, London. *c.*1790.

Mahogany eight-day striking longcase clock. Same style of dial and spandrels as the Holmes clock on page 224, but different hands. The break arch hood has fluted pillars with metal strip inserts in the lower parts, repeated on the trunk. Single finial. The movement has a dead beat escapement, and, according to Britten, maintaining power. Height 7ft 2in (2.18m) Dial 12 by 16in (30 by 41cm).

209 Vulliamy, London. *c.*1790.

Mahogany eight-day striking longcase clock in an architectural style case with a square one-piece dial, silvered all over, which has no corner decoration; the name and place signed below the centre. Minute ring and date aperture. Height 7ft 2in (2.18m) Dial 12in (30cm) square.

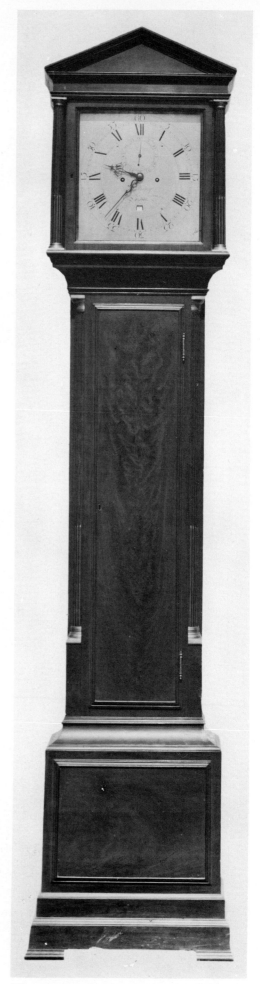

209

210

210 Thomas Mudge and William Dutton, London. *c*.1790.

Mahogany striking longcase clock. The break arch dial has the same pattern of spandrels as the Holmes and Iles clocks on pages 224 and 226, but this clock has a one-piece zone and chapter ring, silvered all-over, engraved with the makers' names and place and with a seconds dial and date aperture. A circle is engraved under the chapters; it was often omitted on contemporary clocks. Strike/Silent in the arch. Height 7ft 2in (2.18m) Dial 12 by 16in (30 by 41cm).

211 James Moore, Salisbury, Wiltshire. *c*.1790.

Mahogany eight-day striking longcase clock in the Sheraton style with inlaid fan motifs and shallow pagoda top. According to Britten, it also strikes the quarters, but there is no sign of a third winding hole anywhere on the dial. The painted one-piece iron dial has simple corner ornaments and a coloured female figure in the arch. The date aperture is curved, with a point at the centre to show the day's date, a favourite style of provincial makers. Height 7ft 6in (2.29m) Dial 12 by 16in (30 by 41cm).

212 James Gray, Edinburgh. *c*.1790.

Mahogany eight-day striking longcase clock in the Sheraton style, with horned cresting on the hood and free standing fluted pillars, a theme continued on the trunk. Silvered break arch one-piece dial with simple engraved corner motifs and the maker's name and place in a circle in the arch. The case has solid feet. Seconds dial and round date aperture. Height 7ft 6in (2.29m) Dial 12 by 16in (30 by 41cm).

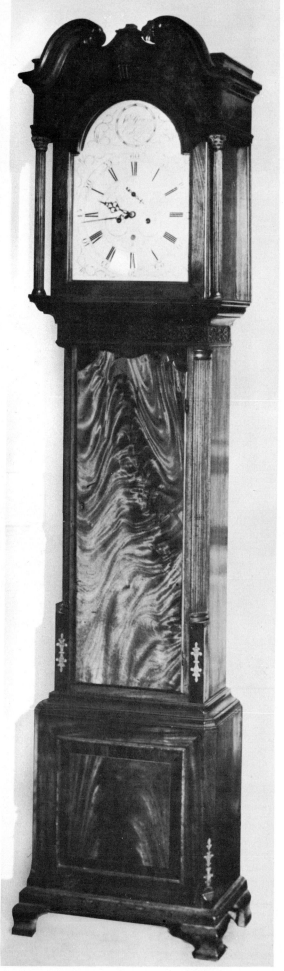

211

212

213

213 Alexander Cumming, London. *c*.1790.
Mahogany eight-day longcase clock with floral inlays in panels and a pagoda topped hood with reeded pillars and a tapered and aproned foot. The inlays (or marquetry) do not look right. Acanthus spandrels, Strike/Silent in the dial arch, large seconds ring, maker's name and place on a cartouche in the arch, and date aperture. The foot is like many applied to Wetherfield's clocks. Height 8ft (2.44m) Dial 12 by 16in (30 by 41cm).

214 John Arnold and Son, London. *c*.1800.
Mahogany longcase regulator. Flat topped hood without pillars. Square silvered dial with hour sector immediately under the centre of the minute pointer. Seconds pointer at the top and winding hole left of centre. Height 6ft 5in (1.96m) Dial 12in (30cm) square.

215 James Sweetman Eiffe, London. *c*.1850.
Mahogany longcase regulator with flat top, silvered circular dial, and mercurial pendulum. The dial has hours from 1 to 24 indicated by a lower subsidiary dial, seconds on an upper one and minutes on the main ring, indicated by the central hand. Height 6ft (1.83m) Dial 11in (28cm) diameter.

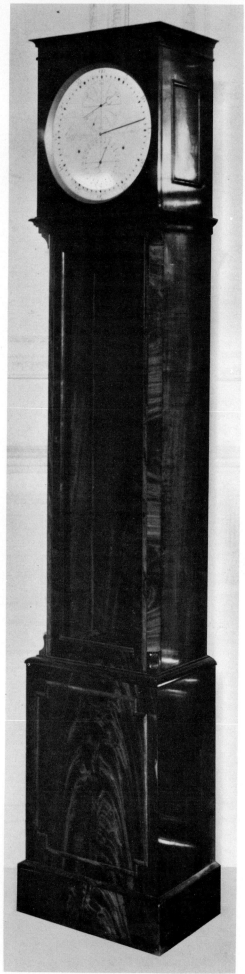

214

215

216 John Evans, London.

Eight-day three-train striking and chiming longcase clock in a mahogany case with flat topped hood with cresting and finials and reeded pillars. The door has brass strap hinges and the plinth brass feet. The square dial is traditional, with dial plate and silvered chapter ring, which has quarter divisions and half hour ornaments, through which screws have been inserted, indicating a 'cannibalised' dial. The chapter ring is signed 'John Evans London No 89 Mount Street S London' in a crowded style suggesting an addition. The movement has a three-legged gravity escapement and a three-part chime, according to Hurcomb. It was described by Vernay as 'the only modern clock in the collection', and dated *c*.1890. Height 7ft 11in (2.41m) Dial 12in (30cm) square.

217 No name. A 'marriage', impossible to date.

Thirty-hour striking and musical longcase clock in an oak case with painted decoration in the case, according to Hurcomb, although it looks like inlay on the print. The dial in the case is of earlier style, with earlier hands and is almost certainly eight-day.

218 No name. Impossible to date. The dial could even be a German reproduction of *c*.1900.

Mahogany eight-day striking longcase clock in a provincial style broad case with a flat topped hood which has free standing pillars and inlaid banding and motif on the case, repeated on the hood. The case maker has reverted to a form of the early convex moulding under the hood. The break arch dial has the orthodox silvered chapter ring with acanthus pattern spandrels on the dial plate, but the zone is silvered and engraved instead of being matted brass. Wavy minute hand . Phase of the Moon dial in the arch with the Moon's age indicated round it. Height 7ft (2.13m) Dial 13 by 18in (33 by 45.5cm).

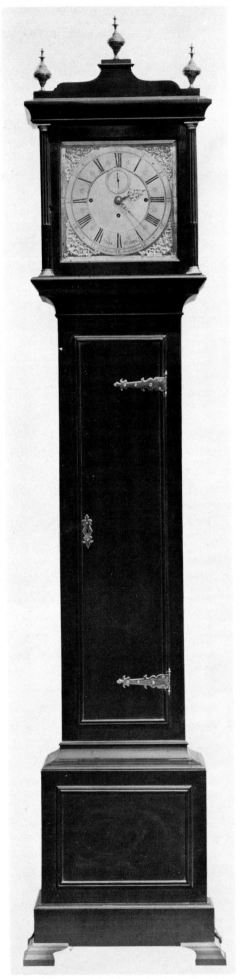

216

217

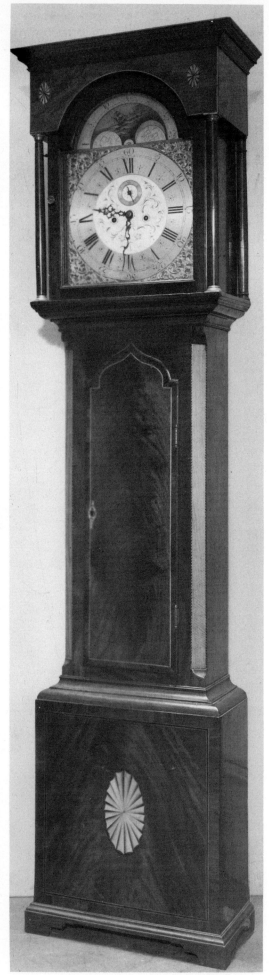

218

219 No name.
In the catalogue and illustrated by Vernay, but a 'mixed marriage'.

219

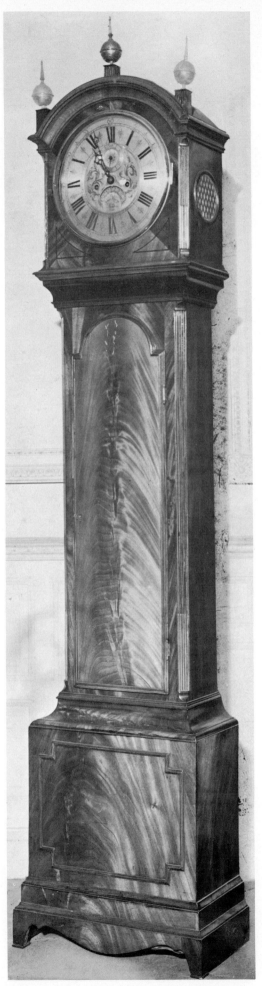

220 'Thomas Mudge, London.'
Catalogued and in Hurcomb as by Mudge but nothing of the kind.

220

Notes concerning Makers of the Clocks illustrated

Illustrations are indicated by serial numbers

Abbott, Philip, *London*, was apprenticed in 1695 to Thomas Stone for seven years and gained his Freedom of the Worshipful Company of Clockmakers in 1704. He remained in the Company, and therefore as a maker, until 1733.   181

Adamson, Humfry, *London*, is not in the Clockmakers Company register of apprentices, but is known to have been working from 1668 to 1682 at least. He built a clock for Whitehall Chapel, London.   19

Allett, George, *London*, was apprenticed to Solomon Bouquet in 1683. He appears in the register of apprentices as Allatt. At the time, names were often spelled in different ways, and he also appears as Allet. He was a Freeman in 1691, but little else is known about him.   41

Andrews, Thomas, *London*, was probably a clockmaker who worked in Leadenhall Street, apprenticed in 1686 and was a member of the Clockmakers Company from 1705 to 1722.   147

Arnold and Son, *London*. John Arnold (1735(6)–1799) was one of the greatest English makers, particularly of marine chronometers, famed for his ingenuity and craftsmanship. He had a fashionable 'court business', but apparently gave it up to devote himself to precision timekeeping. He was a friend of the celebrated A-L. Breguet, who much admired him. In 1783, he took into partnership his son, John Roger (1769–1843), who was only 18 and still serving his apprenticeship to his father. John Roger went to work for Breguet in Paris, but was unable to stay there long because of the Reign of Terror. The business was at 102 Cornhill until 1812–13, then was moved to The Strand. The Wetherfield clock was made at about the time that John Roger Arnold was using his house in Chigwell, Essex, as a temporary workshop.   214

Barnett, John, *London*, was apprenticed to John Ebsworth in 1675 and admitted to the Freedom in 1682. He carried on his business at Ye Peacock in Lothebury. Most businesses were indicated by a trade sign in the 17th and 18th centuries. Clockmakers usually showed a dial and often another symbol, which was sometimes one or more crowns – because of the crown in the arms of the Clockmakers Company – or Father Time. He was in the company until 1700.   104

Bennett, Thomas, *London*, was apprenticed to Katherine, widow of Richard Wallitt, for seven years from 1710 and became a Freeman in 1720–2. (There was another Thomas Bennett apprenticed in 1696.)   174

Betts, Samuel, *London*, who was referred to in 1645 and is believed to have been dead by 1675, was regarded as a maker of repute. As well as the bracket clock in the Wetherfield Collection, there are watches of his make in the Guildhall Museum (Clockmakers Company Collection) and British Museum (Ilbert Collection).   16

Bonner, Charles, *London*, was apprenticed to Daniel Beckman in 1693. He was a member of the Clockmakers Company from 1705 to 1717 and his clock in the collection is signed 'Bonnor' although he was apprenticed as 'Bonner'.   151

Bradley, Langley, *London*, is best known by clockmakers as the constructor of the original great clock of *c.*1706 in the south-west tower of St Paul's Cathedral, that struck the hours in 'Great Tom', which does broadcasting duty when 'Big Ben' is out of action. He also made the tower clock at St. Giles', Edinburgh. After apprenticeship to Joseph Wise in 1687, he was admitted to the Company as a Freeman in 1695, was Master in 1726 and was a member until 1738. Bradley was technical adviser to Dr. Derham, author of one of the earliest books on the craft, 'The Artificial Clockmaker', who gave Bradley's address in 1696 as Whitechapel. For most of his career, however, he worked at The Minute Dyall in Fenchurch Street.   117

Bridge, Thomas, *London*. Little is known of this maker. He does not appear in the Worshipful Company of Clockmakers' register of apprentices, so was probably apprenticed outside London, since the Company only had authority in the City of London. Britten commented that he had seen only one other production by this maker, which was later than the longcase clock in the collection.   145

Burges, Elias, *London*, was apprenticed to Edward Enys in 1673 and was a member of the Company from 1681 to 1702. The spelling of his name is as in the register; it also appears as Burgess and Burgis.   115

Clare, Thomas, *Warrington*, one of the provincial makers represented in the Wetherfield Collection, is not in the register of apprentices and undoubtedly learned the craft outside London. The longcase clock in the collection is the main means of dating him around 1790. It is very unusual in having a Battersea enamel dial.   206

Clarke, George, *London*, worked in Leadenhall Street. From 1787, he was a Liveryman of the Clockmakers Company, meaning that he had sworn allegiance to the King and was allowed to carry arms. Baillie lists a watch by him in the Guildhall Museum, but it does not appear in the 1975 catalogue of the Clockmakers Company, as well as a longcase clock in the Virginia Museum, USA, and a sheepshead clock – a lantern clock with an extra large chapter ring.   56

Clay, Charles, *London*, first worked in Stockton and was known there before he moved to the Strand, then St. James's, London. He was certainly working in London in 1736. His petition for a patent on repeater and musical watches was opposed by the Clockmakers Company. He died in 1740.   166

Clay, William, *Westminster*. There was a William Clay working in London at least from 1652 to 1680 and there are watches by him in the Guildhall Museum and Taunton Museum. The clock by him in the Wetherfield collection could be *c.*1660, twenty years earlier than at first thought when preparing the illustrations for this book.   8

Clement, William, *London*, an eminent maker closely associated with the development of the longcase clock, was born in Rotherhithe in 1638–9, where he became a blacksmith and anchorsmith. In 1677, he was made a Brother of the Clockmakers Company, which means he was a Freeman of another City Company, presumably the Blacksmiths, to which a number of earlier clockmakers belonged. He was in the Company until 1699 and was elected Master in 1694. He made lantern clocks and tower clocks, which included a special birdcage clock for King's College,

Cambridge, that incorporates an anchor escapement, which he has been credited with inventing, but it is now generally accepted that this escapement is an 18th century renewal. The clock is stamped 'Guliemus Clement Londini Fecit' with the date 1671 and is now in the Science Museum, London. Joseph Knibb made a clock with anchor escapement for Wadham College, Oxford, which is not dated on the movement, but was made in 1670 according to documentary evidence. The anchor escapement made the longcase clock the most accurate clock of all types of clock, and it has been used, virtually unchanged over the years. The success of the 39 inch seconds pendulum was such that Clement was convinced a longer pendulum would perform very much better. He therefore specialised in longcase clocks with pendulums about 60 inches long, that beat $1\frac{1}{4}$ seconds and hung to near the bottom of the case, but they were not generally popular and the original seconds pendulum became almost universal, at least on eight-day clocks. His first pendulum had spring suspension, which he may also have introduced, and some had a fine adjustment. The register of apprentices lists a William Clement, presumably his son, being apprenticed to him in 1684. He died in 1704 and is buried in what is now Southwark Cathedral. 88

Clift, Thomas, *Hull*, is another provincial maker represented in the collection. His name also appears on a watch. Loomes lists a Thomas Clift of Hull as working from *c.*1740 and dying in 1781. 180

Closon, Peter, *London*, subscribed £5 to the incorporation of the Worshipful Company of Clockmakers in 1630, the year before it received its charter from Charles I, and was Senior Warden in 1636. Several lantern clocks of his are known, one in the James Arthur collection at New York University. There are two in the Clockmakers Company collection in the Guildhall, both converted to anchor escapement and long pendulum, as nearly all such clocks still existing were. One gives his address as 'Neere Holburn'. He died *c.*1653. I

Clowes, James, *London*, was a fine maker, admitted to the Clockmakers Company in 1670 as a Brother because he was already a Freeman of another Company. He was still in the Company in 1689. 112

Colley, Thomas, *London*, who worked in Fleet Street, was an apprentice of the celebrated George Graham, FRS, and after Graham's death in 1751, set up in business with Samuel Barkley, another apprentice, who became Graham's foreman and then his executor. They called themselves 'Barkley and Colley, Graham's Successors'. The partnership lasted until 1754 and thereafter Colley worked on his own. The Wetherfield clock inscription declares Colley alone to be Graham's successor. He died in 1771. 202

Collyer, Benjamin, *London*, was apprenticed in 1684 and in the Clockmakers Company from 1693 to 1730. He acquired a reputation as a reputable maker. His name is also spelled 'Collier'. There is a watch by him in the Guildhall Museum, London. 125,164

Colston, Richard, *London*, was in the Clockmakers Company from 1682 until 1709. There is another of his clocks in Battle Abbey, Sussex, and watches in the Victoria and Albert Museum, London, and Metropolitan Museum of Art, New York. 162

Comber, Richard, *Lewes, Sussex*, was described by Britten as a 'remarkably efficient horologist', who quoted another Lewes clockmaker as saying about his work, 'I have never met with a bad or imperfect specimen'. He was born in 1742 and died at the age of 82.   199

Cowan, James, *Edinburgh*, was one of the most famous Scottish makers, who was apprenticed to Archibald Straiton in 1744 and, when released from his indentures, worked for a short time with the famous Julien Le Roy in Paris. He died in 1781. One of his apprentices, Thomas Reid, wrote 'Treatise on Clock and Watchmaking' in 1826.   62

Coxeter, Nicholas, *London*, had a workshop 'neare Goldsmiths Hall'. He was a celebrated maker who had been apprenticed to Richard Masterson in 1638, then turned over to John Pennock, and made lantern and longcase clocks. He was a Freeman of the Clockmakers Company in 1646, and was Master twice, in 1671 and 1677.   3,78

Cumming, Alexander, *Edinburgh and London*, was a very renowned maker and one of the clockmakers distinguished enough scientifically to become Fellows of the premier scientific body, The Royal Society. Born in Edinburgh about 1732, he was elected an honorary Freeman of the Clockmakers Company in 1781 after he moved his business to London, first to The Dial and Three Crowns in New Bond Street, then to Clifford Street, and finally to Fleet Street. There is a fine clock incorporating a barometer made by him for George III, at a price of £2,000 plus £200 a year for maintaining it, in Buckingham Palace. He was appointed, by Act of Parliament, 1761, as one of the experts to report on John Harrison's remarkable No.4 marine timekeeper, and also wrote 'The Elements of Clock and Watch Work', first published in 1766.   60,213

Davis, Andrew, *London*, was apprenticed to Robert Nemes in 1679 and admitted to the Freedom of the Clockmakers Company after completing his indentures. The Company's register gives his Christian name as Awbery.   176

Day, Edmund, *London*, was apprenticed in 1684 and a member of the Clockmakers Company from 1692 to 1710. Little else is known about him.   157

Delander, Daniel, *London*, was a famous maker who was apprenticed in 1692, made Free of the Company in 1699, and died in 1733. He moved from Devereux Court to a house between the two Temple Gates (Fleet Street) about 1714 and had been 'servant' to Thomas Tompion, according to *The Spectator*. That does not mean the same as 'servant', today. In 1714, he advertised a reward of '10L and no questions asked' for the return of a large jewelled watch made by Daniel Quare to his workshop, 'where all sorts of repeating jewel watches and other are made and sold'. One of his clocks in the Wetherfield Collection is particularly fine, as it goes for a year and has equation work. There are watches by him in the Victoria and Albert Museum, British Museum and Guildhall Museum, London, and Metropolitan Museum of Art, New York, and three clocks in the Virginia Museum, USA.   10,48,178,184

Dutton, Matthew and Thomas, *London*, was a partnership from a family of clockmakers. The most famous Dutton – William – was partner of and successor to Thomas Mudge. His son Matthew, apprenticed in 1771, and Company Master in 1800, was one partner. The other, Thomas, was apprenticed in 1776.   200

Dwerrihouse and Carter, *London*, worked at 30 Charles Street, Berkeley Square from 1809 to 1818, and then moved to 27 Davis Street in the same area until 1823.

John Dwerrihouse (or Dwerryhouse), who was described by Britten as a 'clever man', was elected an honorary member of the Clockmakers Company in 1781. From about 1820, the firm was Dwerrihouse, Carter and Son.   68

Eagle, John, *London*, was apprenticed in 1683 and a member of the Clockmakers Company from 1690 to 1712.   161

East, Edward, *London*, most celebrated of the earliest English makers, was born in Southill, Bedfordshire, only a few miles from Northill, where Thomas Tompion was born. He lived to the great age, for that time, of 95, and until the fact was discovered was thought to be two makers. He was apprenticed at the age of 15½ to a goldsmith for eight years and, only four years after gaining his Freedom, became junior member of the Court of Assistants (management committee) of the Clockmakers Company on its formation in 1631. In 1645, he was elected Master and occupied that position again in 1652. Charles I appointed him Royal Clockmaker and his watches were awarded as prizes for tennis played in The Mall. After the Restoration, he was reappointed by Charles II. He worked in Pall Mall, moved to Fleet Street, and spent his later years in Hampton, Middlesex, presumably to be near Hampton Court Palace. There are watches by him in the British Museum, Victoria and Albert Museum, and Guildhall Museum, London, and Metropolitan Museum of Art, New York. He made the only known example of a longcase night clock (in which pierced moving hour numerals were illuminated by an oil lamp from the back).

11,15,81,89,93

Ebsworth, John, *London*, was a good maker of lantern clocks, then bracket and longcase clocks. After apprenticeship from 1657, and Freedom of the Company in 1665, he became the Master in 1697. He remained in the Company until 1703.   101

Eiffe, James Sweetman, *London*, was a clever maker of chronometers and precision clocks. He was born in 1800, worked at 48 Lombard Street, and died in 1880.   215

Ellicott, John, *London*, was one of the most eminent of English makers, inventor of a temperature compensated pendulum and publisher of an Equation of Time table. He was born in 1706 and, from about 1728, he had a business in Sweetings Alley, near the Royal Exchange, and in 1738 became one of the exclusive few clockmakers to be elected to the most august scientific body, The Royal Society. Among his sponsors were John Senex, the celebrated globe maker, and John Hadley, the astronomer. He was on the council of the Society for three years. At his home in St. John's, Hackney, he had a private observatory where he conducted scientific experiments. He was also appointed Royal Clockmaker. Among Ellicott's public clocks was one for the London Hospital. He died in 1772 after he fell from his chair, and was succeeded by his eldest son and partner, Edward. From 1785 to 1811, the firm was called Edward Ellicott and Sons. The longcase clock on page 223 was perhaps in the making when he died. His father, also named John, was a fine craftsman too.   52,53,54,197,203

Elliott, Henry, *London*, became a Brother of the Clockmakers Company in 1688, which meant he was a Freeman of another Company, perhaps the Blacksmiths, like a number of other early clockmakers. Baillie mentioned a bracket clock by John or Joseph Mosely Elliott in the collection, but it was not in the sale. Three bracket clocks were catalogued (numbers 123, 137 and 154) as by 'John Elliott'; in fact all were by Ellicott.   128

Emery, Josiah, *London*, was a watchmaker from Geneva in Switzerland who became eminent as a clock and watchmaker in England, carrying on business from 33 Cockspur Street, Charing Cross. He was elected an honorary Freeman of the Clockmakers Company in 1781, a rare distinction. (For some reason there was a large number of elections to the Company in 1781.) There is an unusual balloon style bracket clock by him in the Ilbert Collection in the British Museum, but he is noted mostly for his 30 or so lever escapement watches, as he was first to employ the invention after the inventor, Thomas Mudge. He was born about 1725 and died in 1797.   63

Evans, John, *London*, worked at 89 Mount Street, is not recorded, although there were many clockmakers named Evans with a few Johns amongst them.   216

Finch, John, *London*, was apprenticed in 1668 to Nathaniel Barrow and became a Freeman in 1675. In 1706 he was Master of the Company and died about 1713. Little else is known about him.   142

Fleureau, Esaye, *London*, was probably French, but worked in London in the earlier 18th century. There is a watch by him in the James Arthur Collection in New York University.   160

Fromanteel, John, *London*, was the son of Ahasuerus Fromanteel, who first made and advertised the longcase pendulum clock, in England. Born in 1638, and apprenticed to his father in 1651, John became a Freeman of the Company in 1663. His father sent him to Holland to study under Salomon Coster. He arrived only 11 days after the patent for pendulum clocks was granted to Christiaan Huygens. The clockmaker licenced to make them was Coster. Details of construction were passed by John to his father in England with the agreement of Huygens or Coster, and when John returned in 1658, his father had already made and sold some. The making of longcase, bracket and lantern pendulum clocks was taken up in England at an incredibly rapid pace for the time and never developed with anything like the same speed and energy in Holland or any other country until later. About 1680, John Fromanteel returned to Holland, but to Amsterdam instead of The Hague, where Coster had worked, accompanied by his brother Ahasuerus the second, but died soon afterwards, it is believed.   74

Fromanteel and Clarke, *Amsterdam*. After Ahasuerus Fromanteel the second went to Amsterdam, *c.*1680, as related above, his daughter married a Christopher Clarke there in 1694. Fromanteel took his son-in-law into partnership and the clocks they produced are called 'Dutch Fromanteels' in the antiques trade. Ahasuerus the second was born in 1640, apprenticed to his father, the first Ahasuerus, was Free of the Clockmakers Company in 1663, and died in 1703. Loomes gives the period of the business as from *c.*1694 to *c.*1722 as Clarke carried on alone. Later he took a Roger Dunster into partnership.   127

Goode, Charles, *London*, was admitted as a Brother of the Clockmakers Company in 1686, which means he was already Free of another trade guild. Although there were both a longcase and a bracket clock of his in the collection, his other known works are watches. He worked in The Strand and died in 1730.   40,103

Gould, Christopher, *London*, was a maker of great repute, particularly of longcase clocks, of which there were three in the Collection. He became a Freeman of the Company in 1682 and died in 1718.   95,100,129,140,167

Graham, George, *London*, was one of the most eminent makers of all time of clocks, watches and scientific instruments. A Quaker, born in Rigg, Cumberland, in 1673, he tramped to London, where he became apprenticed to Henry Aske in 1688. On completing his indentures and becoming a Freeman of the Company in 1696, he was invited by the great Thomas Tompion to join him at the The Dial and Three Crowns. The two men became close friends and ten or twelve years later, Graham married Tompion's niece, Elizabeth Tompion. At this time, Edward Banger, who married another niece, was also working for Tompion. After Banger was dismissed (see Tompion and Banger), Graham became Tompion's chief assistant and succeeded to his business when he died. In 1720, Graham moved from Tompion's old premises to the east corner of the entrance to Peterborough Court in Fleet Street, which was not numbered in his lifetime but subsequently became number 135. It is now part of the site occupied by *The Daily Telegraph*. He shared the premises with Thomas Wright for the first nine to 12 years and afterwards with others, staying there until he died. The next occupants were Samuel Barclay and Thomas Colley then Thomas Colley alone. Thomas Mudge, who was one of Graham's best apprentices and worked for him from time to time after setting up on his own, did not take over the premises at 135 Fleet Street, as often stated, but had his own at what became number 151 from 1750 until he left London in 1771. Graham was elected to the august Royal Society in 1720, promoted to the council only two years later, and contributed 21 papers to the *Philosophical Transactions*. He was elected Master of the Clockmakers Company in 1722, but devoted more and more time to astronomy, in co-operation with the astronomers Halley and Bradley. He invented the accurate dead-beat escapement for clocks, and the cylinder escapement that superseded the verge, for watches. He died in 1751 and was buried in the same grave in Westminster Abbey as his former Master and friend, Thomas Tompion.

43,44,154,169,170,177,185,186

Gray, Benjamin, *London*, was a fine maker who became Clockmaker to George II in 1744. Born in 1676, he established a business in Pall Mall in 1727, and later went into partnership with his son-in-law, Justin Vulliamy, as Gray and Vulliamy, in Pall Mall, from 1743 to 1762.

Gray, James, *Edinburgh*. A fine maker, who was apprenticed in 1765 and was working until about 1806. He – or possibly his son of the same name, who was known to have been working at least from 1805 to 1836 – made the Wetherfield clock.   212

Gray and Vulliamy, *London*. A partnership of two excellent makers, Benjamin Gray and Justin Vulliamy. See separate entries.   193,194

Gregg, Francis, *London*, was apprenticed in 1691 and was still living at least until 1747. In 1714, he moved from Covent Garden (where he made the clock movement in the collection) to The Dial in St. James Street 'over against the Palace Gates', until 1729, when he was bankrupted. He was still insolvent when he was working in York Street in 1743. Watches by him are in the Ilbert Collection at the British Museum and in the Clockmakers Company Collection at Guildhall, London.   168

Gretton, Charles, *London*, apprenticed to Lionel Wythe in 1662, was a Freeman of the Company ten years later and Master in 1700. A fine maker of clocks and watches, he worked at The Ship in Fleet Street, probably from 1697, the same year that Henry Sully, who became a famous maker in Paris, became apprenticed to him. He was a member of the Company until 1733.   4,46,105,113,118

Haley, Charles, *London*, worked in Wigmore Street and became a celebrated maker. He was apprenticed in 1762 and in the Company from 1781 to 1825. His chronometers are in several collections, including that at the British Museum, and there is a watch by him in the Victoria and Albert Museum, London.   204

Hawkins, William, *Bury St. Edmunds*, was born in 1703 and died in 1775, having become bankrupt in 1747.   191

Herbert, Cornelius, *London*, worked near London Bridge, was apprenticed in 1690, made Free in 1700, and Master of the Company in 1727. He died in 1751, having established a reputation as a fine maker. The bracket clock in the Collection gives his business as in Whitehall. There are watches in existence signed by his father, whose name was the same. The surname was also spelled Harbert and Harbottle.   33,138

Hodges, James, *London*. Nothing is known of this maker except for the longcase clock in the Collection. According to Baillie, a bracket clock by Nathaniel Hodges was in the collection, but it was not in the sale.   196

Holmes, John, *London*, was a member of great repute working from *c.*1762 to *c.*1815 at 156 Strand near Somerset House. His home was pulled down to make way for Waterloo Bridge. He was one of the committee appointed by the House of Commons in 1763 to report on Mudge's timekeepers.   198,205,207

Iles, Thomas, *London*, was working at least from about 1778 to 1790, and made longcase and bracket clocks as well as watches, but little else is known of him.   208

Jackson, William, *London*, was apprenticed in 1725 and in 1735 was made Free of the Clockmakers Company, of which he became a Liveryman. He died in 1776.   50

Jarrett, Richard, *London*, worked in Lothbury and was a member of the Clockmakers Company from 1670 to 1695. He was Master in 1685. Also spelled Jarratt.   20

Jenkins, James, *London*, worked in The Strand. Apprenticed in 1683, he was in the Company from 1692 to 1708.   182

Johnson, John, *London*, was working from about 1770 to 1799 in Gray's Inn Passage, which was a 'very unpretentious neighbourhood' according to Britten, although 'he did, I believe, good business among the lawyers of Lincoln's and Gray's Inns'. Baillie says he worked in Holborn (which borders the Inn).   58

Kipling, William, *London*, who worked from at least 1705 to 1737, was considered a fine maker of complicated bracket and longcase clocks as well as watches. There are examples of his work in the Victoria and Albert and Guildhall Museums in London, the Liverpool Museum, and the Virginia Museum, USA.   183

Knibb, John, *Oxford*, the younger of two clockmaking brothers, lived from 1650 to 1722 and made many clocks, probably mainly for his brother Joseph, to whom he had been apprenticed. He employed as many as ten apprentices at different times. His brother moved to London, but he remained in Oxford, where he became prominent in civic life and served as the Mayor of Oxford twice. It seems that he ran his brother's business for a time, because one of his later clocks is signed 'John Knibb, Hanslop', which was the Buckinghamshire village to which Joseph retired before he died.   6,26,73

Knibb, Joseph, *London*, who was born in 1640 and died in 1711, became one of the finest of all makers of lantern, bracket and longcase clocks, but nevertheless had much trouble in establishing himself as a clockmaker in Oxford. He may have learned his craft in London from his cousin Samuel Knibb, but this is supposition. At any rate, he took on his younger brother John as his apprentice in 1664 and moved to Oxford, first outside the 'city liberties', and then to a shop at Holywell, outside the walls, but within the city jurisdiction. His landlord was Merton College. Soon the Great Plague of London was raging and Charles II moved to Oxford with his court. Local tradesmen resented the 'foreign' tradesmen from London who tried to invade their territory and presented a petition in 1667, after which the City Council agreed to suppress 'offenders'. Joseph Knibb was included among these and it was demanded of him that he 'suddenly shut down his windows and remove either to St. Clement's (where he had started) or else to some other place out of the City liberties'. Knibb tried to avoid the order by applying for the Freedom of the City. He was proposed by the Mayor, but his application was refused by the Council. He had a way out, however; within a month he had matriculated at Trinity College, which enabled him to claim to be a priviledged employee. Inexplicably, he was described as 'Gardener to Trinity College' in his next application for the Freedom of the City. He asked for 'a freedome waveing the power of the University who endevoured to Maynteyn him to keepe shopp . . .'. This time the Council agreed, on payment of 20 nobles and a 'leathern buckett' by him. There were frequent disputes between the City Council and University, but the Council would stop short of expelling a member of the University. In less than two years, Knibb had forgone his new priviledges and had moved to London and become a Freeman of the Clockmakers Company. It was not through pique, however, but most likely to take over the business of his cousin Samuel, who seems to have died about this time. John remained in charge of the Oxford business. Joseph carried on until 1697, when, probably because of illness, sold the business and retired to Hanslop, Buckinghamshire, where he died at the age of 71. He introduced Roman striking, described on page 36.   2,7,14,21,25,69,70,71,72,82,84,85,94,96,108,110,150

Knottesford, William, *London*, apprenticed in 1680, was the maker of the longcase clock in the Wetherfield Collection, not his more famous father William Knottesford (also spelled Knutsford), who was Master of the Clockmakers Company in 1693.
141

Lambert, Nicholas, *London*, was working at least from 1710 to after mid-century. Little else of him is known.   163

Lee, Samuel, *London*, was apprenticed in 1687 and a member of the Company from 1694 to 1719.   175

Lindsay, George, *London*, worked in The Strand and made one of the two musical longcase clocks in the Wetherfield Collection. Although he was Watchmaker to George III, little is known of his life except that it ended in 1776.   192

Lowndes, Jonathan, *London*, was a famous maker working at The Dyal in Pall Mall, whose clocks were often referred to in the *London Gazette*. His name was sometimes spelled Loundes. As well as longcase and bracket clocks, represented in the collection, he made lantern clocks and watches. He was admitted to the Clockmakers Company in 1680 and remained in it until 1710.   30,114,144

Lowndes, Isaac, *London*, also worked in Pall Mall and was sometimes called Lownds. He was a member of the Clockmakers Company from 1682 to 1702. His relationship to Jonathan Lowndes is not known. 122,132

Maclennan, Kenneth, *London*, was in business from 1776 to 1825, at least. He is known to have made a planetarium (showing the motions of the planets) for the Royal Institution. 65

Markwick, James, *London*, was in the Company from 1666 to 1698, having been apprenticed in 1656. He made bracket clocks (represented in the collection) and watches, now to be seen in several collections, including the National Museum, Stockholm. His son, also called James, became more distinguished. (See below.) 39

Markwick-Markham, *London*. James Markwick the second was in the Clockmakers Company from 1692, was Master in 1720, and died in 1730, accepted as an eminent maker. He went into partnership with his son-in-law, Robert Markham (*c.*1725–1780) and they traded under the name of Markwick-Markham. However, Markham also traded under his own name and with Francis Perigal. To confuse the situation more, the partnership also traded with other makers and all three names were used, such as Markwick, Markham, Perigal. Other third names were Story, Borrell and Rogers, but mainly for watches. The partnership specialised in clocks and watches for the Turkish market, with Turkish numerals on the dial, as represented by the unusual small clock in the Wetherfield Collection. 9,17

Marriott, John, *London*, worked in Fetter Lane. He entered the Clockmakers Company in 1768, was a Liveryman in 1776, and Master in 1799. He specialised in musical clocks, one of these now being in the Palace Museum, Pekin. He died in 1824. 66

Marshall, John, *London*, was a member of the Company from 1689 to 1716, after being apprenticed in 1682. Baillie records him as inventor of a 'magic night watch'. 111

Martin, John, *London*, was apprenticed in 1672, and a member of the Clockmakers Company from 1679 to 1701. 34

Martin, Thomas, *London*, who was apprenticed in 1692, worked near the Royal Exchange. He was in the Clockmakers Company from 1699 to 1714. 35

Moore, James, *Salisbury*, was a Wiltshire maker of whom little is known, except that he was working around 1790, the estimated date of the Wetherfield clock. 211

Mudge, Thomas, *London and Plymouth*, one of the greatest makers, was born in 1715 in Exeter. He showed such early aptitude for horology that his father, a clergyman headmaster, managed to place him as an apprentice with 'Honest' George Graham in London. He did so well, that Graham gave him a place of importance when he had completed his indentures. He continued to work for Graham until Graham's death in 1751. His premises were at what became 151 Fleet Street, near Graham's at 135. He often made special pieces for George III and was appointed Royal Watchmaker in 1776, when the previous incumbent, George Lindsay, died. His most important invention was the lever escapement, still used in millions upon millions of watches and clocks. The first lever watch was presented to Queen Charlotte and is still in the Royal Collection. There is a Mudge bracket clock with a lever escapement in the Ilbert Collection at the British Museum. Mudge became a

Freeman of the Clockmakers Company in 1738 and a Liveryman in 1766. In 1755, he entered into partnership with Thomas Dutton, another of Graham's apprentices, but in 1771 moved to Plymouth to devote himself to the development of the marine chronometer. He died at his son's house in Walworth in 1794.   201,220(!)

Mudge and Dutton, *London*. Thomas Mudge and William Dutton, ex-apprentices of George Graham, were partners from 1755 to 1790 and made both clocks and watches, although the watches were not signed by both names until 1765.   57,210

Nickals, Isaac, *Wells, Norfolk*, was working around mid-18th century. The longcase clock in the collection has a centre seconds hand, which is unusual.   187

No name.   102,134,217,218,219

Oosterwijk, Abraham, *Middelburg, Holland*. The longcase clock in the collection is very much in the English style. Curiously, a Severijn Oosterwijk was employed by Huygens, inventor of the pendulum clock, after the death of Coster, who made the first one for him.   158

Papavoigne, Isaac, *London*, was admitted to the Clockmakers Company in 1687, when it was noted that he was French, and remained a member until 1710.   135

Parker, Daniel, *London*, was active around the end of the 17th and beginning of the 18th centuries, working in Fleet Street. Britten points out that there was no Daniel Parker among early makers attached to the Clockmakers Company, but a number of Johns. He added that 'John' was often used when a Christian name was unknown.   86

Paulet, John, *London*, was apprenticed in 1728 and is known to have been a member of the Company in 1740. There are watches by him in the Victoria and Albert and Guildhall Museums.   131

Peckover, Richard, *London*, was apprenticed in 1700 and took premises in Change Alley in 1735, removing to the Royal Exchange in 1751, and continuing until about 1754. He took over the Quare and Horseman business in 1733, according to a trade label pasted in a Quare clock.   49

Pepys, John, *London*, who was apprenticed in 1672 to John Harris, and in 1680 admitted to the Freedom of the Clockmakers Company, of which he was Master in 1707. He was working at least until 1715, and there is a watch by him in the British Museum.   139

Puller, Johathan, *London*, was apprenticed to Nicholas Coxeter in 1676 and made a Freeman of the Company in 1683. He became an assistant of the Court, the governing body, in 1705, but seems to have died in the following year. One of his watches is in the Ilbert Collection, now in the British Museum.   123,136

Quare, Daniel, *London*, who was born in 1649, entered the Clockmakers Company as a Brother in 1671, indicating that he was already Free of another trade guild. He became a very celebrated maker of clocks, including several running for a year at a winding (one once in the Wetherfield Collection and others at Hampton Court Palace, and in the Ilbert Collection, British Museum) and watches, for which he invented a form of repeating work about 1680. There are many examples of his complicated work in collections in several countries. Some of his earlier work is signed with the address St. Martin's Le Grand, London. His address from about 1680 to his death in 1724, was the Kings Arms, Exchange Alley. Quare was a Quaker and the books of the Society of Friends show that he refused the office of Clockmakers to George I because his conscience would not allow him to take the oath of allegiance. However, the King 'bent the rules' by allowing him to be admitted through the back door, where the Yeoman of the Guard, as Quare put it, 'lets me frequently go up without calling anybody for leave, as otherwise he would tho' persons of quality'. He was in partnership from 1718 with Horseman, and, after his death, Horseman carried on under the same names until 1733. He is buried in the Quaker ground at Bunhill Fields, Finsbury, London.

36,98,99,107,109,126,137,146,148,149,155,156,172

Rainsford, John, *London*, worked in New Street Square and was in the Clockmakers Company from 1721 to 1757, having been apprenticed in 1714. Seemingly, he was not a good businessman and went bankrupt. 188

Rant, Jonathan, *London*, was apprenticed in 1680 to Francis Munden and was a member of the Company from 1687 to 1725. 45

Scott, John, *London*, was a member of the Clockmakers Company from 1781 to 1794 and worked in Red Lion Square. 64

Seignior, Robert, *London*, established a considerable reputation as a watch and clockmaker. He worked in Exchange Alley, after having been admitted to the Freedom of the Company in 1667. In 1673, the famous maker Henry Jones accused him of putting his name on a clock by Jones he repaired. In 1682, he received £20 for a clock set up in the Treasury Chambers. He died before 1692. 12,77

Shelton, John, *London*, was apprenticed in 1711, became a Freeman of the Company in 1720 and was a Liveryman in 1766. He is principally known for his astronomical regulators, one of which was presented to Gottingen Observatory by the King, journeyman clocks, and table regulators, and made few domestic clocks. He described himself as 'Operator to the late Mr Graham' (i.e. George Graham). He made several of Graham's regulators and continued after Graham's death in 1751.

55,195

Smith, Thomas, *London*, was apprenticed in 1691 to Stephen Wilmott for seven years, after which he was admitted to the Freedom of the Company. 153

Stanton, Edward, *London*, who also spelled his name Staunton, was apprenticed to Francis Bowen or Nathaniel Allen in 1655 and was made Free in 1662. He was Master of the Company in 1696, and remained in it until 1707. 13

Taylor, Thomas, *London*, was apprenticed in 1678 to his father, also Thomas by name. He was in the Clockmakers Company from 1685 to 1723 and was Master in 1710, and may have worked 'at the upper end of Fetter Lane in Holborn' as given in the *London Gazette* of 1692. 32,119

Thompson, Joseph, *London*, worked in Fleet Street. Little else is known about him. 67

Tomlinson, William, *London*, was in the Clockmakers Company from 1699 to 1741 and was Master in 1733. He worked in Birchin Lane until 1719, when he removed to White Hart Court, and there are (or were) examples of his work in the Victoria and Albert, British, and Guildhall Museums in London, and Metropolitan Museum of Art, New York, and the Chamberlain Collection (which was stolen) in Chicago. 38

Tompion, Thomas, *London*, is regarded as the greatest of all English clock and watchmakers and attained this fame in his own lifetime. He was born in Ickwell Green, Northill, Bedfordshire, in 1639, and after that little is known of him until he was admitted as a Brother by the Worshipful Company of Clockmakers in London, on payment of a fine of 30 shillings in 1671. During the intervening 32 years he must have been apprenticed and learned the craft somewhere. It is curious that another famous early clockmaker, Edward East, was born in a neighbouring village, Southill, but no connection between them is known. Tompion's father, like his grandfather, was a blacksmith, but the business was left to Thomas Tompion's younger brother, James, which suggests that Thomas had established himself elsewhere. He is unlikely to have been apprenticed to his father, although he probably worked as a blacksmith somewhere and learned how to make large wrought iron turret clocks before making domestic ones. Thomas Hearn, in his diary for November 27, 1713, stated that Tompion had died the previous week, adding that he was the most skillful clock and watchmaker in the world, was originally a blacksmith and first set up as a clockmaker in Buckinghamshire. In the entry in the Court minute book of the Clockmakers Company of 1671, he is referred to as a 'Great Clockmaker', suggesting that he was a Master blacksmith-clockmaker making large iron clocks. In London, by 1674 he was living at The Dial and Three Crowns in Water Lane (now Whitefriars Street), Fleet Street, and became acquainted with Robert Hooke, the brilliant first Curator of Experiments for the Royal Society, who, in the same year, commissioned Tompion to make a quadrant. Thereafter, they worked on many experimental projects and Tompion's reputation for fine clocks grew rapidly. In 1691, he was elected as one of four new members of the Court of Assistants, part of the governing body of the Clockmakers Company. Four years later, a rating assessment (to gather money by taxing marriages, births, burials, batchelors and widowers to further the war against France; Tompion was a batchelor) showed the Tompion household to comprise 14 men and five women. All of the males, except for two men and a boy, were horological apprentices or craftsmen. The females were a niece, wives and two servants. The house also contained a tenant family numbering eight. One member of the household, Edward Banger, married a neice of Tompion's (it seems to have been a 'shot-gun wedding') and from 1701, when Tompion's health was declining, many clocks and watches were signed Tompion and Banger. This lasted until about 1708, when there was a quarrel and Banger was dismissed. Nothing more was heard of him, except in Tompion's Will, which stipulated, when leaving property to his neice, that it should not be subject to the debts and 'Intermedling Disposition' of her husband. In the meantime, another apprentice, George Graham, had become Tompion's chief assistant, and, from about 1710, many clocks were signed Tompion and Graham until Tompion's death in 1713. Although he made many clocks for Charles II and William III and some for Queen Anne, he never received the Royal appointment because of the longevity of the incumbent, Thomas Herbert, who was Clockmaker to James II, William III and Queen Anne. Two of Tompion's finest clocks were in the Wetherfield Collection, the William III ('Record') and the Tulip Tompions. Others he made were two for the Royal Observatory, Greenwich, and the Bath clock, given after he had taken a cure there. Apart from technical innovation, he was often ahead in fashion, and pioneered batch production. Altogether, he and his craftsmen produced about 650 clocks, about 5,500 watches and many barometers and instruments. Graham married another niece and became Tompion's close friend. He was referred to as 'my loving Nephew' in Tompion's Will, which left him and his wife the business. Graham had been running it for four years before Tompion's death at the age of 75. Both were buried in Westminster Abbey. There was another Thomas

Tompion (see page 194), who was apprenticed in clockmaking, but was a waster.
5,18,22,23,24,27,28(!),31,37,75,76,79,80,87,90,92,97,120,121,130,143,165(!)

Tompion and Banger, *London*. See previous entry, and also Graham.   152

Tregent, James, *London*, was a celebrated maker who became Watchmaker to the Prince of Wales. He was a member of the Clockmakers Company from 1781 to 1808 and there are watches by him in the Victoria and Albert, Science, and British Museums.   61

Trubshaw, John, *London*, was apprenticed in 1679, and became a Freeman of the Company in 1686 and a Warden in 1714. He made watches as well as clocks, one of them being in the Victoria and Albert Museum, London.   29

Tutet, Edward, *London*, was apprenticed in 1754, Free of the Company in 1765, and Master in 1786. He died in 1792.   59

Tyler, George, *London*, worked at Pope's Head Alley, Lombard Street, and was a member of the Clockmakers Company from 1699 to 1723, having been apprenticed in 1692.   51

Vulliamy, Justin, *London*, was a Swiss who became a very fine maker from 1730 to about 1790. He joined Benjamin Gray as a partner after marrying his daughter. There are watches by him in the British, Victoria and Albert, Science, and Guildhall Museums in London. He worked in Pall Mall.   189,190,209

Watson, Samuel, *Coventry and London*, was a fine maker of astronomical clocks for the King – he was 'Mathematician in Ordinary to His Majesty' – and Sir Isaac Newton. He worked in Long Acre and was a member of the Clockmakers Company from 1687 to about 1710.   42

West, Thomas, *London*, was apprenticed in 1688 to John Edlin and was made Free of the Company in 1698.   116

Wheeler, Thomas, *London*. Nothing is known of this maker except that he was working around the turn of the 17th to 18th century.   106

Williamson, Joseph, *London*, was an eminent maker who became Watchmaker to the King of Spain and claimed to have made every Equation of Time clock produced in England up to 1719. There is a pair of watches by him in the Palace Museum, Pekin. He was apprenticed in 1686, was Master of the Company in 1724, and worked in Clements Lane. He died in 1725.   171,173,179

Willson, Joshua, *London*, was apprenticed in 1688 and in the Company until 1733. He was in Lombard Street in 1712 and Clements Lane in 1720. There is a watch by him in the Victoria and Albert Museum. His name was also spelled Wilson according to Baillie.   133

Windmills, Joseph, *London*, was a very fine maker of clocks and watches, who worked in Tower Street. Free of the Clockmakers Company in 1671, he became Master in 1702. He was in partnership with his son Thomas from about 1700, after which his watches were signed just Windmills. There are pieces by him in the British and Guildhall Museums, London, and Metropolitan Museum of Art in New York. He was in the Company until 1723.   47,83,124,159

Wise, John, *London*. There were three makers of this name in the Clockmakers Company who could have made the Wetherfield clock.   91

Appendix One Marquetry and Veneering

M V Tooley

Marquetry is the cutting and inserting of veneers into other veneers in intricate designs, of which birds and flowers, seaweed and arabesque are the most usual. Parquetry is a cruder and earlier form; the inserts are chopped in or chiselled in, the design generally being geometric. Marquetry was most in evidence during the period 1675–1730.

The making of marquetry is a very prolonged and skilful operation. It starts with a drawing on card. The lines are then pricked out with needles, usually by women. The finer and closer the pricking, the better will be the finished line. A thin paper is put under the pricked card and the card dusted with powdered pumice or asphalt, which passes through the pricked holes and is warmed so that the resulting lines of dots are fixed when cold. A sandwich of veneers is then prepared with a scrap veneer between each sheet of veneer and the paper pattern glued to the top sheet. The veneers are in pairs of lighter and darker woods, so that one can be used as ground and the other as patterns.

The sandwich is cut on a wooden donkey, which is a special bench with a horizontal saw slide on the top. The pattern is sawn along the lines using very fine jeweller's saws. The donkey has a clamp controlled by the feet, to enable the sandwich to be

Methods of laying
veneers on a carcase

1 Vertical butt and
horizontal book-leaf
match

2 Book match

3 Slip match

4 Four-way centre and
butt

5 Random match

6 Diamond

7 Reversed diamond

8 Vee

9 Herringbone

constantly turned. The saw slide has to be very accurately set up with the clamp, so that the cut is perfectly square. The donkey illustrated below is French.

After sawing, the slices of the sandwich are parted. The purpose of the scrap veneers in between is to prevent chipping. All the pieces are pushed out into trays (see illustration), and the appropriate pieces of light coloured wood are matched with the dark wood. Each finished picture sheet is then laid on the case boards.

Many rare and exotic woods and ivory are used in the pictures. I have one clock with 26 woods in the door, including tulipwood, snakewood, sycamore, maple, laburnum, padouk, pear, yew and mulberry.

The most accurate pair for veneering, at the top of the sandwich, is called the 'prime cut' and is reserved for the best case. The remainder pairs of veneers are called the 'contra-cuts'. A pair of large cupboards in Boulle are probably the best examples of pairs, both prime cut and contra-cut, known. They can be seen in the Wallace Collection in London. In Boulle, brass and tortoiseshell are used instead of wood as veneers.

Photo: Courtesy of Richard Graeje Ltd, High Wycombe, Bucks.

Paper patterns glued to sheets of veneer are shown on the right, partly sawn at the top. After being sawn out, the pieces of marquetry pattern are grouped systematically in trays, as shown on the left. At bottom left, part of the marquetry pattern is assembled.

Appendix Two Cross-reference Guide

The first column gives the serial numbers of clocks illustrated, which are in three groups, each group being in estimated chronological order. These numbers serve as figure numbers in the text and index.

The second column gives approximate dates, which are in many cases different from those given by Britten, Hurcomb and Vernay. A date followed by another in brackets means that the first is that of the movement and the second that of the case; m/m indicates that the date refers to the movement only and (?) means that the date is very approximate because it was difficult to determine, or is impossible to guess for some reason, such as the clock is a 'marriage' several times over.

The Hurcomb page numbers, thus 29.3, indicate that the clock is the third illustration on this page of his book.

A maker's name in quotation marks in the last column, indicates that the clock is suspect.

To find how many clocks by a particular maker are represented, turn to the brief biographies on pages 237–250. The serial numbers of the clocks appear after each entry.

Serial number	Approx date	Catalogue lot number	Hurcomb page number	Vernay figure number	Britten figure number	Maker

Lantern

Serial number	Approx date	Catalogue lot number	Hurcomb page number	Vernay figure number	Britten figure number	Maker
1	1650	96	37.2	95	2	Closon
2	1670	95	29.3	—	—	Jos. Knibb
3	1675	81	37.3	—	3	Coxeter
4	1680	83	37.1	—	—	Gretton
5	1680	93	33.1	76	1	'Tompion'
6	1680	162	31.3	—	—	John Knibb
7	1680 m/m	222	70.1	—	—	Jos. Knibb
8	1680 m/m	221	31.1	—	—	Clay
9	1730(?)	164	29.2	94	—	'Marwick-Markham'
10	1730(?)	161	29.1	—	—	'Delander'

Bracket

Serial number	Approx date	Catalogue lot number	Hurcomb page number	Vernay figure number	Britten figure number	Maker
11	1665–70	121	34.1	74	—	East
12	1670	118	35.2	—	15	Seignior
13	1670	119	60.3	—	7	Stanton
14	1670	120	67.1	—	—	Jos. Knibb
15	1670	133	65.3	—	5	East
16	1670–75	153	38.3	—	—	Betts
17	1670–75	155	35.3	—	—	Markwick

Serial number	Approx date	Catalogue lot number	Hurcomb page number	Vernay figure number	Britten figure number	Maker
18	1675	143	64.3	—	—	Tompion
19	1680	92	61.1	78(1)	—	Adamson
20	1680	97	30.1	77	16	Jarrett
21	1680	112	36.1	—	—	Jos. Knibb
22	1680–85	85	28.1	—	—	Tompion ('Tulip')
23	1680–85	122	32.1	—	53	Tompion
24	1680–85	159	63.1	—	52	Tompion
25	1685	84	32.2	—	—	Jos. Knibb
26	1685	139	61.3	—	—	John Knibb
27	1690	125	64.1	71	77	Tompion
28	1690	129	63.3	72	51	'Tompion'
29	1690	130	30.2	—	24	Trubshaw
30	1690	131	30.3	99	17	J. Lowndes
31	1690 m/m	152	66.3	—	—	Tompion
32	1690–95	158	35.1	90	47	Taylor
33	1700	12	61.2	—	—	Herbert
34	1700	124	59.1	—	48	J. Martin
35	1700	126	38.1	—	—	T. Martin
36	1700	145	62.3	—	49	Quare
37	1705	94	33.3	—	—	Tompion
38	1705	128	32.3	86	—	Tomlinson
39	1705	136	62.1	89	—	Markwick
40	1705	157	59.3	96	—	Goode
41	1710	147	59.2	—	78	Allett
42	1710	132	63.2	100	50	Watson
43	1715	144	70.2	—	101	Graham
44	1715	146	70.3	75	—	Graham
45	1720	127	69.1	—	—	Rant
46	1720	134	66.1	—	99	Gretton
47	1720	149	65.1	—	—	Windmills
48	1720	151	65.2	85	100	Delander
49	1735	165	29.4	—	—	Peckover
50	1740	135	64.2	—	—	Jackson
51	1740	141	36.3	—	103	Tyler
52	1740	123	69.2	73	—	Ellicott
53	1760	137	38.2	—	—	Ellicott
54	1760	154	66.2	91	115	Ellicott
55	1760	4	60.2	83	—	Shelton
56	1770	78	39.1	—	—	Clarke
57	1770	138	67.3	93	119	Mudge & Dutton
58	1770	140	68.2	—	129	Johnson
59	1770	148	68.1	79	—	Tutet
60	1770	169	69.2	82, 88	—	Cumming
61	1770	8	31.2	87	—	Tregent
62	1780	55	33.2	—	—	Cowan
63	1780	142	67.2	—	128	Emery
64	1780	150	62.2	80, 92	—	Scott
65	1790	160	34.2	84	—	Maclennan
66	1810	82	36.2	81	—	Marriott
67	1820	2	68.3	—	—	Thompson
68	1820	156	60.1	98	130	Dwerrihouse & Carter

(1) Also Fig. 97, wrongly attributed to Jarrett.

Serial number	Approx date	Catalogue lot number	Hurcomb page number	Vernay figure number	Britten figure number	Maker

Longcase

Serial number	Approx date	Catalogue lot number	Hurcomb page number	Vernay figure number	Britten figure number	Maker
69	1668	75	55.2	32	—	Jos. Knibb (1)
70	1670	115	54.2	13	28	Jos. Knibb
71	1670–75	79	40.1	45	29	Jos. Knibb
72	1670–75	80	40.3	47	27	Jos. Knibb
73	1670 (80)	108	16.3	46	26	John Knibb
74	1675	14	20.2	—	8	J. Fromanteel
75	1675	52	74.1	—	11	Tompion
76	1675	117	51.3	3	9	Tompion
77	1675–80	27	21.3	12	23	Seignior
78	1675–80	53	82.3	16	12	Coxeter
79	1675–80	56	26.3	5	25	Tompion
80	1675–80	59	79.3	1	20	Tompion
81	1675–80	110	—	41	10	East
82	1675–80	189	45.3	21	31	Jos. Knibb
83	1680	106	45.1	14	22	Windmills
84	1680	182	41.2	—	13	Jos. Knibb
85	1680	63	14.1	—	21	Jos. Knibb
86	1680	107	45.2	—	19	Parker
87	1680	13	55.3	10	54	Tompion
88	1680	100	54.1(2)	—	6	Clement
89	1680	109	52.1	54	18	East
90	1680	111	11.3	—	4	Tompion
91	1680	218	72.2	—	—	Wise
92	1680–85	72	56.2	—	—	Tompion
93	1680–85	114	46.1	42	14	East
94	1680–85	197	49.2	35	39	Jos. Knibb
95	1685	29	85.1	—	—	Gould
96	1685	57	84.1	33	—	Jos. Knibb
97	1685	205	26.1	26	56	Tompion
98	1685–90	99	55.1	11	32	Quare
99	1690	70	51.1	38	35	Quare
100	1690	116	18.2	43	37	Gould
101	1690 m/m	170	56.1	—	—	Ebsworth
102	1690 m/m	171	27.2	56	—	No name
103	1690	86	74.3(3)	—	36	Goode
104	1690–95	33	20.1	—	33	Barnett
105	1690–95	67	54.3	27	34	Gretton
106	1690–95	184	17.1	—	55	Wheeler
107	1695	31	26.2	—	58	Quare
108	1695	64	17.2	31	30	Jos. Knibb
109	1695	66	15.3	18	59	Quare
110	1695 (1740–50)	105	27.3	—	45	Jos. Knibb
111	1695–1700	62	41.1	—	62	Marshall
112	1695–1700	74	18.3	6	43	Clowes
113	1695–1700	77	76.3	—	40	Gretton
114	1695–1700	102	11.1	15	60	J. Lowndes
115	1695–1700	103	12.1	—	66	Burges
116	1695–1700	163	12.3	—	64	West
117	1695–1700	179	47.3	29	67	Bradley

(1) Vernay says John Knibb. (2) Wrongly attributed to Goode. (3) Wrongly attributed to Clement.

Serial number	Approx date	Catalogue lot number	Hurcomb page number	Vernay figure number	Britten figure number	Maker
118	1695–1700	187	41.3	—	38	Gretton
119	1695–1700	194	13.2	23	41	Taylor
120	1700	1	80.3	—	95	Tompion
121	1700	3	21.1	2	93	Tompion
122	1700	6	22.2	—	63	I. Lowndes
123	1700	7	22.1	—	76	Puller
124	1700	9	23.2	—	74	Windmills
125	1700	24	24.1	—	—	Collyer
126	1700	30	53.1	—	72	Quare
127	1700	40	22.3	—	88	Fromanteel & Clarke
128	1700	47	77.2	—	—	Elliott
129	1700	58	57.1	—	87	Gould
130	1700	60	Frontis	—	—	Tompion ('Record')
131	1700	61	53.3	—	44	Paulet
132	1700	68	43.1	30	71	I. Lowndes
133	1700	75A	13.3	—	84	Willson
134	1700	87	76.2	—	82	No name
135	1700	177	83.3	4	68	Papavoigne
136	1700	178	46.2	44	65	Puller
137	1700	188	00.0	37	61	Quare
138	1700	190	49.1(1)	—	—	Herbert
139	1700	199	50.3	49	46	Pepys
140	1700	202	84.3	—	42	Gould
141	1700	203	52.5	—	69	Knottesford
142	1700	215	16.2	19	—	Finch
143	1700	204	83.1	—	73	Tompion
144	1705	28	81.3	26	86	J. Lowndes
145	1705	41	24.2	—	75	Bridge
146	1705	45	23.3	—	83	Quare
147	1705	46	13.1	—	—	Andrews
148	1705	49	40.2(2)	28	91	Quare
149	1705	90	77.1	—	80	Quare
150	1705	113	42.3	8	—	Jos. Knibb
151	1705	168	57.2	—	—	Bonner
152	1705	36	15.1	—	97	Tompion & Benger
153	1710	32	82.1	—	96	Smith
154	1710	48	24.3	—	—	'Graham'
155	1710	51	10.3	39	—	Quare
156	1710	54	20.3(3)	7	89	Quare
157	1710	76	50.1(4)	17	92	Day
158	1710	88	25.3	—	94	Oosterwijk
159	1710	89	12.2	—	85	Windmills
160	1710	104	25.2	—	98	Fleureau
161	1710	191	73.3	—	57	Eagle
162	1710	195	79.1	40	90	Colston
163	1710	212	48.2	—	—	Lambert
164	1710	220	48.1	20	—	Collyer
165	1714	35	53.2	24	109	'Tompion'
166	1715	10	17.3	—	—	Clay
167	1715	91	57.3	—	81	Gould
168	1720	167(3)	71.1	—	108	Gregg m/m
169	1720	21	48.3	48	—	Graham
170	1720 (90)	23	72.3	52	—	Graham

(1) Wrongly attributed to Day. (2) Also page 51.2 with later date. (3) Also page 19.1 wrongly attributed to East.
(4) Wrongly attributed to Herbert.

Serial number	Approx date	Catalogue lot number	Hurcomb page number	Vernay figure number	Britten figure number	Maker
171	1720	209	84.2	—	—	Williamson
172	1720	216	16.1	53	—	Quare
173	1725	39	47.1	34	107(1)	Williamson
174	1725	43	25.1	—	111	Bennett
175	1725	50	14.3	—	105	Lee
176	1725	101	52.3	—	104	Davis
177	1725	213	73.1	51	—	Graham
178	1725	217	80.1	9	—	Delander
179	1725	44	81.2	22	106	Williamson
180	1730	174	46.3	—	—	Clift
181	1730	173	47.2	68	113	Abbott
182	1730–35	207	44.1	—	—	Jenkins
183	1735	37	15.2	—	—	Kipling
184	1735	38	19.3	—	110	Delander
185	1735	214	78.2	—	—	Graham
186	1740 (90)	65	79.2	50	112	Graham
187	1740	73	11.2	—	—	Nickals
188	1750	192	73.2	64	—	'Rainsford'
189	1750 m/m	198	43.3	67	—	Vulliamy
190	1750(?)	210	72.1	69	—	Vulliamy
191	1750–60	98	10.2	—	—	Hawkins
192	1755	22	42.2	—	—	Lindsay
193	1760	201	44.2	25	—	Gray & Vulliamy
194	1760	206	50.2	—	—	Gray & Vulliamy
195	1765	71	14.2	66	—	Shelton
196	1770 (1900)	193	44.3	70	—	Hodges
197	1775	42	75.2	—	120	Ellicott
198	1775	25	85.2	—	—	Holmes
199	1778	5	21.2	60	117	Comber
200	1780	15	81.1	—	127	M. & T. Dutton
201	1780	16	80.2	—	125	Mudge
202	1780	26	10.1	—	—	Colley
203	1780	196	49.3	57	114	Ellicott
204	1780	219	82.2	—	—	Haley
205	1780	211	75.1	—	—	Holmes
206	1790	11	78.3	—	116	Clare
207	1790	17	23.1	—	123	Holmes
208	1790	18	42.1	—	124	Iles
209	1790	19	74.2	59	131	Vulliamy
210	1790	20	75.3	61	126	Mudge & Dutton
211	1790	175	27.1	—	118	Moore
212	1790	181	83.2	—	122	J. Gray
213	1790	186	77.3	—	121	Cumming
214	1800	69	56.3	58	—	Arnold and Son
215	1850	34	19.2	55	—	Eiffe
216	1890	185	76.1	63	—	Evans
217	(?)	183	78.1	—	—	No name
218	(?)	200	43.2	65	—	No name
219	(?)	180	00.0	62	—	No name
220	(?)	172	18.1	—	—	'Mudge'

(1) Dial only.

Not identified: Unnamed oak 8-day longcase clock in Hurcomb (page 85.1).
Not in sale: Tompion stained oak 8-day longcase clock, *c.*1700 (Fig. 70), Tompion burr walnut longcase clock, *c.*1705 (Fig. 79), and Thomas Moore, Ipswich, bracket clock with pull repeat on six bells (Fig. 106) in Britten.

Index

This index covers the text with only a few references to illustrations. The pictures of clocks are in chronological order.

To find makers in a particular period, refer to the chart on pages 254 to 258.

To find makers' names and clocks by them in the collection, refer to the biographies on pages 237 to 250.

A page number in the index in italics (e.g. *114*) refers to an illustration on that page.

Adamson, H.   12
Age of Moon dial   38, *52*
Alarm work   18, 20, 22, 24, *61*
Allix, Charles   14, 15
Amboina case   42, 46
Anchor escapement   21, 27, 28, 32, 34, 46, *53*
Annual calendar   37
Apron on backplate   28, *102*
Arch top   30, *75*
Architectural top   43, 46, *72, 122*
Auxiliary dial   33, 37

Baillie, G. H.   16
Balloon case   30, 33, *75*
Balance   19
Banding   43, 45
Banking pin   19
Barlow, William   28
Basket top   29, *73*
'Bed-post' frame   17
Bell top   42, *73*
Bezel   30
'Bird cage' frame   17
Bob, Lenticular   32
Bolt and shutter maintaining power   35, 48, *51*
Bonner, C.   43
Bracket clock   24–33, *72–119*
Bracket, Wall   26, 32
Brass basket top   30, *73*
'Brass clock'   18
Brass construction   18
Break-arch dial   23, 30, 42
Break-arch top   43, 47, *73, 74*
British Museum   9, 15
Britten, F. J.   14, 15, 16
Bull's eye   47
Burr elm case   4, 46

Burr walnut case   15, 42
Burr wood pattern   42

The Cabinet Maker   45
Cabinet style case   46
Case door   47
Centre wheel   28
Cescinsky, H.   14, 29, 30, 44
Chamber clock   17
Chamber top   33, *76*
Chapter ring   31, 38, 39, 47, *50*
Chiming train   26
Chippendale   43, *114*
Chops   27
Clare, T.   40
Clement, W.   36
Clerkenwell clock factory   45
Click   22
Clift, T.   43
Clifton, J.   41
Clockmakers' Company   13
Closon   18
Cocus wood case   46
Comber, R.   40
Continental lantern clock 17, 18, 20, 21
Contrate wheel   21, 28
Conversion   21, 22, 27
Conversion, Balance to pendulum   21, 22
Conversion to Westminster chime   27
Coster, Salomon   24, 33
'Cottage' clock   35
Count wheel   20, 28, 36, 48, *52, 86*
Count wheel, Outside   36, *52*
Cresting   42, 46, 47
'Cromwellian' clock   19
Cross-banding   45
Crown wheel   19, 20, 21, 28, *53*
Crutch   24, 28, *53*

Cuban mahogany   44
Cumming, Alexander   12, 15
Cushion basket top   30, *73*

Date aperture   37, 41
Dating, Systematic   17
Dawson, Percy   12, 15
Day, Edmund   15
Day of the month   31, 37, 41
de Carle, Donald   9
Dead beat escapement   46, 48
Detent   20
Dial, All-over silvered   40, 46, 47
Dial, Enamelled   40
Dial engraving   31, 33
Dial, One-piece   40, 46, *50*
Dial, Painted (one-piece)   40, 48, *50*
Dial plate   31, 38, 40, *50*
Dial plate, False   *50*
Dial shape   32
Dial, Size of   39
Dial, Two-piece   31, 38, *50*
Domed top   42, 46, 47, *72*
Double basket top   30, *73*
Dunn, G.   13
Dutch architectural case   *72*
'Dutch Fromanteel'   242
'Dutch' bell hammer   48
Dutch marquetry   43
Dutch striking   36
Dwerrihouse, J.   15

Early architectural case   *72*
East, Edward   15, 29, 41
Ebonising   29, 41, 42
Ebony case   29, 32, 41, 42, 45
Ebsworth   15
Eight-day clock   26
Electro-gilding   31
Ellicott, J.   15
Elliott   15
Emery, J.   30
Endless rope drive   22, 23, 34, 35
Engraved back plate   *96*
Engraved borders to plates   41
English Domestic Clocks   14, 29
Engraving in dial plate corners   24, *81*
Equal hours   37
Equation kidney   38
Equation of Time   37
Escape wheel   35

Factory, Embryo clock   33
Feet of bracket clock   32

Fifty year rule   13
Finial   47
Fire gilding   31
Five Centuries of British Timekeeping
   (Exhibition)   13
Flat top   42, 46, *72*
Fly   20
Foot   32
Frame construction   18, *50*
Fret   18, 29, 46
Fromanteel, Ahasuerus   24, 33, 34, 41
Fromanteel, John   24, 33
Fromanteel & Clarke   38
Former Watch & Clockmakers and their
   Work   14
Four-glass case   *76*
Four-wheel train   27
French factory clocks   30
French striking   27, 36
Fusee   25, *51*

Gadrooned top   33, *76*
Grande sonnerie striking   36
Gardner, Malcolm   14
Garvan, Francis P.   13
Garrard & Co.   9
Greenwich Mean Time   37
Gretton, C.   31
Going train   19, 25, 26, 34, 35
Gothic style   31
Gould, C.   36
Graham, George   40, 46
Grained case   46
Great wheel   19, 22, 28
Gregg, F.   37
Gregorian calendar   37
Gridiron pendulum   46
Grotesque   43
Gut line   34

Hands   17, 18, 20, 21, 33, 40, 46, 47,
   48, *55*
Handle for case   29, 32
Haley, C.   40
Half-hour division   39, 47
Half-quarter division   31, 39, 47, *54*
Handle, Bracket clock   29, 32
Hanging clock   18
Harrison maintaining power   35, 46
Height of longcase clock   24
Herbert, Corn.   15
Holmes, J.   43
Honduras mahogany   44
Hood, Bracket clock   *72*

Hood, Longcase   42, 43, 46, 47
Hooded wall clock   23
Horological Journal, The   10, 13
Hour wheel   19
Hurcomb, W. E.   10, 11, 14, 15
Hutchinson, Beresford   15
Huygens, Christiaan   24, 33, 34

Ilbert, C. A,   9
Inlay   45
Inverted bell top   30, 42, *73*

Japanning   44
Jumper   37

Keyhole   30
Key, Winding   34, 35, *51*
Kipling, W.   36
Knibb   10, 12, 30
Knight, Frank & Rutley   10

Laburnum case   46
Lacquered case   29, 32, 44
Laiton (Latten)   18
Lancet top   30, 31, *76*
Lantern clock   17–24, *61–68*
Lazarus, Phineas   10, 11
Leap year   37
Lee, Ronald A.   12, 13
Lenticle   37, 47
Lever escapement   26
Lindsay, G.   36
'Locking plate'   20, 28, 36, 48, *52, 86*
Long pendulum   21, 22, 23
Longcase clock   33–48, *124–237*
Loomes, Brian   16
Loomes, Thomas   41
Louis XIV style case   *76*
Lancashire clock   45

Maclennan, K.   15, 30
Mahogany case   29, 32, 44, 45
Mainspring   25
Maintaining power   22, 35, 46, 48, *51*
Mallet, Francis   11, 13
Markwick   29
Marquetry case   15, 29, 43, 44
'Marriage'   23
Matching hands   48
Matting, Dial   31
Mercer, Thomas   10
Mercury pendulum   46

Minute division   23, 24, 33, 47, *54*
Minute wheel pipe   28
Mock pendulum   31, 33, *87*
Month clock   24, 28, 35
Moon dial   38, *52*
Moore, C.   40
Moore, J.   14
Motion work   22, 28, 46
Moulding under hood   41, 47
Moving disc hour   46
Mudge & Dutton   40
Mulberry case   42, 46
Musical clock   27

N.A.G. Press Ltd   17
Neuchâteloise clock   30
Nichols, I.   36, 38

Oak carcase   42, 44
Oak case   41, 44, 45
Ogee top   *76*
Old English Clocks   14
Olive wood case   32, 42, 46
Oyster case   42, 46

Pagoda top   42, *75*
Painted case   46
Pallet   19, 21
Parkes, D. J.   10
Parquetry   43
Pearwood case   41
Pendulum, Bob   21, 32, 34, 48, *53*
Pendulum, Central   21
Pendulum, Fixed   27
Pendulum, Long   21, 22, 34, 35, 36, 46, 48, *53*
Pendulum, Mock   31, 33, *87*
Pendulum, Short   20, 21, 22, 24, 32, 34, 48, *53*
Pendulum, 1¼ seconds   36, 48
Perpetual calendar   37
Pillar   42, 47
Pin barrel   27
Pine carcase   42
Pine case   41, 46
Pinion   19
Plate frame   25, 34, *50*
Plate, Shaped   34, 48
Pollard oak case   44, 45
Portico top   46
Posted (bed-post) frame   17, 22, *50*
Power source   *51*
Practical Watch and Clock Maker   9, 14
Prestige, Sir John   10

Provincial clock   36, 45, 48
Pull-up winding (endless cord)   22, 23, 34, 35, *51*

Quare, Daniel   12, 15, 28, 37, 38
Quarter chiming   26, 36
Quarter hour division   33, 39, 40, 47, *54*
Quarter repeater   29
Quarter striking   26

Rack striking   28, 36, 48, *52*
'Record' Tompion   11, 12, 13
Regency period   30
Regulation dial, Pendulum   27
Regulator   26, 35, 40, 45, 46, *109*
Repeating work   29, 36, *108*
Reproduction clock   24
Rising hood   34, 46, 47, *52*
Roman striking   36
Royal Observatory, Old   15
Royal pendulum   34

Satinwood case   46
Scott, J.   12
Seconds hand   35, 46
Seatboard   34
Sheepshead clock   23
Set-up, Spring   25
Sheraton   45, *75*
Signature of maker   23, 41
Skeletonised chapter ring   47
Snail, Striking   28
Softwood carcase   44
Spandrel   31, 38, 40, 47, *54*
Spanish mahogany   44
Spring barrel   25
Spur, Lantern clock   18
Stanton   29
Strike, Silent   27
Square dial   47
Starting a bracket clock   26
Striking train   19, 23, 25, 26, 27, 36
Stringing   43, 45
Sundial time   37
Swiss factory clock   30
Sykes, J. S.   13
Symonds, R. W.   12, 13

Table clock   17, 25, 32
Thirty-hour longcase clock   23, 26, 35
Thomas Tompion, His Life and Work   12

Three-month clock   *169*
Tic-tac escapement   *53*
Tidal dial   38
Timepiece   26
Ting-tong striking   27
Tompion, Thomas   10, 11, 12, 13, 14, 29, 36
Top of bracket case   29, 32, *72–76*
Tortoise-shell veneer   29, 32, *95*
Train position   26
Tremayne, Arthur   14
Trubshaw, J.   30
Tudor rose engraving   31, 33
'Tulip' Tompion   36
Turkish market   24, 33, *110*

Value of Tompion clock   12
Van Winsum   12
Veneering   42
Verge alarm   20, 21, 22
Verge escapement   19, 21, 28, 32, 34, *53*
Vernay, A. S.   11
Victoria and Albert Museum, London   13
Vulliamy   40

Walnut case   12, 29, 32, 42, 45
Watchmakers and Clockmakers of the World   16, 17
Warning   20
Webster, Malcolm K.   14, 29, 30, 44
Webster, Percy   11, 12, 14
Weight drive   19, 22, 35, *51*
Westminster chime   27
Westminster chime conversion   26
Wetherfield Collection, The   11
Wetherfield Collection of English Clocks, 11
William III   11, 12, 14
William and Mary spandrel   40
Williamsburg Museum, Virginia, U.S.A.   13
Williamson, J.   38
Winding a spring clock   26
Winding holes   26, 41, 47
Winged lantern clock   21
Wood for cases, Periods of   29, 32, 45–46

Year clock   *166, 208*
Yew case   46
Yorkshire clock   45

Zone   31, 38, 41

Selected Bibliography of Books Listing Local Makers

Clockmaking & Watchmaking in Colchester: Bernard Newman (Country Life Books, Feltham, Middlesex, 1969)

Connecticut Clockmakers of the 18th Century: Penrose R.Hoopes (Hartford, Conn., USA, 1930)

Cornish Clocks & Clockmakers:J.K.Bellchambers (Private publication by the author at Midland Bank Chambers, Totnes, South Devon, 1962)

Lancashire Clocks & Clockmakers: Brian Loomes (David and Charles, Newton Abbot, Devon, 1975)

Lancashire: Pigot & Co's Commercial Directory 1822, extract of watch, clock, watch movement and material making trades, etc: (T.&S.Hyde, 59 Scotgate, Stamford, Lincolnshire)

Leicestershire Clockmakers: John Daniell, FMA (Leicestershire Museums Art Galleries and Record Service, 1975)

The Making of Clocks & Watches in Leicestershire and Rutland: J.A.Daniell. (Leicestershire Archaeological Society, The Guildhall, Leicester, 1951)

Clockmaking in Oxfordshire 1400–1850: C.F.C.Beeson (The Antiquarian Horological Society, Ticehurst, E. Sussex, 1962)

Old Scottish Clockmakers: John Smith (Edinburgh, 1921)

Shropshire Clock & Watchmakers: Douglas J.Elliott (Phillimore & Co. Ltd, Shopwyke, Chichester, England, 1979)

Somerset Clockmakers: J.K.Bellchambers (Antiquarian Horological Society, 1968)

Suffolk Clocks & Clockmakers: Arthur J.Haggar FBHI and Leonard F.Miller, CMBHI (Private publication by the authors. Printers: Thanet Printing Works, Ramsgate, 1974)

Clocks and Clockmakers of Tiverton: C.N.Ponsford, J.G.M.Scott and W.P.Authers (Private publication by the authors, Horsdon House, Tiverton, Devon)

Clock & Watch Makers in Wales: Iorwerth C.Peats MA, D.Sc. (National Museum of Wales & Welsh Folk Museum, Cardiff, 1968)

Westmorland Clocks & Clockmakers: Brian Loomes (David and Charles, Newton Abbot, Devon, 1974)

The Clockmakers and Watchmakers of Wigan: Arthur J.Hawkes (Private publication by the author, 95 Dicconson Stuart West, Wigan, 1950)

Yorkshire Clockmakers: Brian Loomes (Dalesman Books, Clapham, Yorkshire, 1972)

Maister der Uhrmacher Kunf: Jurgen Abler (Dusseldorf, 1977)

Watchmakers and Clockmakers in Russia, 1400 to 1850: Valentia L.Chenakal (The Antiquarian Horological Society, Ticehurst, E. Sussex)